CLAY IN THE AGE OF BRONZE

Studies of creativity frequently focus on the modern era, yet creativity has always been part of human history. *Clay in the Age of Bronze: Essays in the Archaeology of Prehistoric Creativity* explores how creativity was expressed through the medium of clay in the Bronze Age in the Carpathian Basin. Although metal is one of the defining characteristics of Bronze Age Europe, in the Carpathian Basin clay was the dominant material in many areas of life. Here the daily experience of people was, therefore, much more likely to be related to clay than to bronze. Through eight thematic essays, this book considers a series of different facets of creativity. Each essay combines a broad range of theoretical insights with a specific case study of ceramic forms, sites or individual objects. This innovative volume is the first to focus on creativity in the Bronze Age and offers new insights into the rich and complex archaeology of the Carpathian Basin.

Joanna Sofaer is a Professor in Archaeology at the University of Southampton. She has published widely on the European Bronze Age and archaeological theory. She is the author of *The Body as Material Culture* (2006), editor of *Children and Material Culture* (2000) and *Material Identities* (2007), and co-editor of *Biographies and Space* (2008).

CLAY IN THE AGE OF BRONZE

Essays in the Archaeology of Prehistoric Creativity

JOANNA SOFAER

University of Southampton

CAMBRIDGE
UNIVERSITY PRESS

CAMBRIDGE
UNIVERSITY PRESS

32 Avenue of the Americas, New York, NY 10013–2473, USA

Cambridge University Press is part of the University of Cambridge.

It furthers the University's mission by disseminating knowledge in the pursuit of education, learning and research at the highest international levels of excellence.

www.cambridge.org
Information on this title: www.cambridge.org/9780521155366

First published 2015

Printed in the United States of America

A catalog record for this publication is available from the British Library.

ISBN 978-0-521-76826-9 Hardback
ISBN 978-0-521-15536-6 Paperback

For GJAS

A creative kid who wanted this book to be about pirates (or ninja). Maybe next time . . .

We know the past by pieces
        by sherds
        broken pieces of pottery found
        beneath the earth's crust
        having once been a part, expressing totality.
Now still a part more and less so
        speaking history to us
        being form in fragment.
What can we name it . . .
        when a way of life still exists
        and itself is a fragment
        being part of the past and
        projecting tenaciously into our time?
Patterns of existence . . . what for?
        this life-way discovered and reported is not a
            hard-fact fragment
        it is a real existence
        flowing
        continuously in today from yesterday
        making tomorrow.
In our totality of today we can see it only
        as a fragment and learn some truth
        in its form. Paradoxically in looking
        we atrophy it making it hard and fast.
But this must be transcended for today was
        yesterday and our living
        will see tomorrow.
Potters are water-carriers of history's truths.

Fragments, Charles Counts (1971)

CONTENTS

FIGURES AND TABLES

Figures

All maps and drawings by Ian Kirkpatrick unless otherwise stated.

x

Tables

PREFACE AND ACKNOWLEDGEMENTS

For more than a decade I have had the privilege of working in Hungary at the Bronze Age tell settlement of Százhalombatta. I had become fascinated by the particular complexity and diversity of Bronze Age ceramics in the Carpathian Basin. I wanted to explore not only the nature of this diversity, but also the human practices and motivations that lay behind it. The HERA-funded project Creativity and Craft Production in Middle and Late Bronze Age Europe (CinBA), which I led from 2010 to 2013 (grant number 09-HERA-JRP-CI-FP-020) (www.cinba.net), offered an opportunity to understand these in new ways through the lens of creativity. The project brought together colleagues from the Universities of Southampton, Cambridge and Trondheim, the National Museum of Denmark, the Natural History Museum in Vienna, the Archaeological Museum in Zagreb, the Crafts Council and Sagnlandet, Lejre. It aimed to explore the fundamental nature of creativity in a critical period of human history by looking at developments in crafts that we take for granted today: pottery, textiles and metalwork. This volume is the fruit of that project.

Addressing creativity in the archaeological record has been both challenging and enjoyable. The intellectual, methodological and interpretive provocations that it offers have gone far beyond what I had anticipated. As a result it has been incredibly rich and stimulating, and has sparked many new ideas and collaborations. Although CinBA is now at an end, my own creative journey is just beginning.

It has been a joy and a privilege to work with all the colleagues involved in CinBA. I greatly value our discussions and friendship. This book could not have been written without the generosity of many archaeologists in the countries of the Carpathian Basin who kindly showed me material, answered queries and provided me with literature. I would like to thank Jacqueline Balen, Alice Choyke, Monica Constantin, Gabriel

Craciunescu, Anna Endrődi, Dragan Jovanović, Carol Kacsó, Viktoria Kiss, Jovan Koledin, Gabriella Kovács, Daria Ložnjak-Dizdar, Dan Pop, Cristian Schuster, Jasna Šimić, Cristian Stefan, Alexandru Szentmiklosi, and Alexandru Vulpe. I am particularly indebted to Snježana Karavanić, Sanjin Mihelić, Nona Palincaş, and Magdolna Vicze, who not only helped with access to objects and literature but also took the time to read and comment on draft chapters. Ian Kirkpatrick patiently listened to my ideas for illustrations and turned them into reality. Conversations with Marie Louise Stig Sørensen and Lise Bender Jørgensen have always been inspiring and thought-provoking. I would also like to thank my brother, Joshua Sofaer, for sharing with me his insights into creativity.

Finally, this book could not have been completed without the fantastic support of my family. Thank you.

CinBA was financially supported by the HERA Joint Research Programme (www.heranet.info), which is co-funded by AHRC, AKA, DASTI, ETF, FNR, FWF, HAZU, IRCHSS, MHEST, NWO, RANNIS, RCN, VR, and the European Community FP7 2007–2013, under the Socio-economic Sciences and Humanities Programme.

Introduction

Creativity is a quality that is highly valued, but not always well understood. Studies of creativity frequently focus on the modern era, yet creativity has always been part of human history. It is impossible to understand the development of the new – the imagination, ideas, and innovations that form our past – without invoking creativity.

At the same time, however, the archaeological investigation of creativity is frequently perceived to be somewhat romantic and perhaps even impossible. Despite an explosion in studies of creativity in other disciplines (e.g. Bohm 1996; Sternberg 1998; Boden 2003; Hallam and Ingold 2007), creativity is often seen to be a disembodied, almost magical quality of individuals that is responsible for radical self-expression and uniqueness (Boden 2009; Gibson 2010; Wilf 2011). It is an intangible 'something' valued in and of itself as a kind of intellectual property (Thrift 2000). This reflects a view of the subject in which creativity is often understood in terms of individual (often artistic) 'creative genius' (Boas 1955), where personal expression has become one of the cornerstones of modern Western capitalist culture (Taylor 1989; Wilf 2011). By locating creativity solely in the mind of the exceptional person and outside the material realm, such a view of creativity would indeed seem to place it beyond archaeological study. As a discipline, archaeology struggles to identify the work of individuals. Instead it has a strong emphasis on social structures and actions constructed through the identification of patterns in material culture. A non-materialist, individualist view of creativity, therefore, does not chime with archaeological investigation.

An alternative view of creativity identifies it in terms of shared cross-cultural cognitive processes in past and present that sit at the heart of what it means to be human. Drawing heavily on recent work in neuroscience and psychology, in this perspective the ability to imagine and to express creativity – defined primarily in terms of artistic vision – sets people aside from the rest of the animal kingdom in a manner akin to the distinctiveness accorded to humans through the notion of *Homo faber* (Arendt 1958). Such a perspective lends itself to exploring the origins of creativity in the deep human past through, for example, the study of cave paintings and portable art (Mithen 1998; Pringle 2013). Yet here too creativity is seen as located in the mind, leaving questions regarding the cultural and material specificities of creativity unanswered. It raises the question as to whether creativity can be explored outside artistic endeavour. In other words, are there other forms and contexts in which creativity might be expressed? Under what conditions might creativity be stimulated? How might creativity be articulated in later prehistory or in settings that archaeologists deal with frequently, including settlements and cemeteries?

In this book I want to address these issues by exploring creativity as a cultural and material phenomenon. At the cultural level (between the extremes of absolute individualism and cross-cultural similarity), creativity is a social phenomenon that emerges from the relationship between people and society (Leach 2004; Gibson 2010). It is not only the momentary flash of individual brilliance that results in an absolutely original idea – there are very few absolutely original ideas (Jeanes 2006) – but it emerges within social settings in which knowledge is cultivated and transferred among people. It can be understood as the ability to see connections and relationships where others have not (Liep 2001; Jeanes 2006). In other words, innovation in the production of cultural forms involves the manipulation, reconfiguration, and recategorisation of familiar forms and ideas (Barnett 1953; Koestler 1964; Boden 1994; Liep 2001; Leach 2004). In this sense, creativity is not a matter of ownership or appropriation. Creativity always emerges from existing understandings and, as such, is contextually specific. The philosopher Gilles Deleuze (1995: 161) put it well when he said, 'It's not beginnings and endings that count, but middles. Things and thoughts advance or grow out from the middle, and that's where you have to get to work, that's where everything unfolds'. This perspective diverges from a traditional archaeological emphasis on the identification of origin points and moves towards a wider understanding of the new.

In terms of materials, creativity is a matter of knowing how to work with them – their potentials and limitations – in order to put ideas into practice. Different materials have different qualities. What can be done in one material cannot be done in another (Pye 1968). In other words, the contrasting innate properties of different materials lend themselves to being worked in different ways. As the sculptor Constantin Brâncșui stated,

> [Y]ou cannot make what you want to make, but what the material permits you to make. You cannot make out of marble what you would make out of wood, or out of wood what you would make out of stone . . . Each material has its own life . . . we must not try to make materials speak our language, we must go with them to the point where others will understand their language.
>
> (Pallasmaa 2009: 55)

Recent work has emphasised how learning these languages – learning to work with materials by listening to them – is not self-evident but is developed through gestures, tools and direct experience of materials by craftspeople (Piazza 1997). In other words, learning material languages is not simply a matter of abstract intellectual thought but of accumulated physical experience (cf Leach 2004). Materials can suggest and inspire ideas, but it is only through working with them that their properties and potentials become clear. It is during the construction of a relationship with materials that possibilities of modification, transformation and structuring present themselves (Piazza 1997). This process of discovery includes the acquisition of a wide spectrum of knowledge including, for example, malleability, texture, shape, form, colour, and weight.

Understanding the relationship between materials and creativity, therefore, is not to argue for material determinism but rather for an investigation of the particular ways that people acted in relation to materials, in both making and using objects. Thus, it may be possible to trace creative practice through a focus on decisions in the ways that people interacted with materials. In this view, objects and their arrangement are the tangible expression of creative action. Emphasising the material expression of creativity offers a methodological avenue for its investigation in archaeology as both process and outcome. At the same time, however, such an approach suggests that the archaeological exploration of creativity demands a considered focus upon specific materials.

In this book I want to explore how creativity was expressed in one specific medium: clay. I want to take a journey into the past to investigate how it was articulated within local and regional contexts in the Bronze Age in the Carpathian Basin. My aim is to explore creativity in the making of objects from clay and in the ways that such objects were employed within specific settings.

The Creative Potential of Clay

Clay had long been a familiar medium to Bronze Age craftspeople (Sofaer 2006; Michelaki 2008). Clay is not, however, a singular material; there is not one clay but many clays, each with different properties and hence implications for the way in which it is worked. It may also be modified in different ways through mixing and the addition of tempers. Such variation in raw material and its manipulation to promote desired qualities is not unique to clay. The same might be said of metal ore and fibres used in the production of textiles. The defining quality of clay, however, is its plasticity, as a result of which an infinite variety of shapes can be formed.

There are many different potential ways to work with clay. For instance, clay can be pinched, thumbed, coiled, squashed, rolled, moulded, incised, impressed, pierced, or joined to other pieces of clay or to other materials. It is possible to make simple and complex, small and large objects from clay. Unlike textiles, which must be woven as a flat sheet and which are determined through the set-up of the loom, or the shaping of bronze, which is predetermined through the forming of a mould, the shape of clay objects need not be pre-planned. In the Bronze Age the search for form took place through the actions of the hand and fingers and, therefore, had the potential to occur in a particularly spontaneous manner since the parameters of the finished object were defined during its production. Clay is thus 'good to think with' (Sennett 2009: 129). There is no inevitability either in the shape of clay objects or in how to form things from clay; different objects can be made using similar techniques, and similar objects can potentially be made using different techniques. Clay thus asks the potter to make creative decisions for which there are potentially many ways of arriving at an answer. It eludes technological and material determinism in which materials and techniques lead to certain forms. This is not to say that working with clay is without constraints – like any other material it also presents these – but, rather, that it is a potentially provocative material.

In making decisions the potter listens to his or her clay and responds to it through direct contact with the material. In this sense the actions of the potter are intimately linked to his or her perception of the material itself. This perception is multisensory and arises from the direct relationship between the body and clay in the making of objects (cf Ingold 2013). Working with clay requires potters to think through their body (cf Merleau-Ponty 1962). This direct relationship also offers possibilities for a qualitatively different kind of creativity to other materials as the plasticity of clay directly mirrors the actions of the body: If I push the clay, I make an indent. If I pull it, I draw it out. If I press down upon it, I flatten it. Working with clay is a matter of probing the limits and possibilities of interaction between maker and materials (Morris 1970). Furthermore, in working with clay there is immediacy between material response and the human body in which the effects of actions are at once perceptible. Objects arise from a constant exchange between the 'objective properties of the material and the subjective, problem-solving capacity of artisanal will' (Adamson 2010: 360, paraphrasing Focillon 1989).

The language of clay, therefore, is open to a wide range of articulations. In a similar way that English has a range of regional and national expressions – as British English, American English, Indian English, various kinds of pidgin English, or local dialects – clay can be worked in distinctive ways in particular cultural settings. In this sense, learning the language of clay is a culturally specific process. Yet the plasticity of clay not only provides its own language, but also lends itself to the transliteration and translation of other material languages. Transliteration and translation differ in that in the former (as for example in the transliteration of Japanese characters into Latin script), the original language is retained but transferred into a different material. In material terms, this means that techniques developed in another material (such as chiselling or jointing techniques in wood, or riveting in metal) can be implemented in clay (see Sofaer 2006; Kacsó 2011). Sennett (2009: 127) terms the application of a technique seen in one material to another a 'domain shift'. Here creativity lies in the imagination of what is produced as an outcome rather than in the development of the technique. By contrast, in translation the original language is reconfigured into another language. Here a different set of techniques or ways for working with material are employed to recreate an existing object in another material, in other words to make a skeuomorph. In this case creativity lies in the application of different material-specific techniques in order to reimagine the original object in a different material. In transliteration and translation creativity thus lies in contrasting locations. Nonetheless, in both cases the making of clay objects is a matter of the dynamic between the constraints and responsiveness of the material and those of the potter.

The qualities of clay are not, however, constant throughout the making process. Clay is plastic when hydrated, leather hard when drying, and when fired a range of hardnesses varying from that which can be scratched with a finger-nail to a very hard glass-like surface. Making things from clay is a matter of managing metamorphosis of substance as well as of form. It requires getting to grips with temporal changes to the material – judging its state – and of temporality in the making process itself. Just as language is not just a matter of stringing sounds together but also involves timing and rhythm, so it is with working with clay. Clay objects are temporal accumulations of actions, effects and pauses, each of which have their own timing, rhythm and duration. Since clay is a plastic additive medium, it accumulates histories of these allowing archaeological access to the creative process itself. Thus the innate qualities of clay not only allowed for creativity in the past, but permit the tracing of past creativity in the present. It is useful, therefore, to explore them in more detail.

The particular qualities of clay lend actions to their own specific timing and these in turn have duration. Like the good telling of a joke, timing is not just a matter of what to say but also of when to pause and the duration of pauses during the joke's delivery. In language the timing and breaks between stressed words or syllables, as well as words and sentences, are what enable the listener to make sense of what is being said. In craft production, the timing of particular actions – when they do and do not take place – is also a matter of listening to the material. In other words, when a particular action takes place in relation to the state of the material. The skilled practitioner understands the importance of timing and chooses their moment with care (Ingold 2011, 2013). For clay this is important with regard to how the material will respond differently to the potter in its different states. These must be anticipated and integrated into different stages of the making process as different kinds of responsiveness of the material to touch and manipulation are both possible and required at different stages of production. For example, vessel forming needs to take place while clay is still damp, but avoiding vessel collapse or sagging when constructing large vessels such as pithoi requires that they be built in stages. In this case it is necessary to let the lower parts of vessels dry before further applying clay, but in order to make sure that the new clay additions adhere properly and to avoid premature shrinkage, it is also necessary to make sure that the existing parts of the vessel to which it will be added are damp (Blandino 2003). This requires the potter to actively manage the state of the clay and to know both when to stop building the vessel and when to resume. Surface treatments must also be timed. For instance, burnishing must be carried out when the clay is at the leather-hard stage. Pots must also be dried prior to firing in order to avoid their sagging in the kiln. Firing leads to colour changes and vessel shrinkage, and these may further need to be factored into the making process if a particular visual effect or size of an object is required.

Working with clay takes time; it has duration. Even if a potter desires to make an object in a single sitting, whatever the object, it is inevitably a somewhat punctuated process with actions preceded and followed by periods of monitoring and waiting. For clay, the preparation of the material may require a substantial period of time, especially if a very fine clay is desired and the clay needs to be soaked. Furthermore, the possibility to move between wet and dry states means that objects (large or small) need not be finished at a single sitting, as long as they are sufficiently protected between working sessions and not allowed to dry out completely (Blandino 2003). Indeed, the positive need to return to large vessels over several occasions in order to successfully maintain the vessel structure means that the process of making such vessels may be quite drawn out. In addition, since clay objects must be dried to a leather-hard state prior to firing, there is inevitably an hiatus between finishing an object and firing it. Firing itself and waiting for a vessel to cool may also be a protracted process. The time taken to make an object from clay, of course, is dependent upon the size and complexity of the object itself and is highly variable.

Potting is thus a matter of understanding how to actively follow the material by remaining alert to sensory clues that reveal changes to it (Ingold 2011). This in turn demands of the potter an awareness of temporality – of the way that the forming of objects is related to 'material flows' by which objects unfold (Ingold 2011) – in other words, an understanding of the ways that objects are made over time. This is related to an understanding of the changing qualities of the material and the sequence and performance of potting tasks, each with its own timing, rhythm and duration. What appears to the observer to be a linear series of steps, or *chaîne opératoire*, is thus 'a complex reciprocal process for the practitioner' (Keller 2001: 37). Each task takes its meaning from its position within a suite of tasks, and each action follows from the previous action yet never quite repeats it exactly (Fogarty 1937; Ingold 2011). When the duration of making is misjudged and actions are mistimed in relation to the material, like interrupting someone speaking, the results seem to jar. For instance, in order to achieve clean-looking incised decoration, the incising must be carried out when the clay is neither too wet nor too dry. Impatience or rushing to incise a pot too early results in jagged edges as the clay piles up at the edge of the line. The number of pots with mistimed actions that enter the archaeological record may be relatively few compared to the number of mistimed interventions since, prior to firing, it is possible for potters to manipulate and manage the state of clay by wetting it or letting it dry and thus to move backward and forward between states. This means that as long as clay does not dry out completely it is possible to correct or erase errors, or to recycle clay scraps. Recycling can also take place following firing as pots can be creatively deployed in a number of ways: they can be ground up for grog or reused as tools or as building materials.

Working with clay thus presents potters with the potential to combine improvisation and spontaneity as a result of clay's responsiveness to body actions, while simultaneously anticipating and predicting changes to the quality of the material. It also provides particular design possibilities since the lack of inevitability in form and decoration offers potters opportunities to play around with these, should they so desire. It is a medium in which on-the-spot creative problem-solving and pre-planning go hand in hand.

The Bronze Age in the Carpathian Basin

The Carpathian Basin is situated at the boundary of central, eastern and southeast Europe. Also known as the Pannonian Basin or, in the case of the lowlands as the Pannonian Plain, it forms a topographically discrete unit ringed by the Carpathian Mountains, the Alps, the Dinarides and the Balkan Mountains. Two major rivers – the Danube and the Tisza – bisect the basin. Today all or

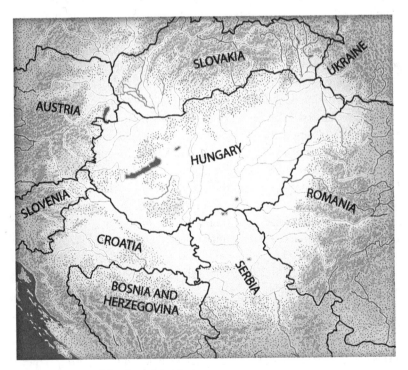

FIGURE I.1 Map of the Carpathian Basin.

part of nine European countries lie within it: all of Hungary, central and eastern Croatia, south-east Slovenia, north Serbia, western Romania, western Slovakia, and small parts of Austria, Bosnia and Herzegovina and Ukraine. It extends from Vienna in the north-west, Zagreb in the south-west, Belgrade in the south-east, and Satu Mare in the north-east (Figure I.1).

Within the region, clay was a key material in all areas of life. In contrast to their neighbours, the inhabitants of the Alps and Swiss lakes to the north and west who lived in a world of wood, and those to the south and east for whom stone was a key material, the people of the Carpathian Basin literally lived in a world of clay (Michelaki 2008; Sofaer 2011). Easy access to local clay deposits, including the loess that makes up much of the Hungarian Plain, meant that clay was used in construction including as daub for walls, beaten earth floors, ovens, or in plasters. Ceramic vessels used for serving food, drinking, storage, or food preparation, are frequently the most prevalent of all items in archaeological contexts. Clay was also used to make other objects such as spoons, loom weights, spindle whorls, roof weights, portable ovens, perforated clay slabs, briquetage and other ceramics related to salt production, anthropomorphic and zoomorphic objects, models such as carts, abstract shapes including stars or crescents, as well as miniature vessels. Clay objects were used in metalworking such as tuyers and crucibles, as well as moulds for casting. There is therefore an enormous number and range of objects made from unbaked and fired clay. Within the region, clay objects are found in settlements and cemeteries. They were used for domestic purposes as well as prestige objects. Indeed, these two categories were not mutually exclusive as high-quality elaborate vessels are also found in houses. In some cemeteries, ceramics have been identified as high status objects, perhaps replacing metal (Vicze 2011).

From the Early to Late Bronze Age (2500–800 BC) there is also a great deal of temporal and regional variation in ceramic forms and decoration. The large number of objects and their variability over space and time lends itself not only to the investigation of contrasting attitudes to clay as a material, but also to an exploration of creativity in how objects were used. Although clay objects are more or less ubiquitous in the European Bronze Age, this does not mean that creativity was present everywhere or that it took place in equal measure wherever such objects are found. Though both culture and people may be in a never-ending state of perpetual creation as people adapt to changing conditions (Wagner 1981; Toren 1999), it is clear that certain places and periods may be 'hot spots' of innovation while in others change is slow and material culture is more homogenous. Thus, there would seem to be spatial and temporal points that have a dynamic that presents more favourable conditions for creativity than others (Liep 2001). Along a spectrum of creativity – from the practice-based solutions and ongoing problem-solving of the everyday to the localised conditions of specific environments that offer the conditions for concentrated bursts of novelty or originality (Liep 2001) – the creative potential of clay was deployed in the Carpathian Basin in different ways and to different ends. Investigating creativity thus requires an understanding of the locations in which creativity takes place and the conditions under which it emerges.

If creativity involves the bringing together of previously unlinked ideas, then the potential for the most striking and novel forms might be expected to be greatest where cultural differences are large (Liep 2001). One such point might be the boundary where two or more cultural groups meet. In the Bronze Age – as in later periods – the Carpathian Basin was a cultural crossroads. It was a dynamic region with a rich, complex and shifting cultural milieu, and a changing balance between receptiveness to influences from outside and the maintenance of local traditions. People thus developed and responded to local demands as well as to broader regional and continental influences. The ceramic evidence, alongside local variations in burial tradition and settlement form, reveals a large number of shifting local and regional cultural groups in the area (see, e.g., Hänsel 1968; Bóna 1975; Visy 2003).

Understanding the differences and relationships between these is a challenging task. Traditionally, a heavy emphasis on typology and on understanding local chronological sequences means that these have frequently been framed within the development of individual national chronological schemes, each with their own terminology for what may, in some cases, be rather similar pottery types crossing modern borders. Furthermore, a lack of radiocarbon dates in some areas precludes the effective knitting together of some chronologies where ceramics are clearly substantially different. Nonetheless, the accumulation of culture-historical knowledge does offer substantial opportunities to address dynamics of similarity and difference between groups through an understanding of creative processes in specific locations. While culture-historical approaches to ceramics commonly identify new cultural groups as emerging either from the blending of two or more pre-existing traditions or as a result of migration, the underlying human actions or processes that underpin such mergers or radical shifts have rarely been explored.

Local variability in ceramics contrasts with the widespread similarity of metalwork throughout large parts of the Carpathian Basin. This means that bronze objects have frequently been used as a proxy for absolute dates (e.g. Mozsolics 1967; Hänsel 1968), but such similarity may also hold social significance. A distinctive Middle and Late Bronze Age Carpathian metalwork style suggests that people fostered a regional identity (Kristiansen 2000). Furthermore, shared metal object types, as well as imported and exported objects, indicate that throughout the second half of the third millennium and the whole of the second millennium BC, the people of the region were connected and integrated with the wider European Bronze Age world (Kristiansen and Larsson 2005; Harding 2013). Yet at the same time, while some people in the region seem to have embraced continental developments, this was not the case for all. The inescapable tension between local ceramic modes of expression and the much larger scale articulation of similarity and difference in metalwork raises questions regarding the scale at which creativity played out and the reasons why it might have been differently articulated in the two materials. Furthermore, the southern and eastern boundaries of a number of widespread Bronze Age cultural phenomena, including the distribution of Beaker, Tumulus, and Urnfield material culture, lie within the region. This raises further questions regarding potential resistance to dominant cultural forces and the ways that this can provoke creative responses.

Yet creativity is not just a matter of responding to large-scale social dynamics. It is also about how objects are configured and reconfigured at a local level. If difference is a mark of novelty, and novelty is a mark of creativity, this provokes consideration of how we identify distinctions between things and in what way these distinctions are meaningful. On one level, difference is the inevitable outcome of the handmade nature of Bronze Age ceramics in the Carpathian Basin. No two vessels are exactly alike, even if their technical signatures suggest that they may have been made by the same potter. On its own, however, this is not necessarily evidence for the expression of creativity. Instead the potential for creativity exists in the space between the attempt to make a faithful copy of an existing object and the development of the new. In other words, creativity lies in the mimetic process: the relationship between original and reproduction and the way that this constructs new realities. Indeed mimesis has sometimes been viewed as the original impulse of all creative activity and as essential in moving from the existing to the new (Benjamin 1933).

The potential for creativity is a matter of social practice in terms of how, and to what extent, the reproduction of objects and ideas are regulated. It is also a matter of imagination, emotional responses, and of the articulation of human action and relations among people. In other words, it is a matter of performance in the particular ways in which creativity was played out through the deployment of objects within specific settings: how clay objects were given social meaning and the extent to which these were socially acceptable.

This Volume

In this volume I attempt to capture some of the complex, polysemic, and sometimes contradictory nature of creativity. Instead of pursuing some kind of global understanding, this book seeks to explore a series of different facets of creativity and how those facets were played out in clay within a range of specific settings in the Bronze Age in the Carpathian Basin. To this end, the volume consists of a series of eight thematic essays arising from the material and contextual concerns described in this introduction. Each essay is directed towards understanding an aspect of creativity by working through a specific case study of ceramic forms, sites, or individual objects.

I have deliberately chosen not to follow chronological order in the presentation of the case studies. This would give a rather misleading impression of creativity as a developmental phenomenon. Instead, I begin with explorations of creativity in working with clay as a material. The first essay, 'Hands', deals with the relationship between the body and clay in the making of objects. Here I consider creativity quite literally in terms of the act of creation and the ways that the plasticity of clay facilitates different body responses from the potter in terms of forms of creative action. My case study explores this through the modelling of miniatures and figurines from throughout the Carpathian Basin. The next essay, 'Recycling', addresses how the reuse of materials and objects, and its counterpart destruction, both offer possibilities for the creation of the new. This creativity in reshaping and rethinking the possibilities of things is explored through my case study of the Early–Middle Bronze Age tell settlement of Százhalombatta, Hungary. Here people lived surrounded by clay, yet they also made striking, deliberate decisions about the recycling of ceramics. 'Design' examines the creative problem-solving and pre-planning implicit in the making of objects. Through a consideration of one particular regional vessel type – so-called Swedish helmet bowls – I look at the ways that these objects were deliberately constructed in order to express cosmological ideas and to colour the experiences of their users through a relationship between shape and decoration.

In 'Margins' I move away from the creativity implicated in the making of objects to explore the relationship between place and creativity. I look at how particular locations can offer conditions under which creativity may thrive. One kind of location for creativity is the geographical margin of cultural phenomena. Margins offer particular possibilities for encounters between people as well as potential freedom from constraints and conservatism felt at the centre. My case study is drawn from the Csepel group of Beaker sites in Hungary. This lies on the southern edge of the Europe-wide distribution of the Early Bronze Age Beaker culture. Following on from this, 'Resistance' examines ways in which people manipulate dominant cultural forces through the creative reappropriation of objects, actions and ideas in ways that at once conform to, but at the same time also reconfigure or resist, dominant paradigms. My focus here is on what Michel de Certeau (1984: xiv) called 'the procedures of everyday creativity' as a means of understanding similarity and difference in material culture. My case study is the late Urnfield cemeteries of Velika Gorica and Dobova in Croatia and Slovenia.

The next two essays address creative processes in terms of a range of practices that inform creativity, rather than the other way around. 'Mimesis' explores how the process of creativity emerges through the relationship between an original object or idea and its reproduction. My case study is the Late Bronze Age and Early Iron Age cemetery of Vukovar Lijeva Bara in eastern Croatia. At this site mimesis was expressed in several different ways including illusions generated through decoration, the use of mimesis to express narrative and cosmology, the subtle revelation of the copy, and the way that the uniqueness of individual vessels was cultivated. 'Performance' examines how creative thought and action can be used as a means of producing knowledge. At the Middle–Late Bronze Age cemetery of Cârna in Romania, deposition of ceramics formed an important part of the burial rite that expressed creativity in conceptualisation and in execution. Individual burials reiterated shared principles with others in the cemetery and with the wider cultural context, but each was also a 'one off' performance in which flexibility and novelty were articulated. Here creativity in the deployment of ceramics was embedded within performance as a social process linked to the community's need to articulate the identity of the deceased and to its emotional needs.

My final essay draws together discussions of creativity in the making of objects and in the social reception of novelty through a discussion of 'Failure'. Not only is failure a persistent risk within the creative process, but it is also the inevitable counterpart to creativity. My case study focuses upon two very different individual objects. The first is an Early Bronze Age Nagyrév jug from the tell site of Százhalombatta in Hungary. Rich in technical errors, this vessel stands as an example of failure in the making of ceramics. The second is a Late Bronze Age vessel from the site of Lăpuș in north-west Romania. This is a technically outstanding and innovative vessel, yet it does not seem to have many counterparts and, therefore, might be regarded as a social failure.

The volume ends with a short Afterword; the material specific, contextual and polysemic nature of creativity precludes some kind of grandiose final statement. Each of the essays can be read individually or as part of the whole. For this reason, and for ease of use, the list of references is organised according to essays. Throughout I have tried to make Bronze Age creativity accessible through discussions of the contemporary world without assuming any correspondence between 'them' and 'us'. Of course, the case studies that I have chosen have been selected for their illustrative value, and it has not been possible to explore all of the rich and complex clay cultures in the Carpathian Basin. Some of the archaeological material in the case studies may be familiar to readers, but I aspire to enable them to see it in new ways. I hope that this book will offer some insights into the creativity of Bronze Age people and how this was expressed through their ceramic objects.

CHAPTER 1

Hands

The Human Body and Clay

The Japanese potter Yagi Kazuo was once asked to name the essence of ceramics. Was it the wheel, the traditional tool of the potter? 'No, it's not the wheel', Yagi replied. 'It's that feeling you get when you take soft clay and squish it between your fingers' (Adamson 2007: 57–58). The plasticity of clay and the way that it is directly formed by the body set clay apart from other materials. This relationship between the physical qualities of clay and the corporeal nature of potting has often become lost among traditional archaeological concerns with ceramics such as typology, style and function. Yet given that in the European Bronze Age the vast majority of ceramics throughout the continent were handmade, the interrelationship between the particular qualities of clay and the ways in which clay could be worked by potters is critical to understanding the potential of clay for creativity in material culture.

In this essay, I want to explore the dialogue between hands and clay in the making of objects. I want to look at creativity in terms of the role of the body in the forming of things – as a literal act of creation. This necessitates an understanding of craft – the process of making by hand – and its outcome, the handmade object (Adamson 2007). It also requires an understanding of creativity as an embodied process in which thinking takes place through the whole body, not only in the mind. In other words, thinking takes place through doing. Such a process is particularly important in potting because of the way the creation of objects takes place through the relationship between the body and materials; creativity is a matter of the 'thinking hand' (Pallasmaa 2009). My case study focuses upon Early and Middle Bronze Age miniatures and figurines created through a diverse range of techniques for modelling in clay from throughout the Carpathian Basin.

Creativity, Craft and the Hands

Making things demands actions of the body, in particular of the hands. It is by taking hold of materials and manipulating them with the hands that they are turned into something new. Craftsmanship thus arises from the hands (Sennett 2009). In pre-industrial societies, including the Bronze Age, the entire material world was 'handmade'. Indeed, it has been argued that the centrality of the body to making things is the defining element of craft (Cardoso 2008). Hands, therefore, are critical to creativity in the production of objects.

The hands are not, however, simply mechanical appendages that form part of a doing body distinct from a thinking mind. Hands create knowledge (Benjamin 1968; Ingold 2013). They tell us if something is hot or cold, sharp or blunt, wet or dry. They form a point of contact that connects a person with the world such that the whole body is a knowing entity (Merleau-Ponty 1992). It is such an embodied understanding of the world that lends us the phrases 'to get a grip', 'hold on', 'to grasp the truth', 'seize the future', and 'place the matter in your hands'; the hand is a political organ (Leslie 1998). In other words, we think through our bodies. As the philosopher Martin Heidegger put it:

> Perhaps thinking, too, is something like building a cabinet. At any rate, it is a craft, a 'handicraft', and therefore has a special relationship to the hand. In the common view, the hand is part of our bodily organism. But the hand's essence can never be determined, or explained, by its being an organ which can grasp ... The hand is infinitely different from all the grasping organs ... different by an abyss of essence. Only a being who can speak, that is, think, can have hands and can handily achieve works of handicraft.... Every motion of the hand in every one of its works carries itself through the element of thinking, every bearing of the hand bears itself in that element. All the work of the hand is rooted in thinking.
>
> (Heidegger 1977: 357)

If we think through our hands, then the hands also provide the link between knowledge, thought, and creativity since it is only by way of a haptic understanding of the world that it becomes possible to imagine something new. The way that the hands seek out materials is critical to understanding the nature of substances. It is only through direct physical experience that it is possible to understand materials. The feel of materials is vital to the ways that craftspeople work with them and explore their innate properties. The Finnish designer Tapio Wirkkala called this process 'eyes at the fingertips' (in Pallasmaa 2009), or as the wheelwright George Sturt put it, '[M]y eyes know because my hands have felt' (Sturt 1923: 24). In discussions of modern design, such close communication with materials at every stage of the making process has been seen as an advantage of craft as opposed to the use of machines (Pallasmaa 2000). The philosopher Gaston Bachelard wrote, 'Even the hand has·its dreams and assumptions. It helps us understand the innermost essence of matter. That is why it also helps us imagine [forms of] matter' (Bachelard 1982: 107). Creativity calls for imagination and, as anyone who has doodled his or her way through a meeting knows, creativity does not reside in our brains alone, but in our entire bodily constitution (Pallasmaa 2009).

The innate potentials and resistances of different kinds of materials lead inevitably to different kinds of interactions with them and thus to different potentials for creativity through different kinds of manipulations. Take, for example, the folding over and creasing hand actions of Japanese origami work, which are enacted on paper but cannot be easily transferred to the making of a wooden bowl. What the hand, arm and body movement can do in relation to flat surfaces is different to what they can do in relation to objects in three dimensions (Morris 1970). In the making of ceramics, the plasticity of clay allows the hands to knead, roll, smooth, pat, bend, push, prod and squeeze. In the particular case of clay, forming takes place through the actions of the hand in a particularly spontaneous manner since the degree of pre-planning for form is much less than that required for some other crafts such as bronze casting or weaving, where the preparation of a mould or loom defines the parameters of the finished object. Although there may be substantial investment in the preparation of clays with anticipation of the kind of object to be made, during the making of ceramic objects there is a search for form with the fingers. The potential range and variation of hand actions may also be greater than in some other crafts as the plasticity of clay means that there are endless potential possibilities of form. For instance, the various actions in making a pot are potentially much greater and less repetitive than those required in weaving. The actions of the hands, therefore, differ in the ways that they probe the limits and possibilities of interaction between maker and materials (Morris 1970).

Thus, the creativity embedded in objects is not just a matter of surface finish or decoration; it also lies within the forming of the object itself and in the responses of the craftsperson to the challenges that the materials pose (Hahn 2012). Objects articulate the boundary between their maker and the world such that the bodily and mental constitution of the maker becomes the site of the work (Pallasmaa 2009), as different creative possibilities arise through different hand and body movements. Within archaeology attempts have been made to capture the dynamics of body movement in woodworking using dance notation, revealing the potential complexity and sophistication of body interactions with materials during crafting in terms of rhythm, speed, force and technique (Høgseth 2013).

The movements involved in making objects entail the hands as both tools and tool-using. The ethnologist and sociologist Marcel Mauss advanced the concept of the *homme total*, where man is himself a tool, a notion re-explored in anthropology and archaeology (Ingold 1998, 2013; Gamble 2007; Budden and Sofaer 2009). As Mauss himself put it, '[T]he body is man's first and natural instrument. Or more accurately ... man's first and most natural technical object, and at the same time technical means, is his body' (Mauss 1935: 83). Influenced by human physical anthropology, recent discussions in the theory of craft have explored the implications of the particular structural anatomy of human hands in the development of craft technique, in particular the distinctive physical experience of grip (Pallasmaa 2009; Sennett 2009). Unlike the blinking of eyelids, grip and the release of grip are voluntary actions (Sennett 2009). Three different basic types of grip have been identified (Marzke 1992, 1997). First is the pinching of small objects between the tip of the thumb and the side of the index finger. Second is the cradling of an object in the palm of the hand and its movement around with pushing and massaging actions between the thumb and fingers. Third is a cupping grip in which a larger object is held, with the thumb and index finger placed at opposite sides of the object, as in holding a ball or a mug of coffee. The cupping grip allows an object to be held securely while it is being worked on by the other hand (Marzke 1992, 1997; Sennett 2009).

Tools can be used to amplify or extend the actions of the hand as, for example, in the use of a hammer. They can distance the hand from the site of action, as in the use of tongs to hold a crucible or to turn meat on a barbeque, or to do things that the hand cannot do, such as using a can opener or using a hide scraper. Some tools require particular kinds of grips or gestures in order to be used. For instance, effective use of a pen to write requires a pinching grip. Other tools are multi-purpose and therefore have several potential holds. The straight-edge screwdriver, for example, can be used to loosen or tighten a screw, in which case a pinching grip along with rotation of the wrist is required. It can also be used as a gouge, awl, cutter or lever, which may require grip and movement of the hands and arms in other ways (Sennett 2009). Using a tool, whether it is a found item such as a stick or a purpose-made object such as an axe, generates additional creative possibilities to using the hands alone. Tools offer particular possibilities for action, and as such they organise imaginative experience with productive results; they guide people in the process of making things (Sennett 2009: 213).

Importantly, what, when and how to execute hand actions – with and without tools – need to be learnt. The saying 'A bad workman always blames his tools' implies that skill lies at the heart of craft. Creativity demands technical ability as well as imagination and understanding of materials. Such technical ability or manual dexterity requires the development of embodied or non-discursive knowledge (Budden and Sofaer 2009; Sofaer and Budden 2013; Sørensen and Rebay-Salisbury 2013). In other words, the learning of practices becomes embedded within the body as motor skills and ways of doing things become 'second nature' (Sofaer 2006; Budden and Sofaer 2009). The classic example of this is riding a bicycle (Knappett 2005). It is possible to understand the principles of how to ride a bike without actually being able to perform the task. Only with repeated practice can one cycle without constant reference back to the articulation of those principles. Similarly, learning to play a musical instrument or a sport requires the constant repetition of actions such that they become engrained in the body. Watching a young child struggle to learn to write is a salient reminder of the complexity of the mechanics of holding a pencil and letter formation, and of the training required by the hands in order to accomplish actions that I take for granted.

The acquisition of embodied knowledge is culturally contingent. Thus, as Marcel Mauss pointed out in his famous essay on the techniques of the body (1935), the capacity to walk is universal, yet people in different cultures are brought up to walk in very different ways. Similarly, in the making of a pot, different suites of actions are required in order to produce different kinds of vessels (Sofaer and Budden 2013), but only some of these may actually be deployed in any given cultural setting. How to do things is culturally situated and socially defined. The possibilities for learning particular kinds of actions (and therefore skills) are held within communities of practice (Lave and Wenger 1991; Lave and Chalkin 1993; Wendrich 2012). These bring people together through shared structures of knowledge and ways of doing which shape the material world (Wendrich 2012; Kohring 2013). Communities of practice are also repositories of cultural interests. For instance, one of the best-selling books in Japan in recent years teaches the reader how to make the 12 animals of the zodiac while peeling citrus fruits (Okada and Kamiya 2010). The success of this volume lies in its cultural resonance. It links to a tradition of paper cutting, or *kamikiri*, and more widely to a persistent cultural value of making ephemeral things by hand. It is difficult to imagine the wild success of such a volume in twenty-first century Britain! What and how to make things, therefore, are expressions of cultural values. Communities of practice both create and circumscribe creative possibilities.

Actions are also given meaning within cultural contexts. The elaborate hand gestures, or *mudra*, of Indian classical dance are used to narrate a story and to refer to objects, weather, nature and emotion (Carroll and Carroll 2012). Likewise, meanings can be sought in the creative act of making an object, not just in the finished object itself. In a recent study of spinning in Bronze Age Europe it has been argued that functionally equivalent regionally specific preferences in the direction of twist in yarn – clockwise (z-twist) and anti-clockwise (s-twist) – may have been related to cosmological notions that led to 'right' and 'wrong' ways of doing things in particular places (Bender Jørgensen 2013). In this case there is no division between the sacred and the profane. The knowledge of making is bound up with knowledge and understanding of the world embedded within the actions of the hands (Lakoff and Johnson 1999; Slepian and Ambady 2012). Furthermore, movements of the hands, especially when in sequence, assist and hold memory (Shusterman 2012; Bender Jørgensen 2013). This is something that we all employ in our everyday life through the establishment of routines such as laying the breakfast table or packing a suitcase (Bender Jørgensen 2013). The work of the hands, therefore, has the power not just to make but to evoke.

Since the crafting of things is not separate from life but is part of it, meaning can exist within the act of making. While the transformative nature of craft has often been understood as magical (Budd and Taylor 1995), the form-giving actions of craftspeople might be understood in terms of a literal making sense of the world. In other words, an embodied means of self-understanding in which imagination does not run riot but is put to a specific disciplined use (cf Adorno 1979). In this perspective, things are not made by chance or in a spirit of fantasy (Bâ 1976). Acts of creation have meaningful reasons and intent that go beyond the need for skilled technical solutions. Furthermore, not only do they involve transformations from raw materials to finished object, but they are intrinsically powerful acts. This is reflected, for example, in the persistent description of God as a potter in Judaic thought or the deliberate imperfections woven into Persian carpets since only Allah is perfect. Ethnographic accounts of craft frequently describe a relationship between the work of craftspeople and religious or other forms of social significance, such that ceramics, metalworking, wood working, leather working and weaving are more than utilitarian, domestic, economic or recreational occupations (Bâ 1976; Wade 1989; David 1990).

In his description of craft in West Africa, the intellectual and politician Amadou Hampâté Bâ (1976) describes how making objects can be simultaneously the expression of cosmic forces and a means of making contact with these forces. Here creativity is a matter of navigating the world with the hands.

In the following section I want to explore these arguments by examining the role of hands in the practice of Bronze Age craft, in particular, the modelling of clay that resulted in miniatures and figurines. My focus is on the processes involved in the forming and shaping of objects rather than on their decoration.

Creativity and the Hands: The Case of Early and Middle Bronze Age Miniatures and Figurines

Ceramic miniatures and figurines are found throughout much of the Carpathian Basin during the Early and Middle Bronze Age (2500–1400 BC). They include items such as wagons, wheels, chariots, boats, axes, chairs, houses, ovens, and miniature vessels. There are also anthropomorphic, aviform and zoomorphic objects including human figurines, human feet (either on their own or as part of other objects), bird rattles and animal figurines. Some of these are one-offs or very rare in the region, such as the house from Karaburma in Serbia (Todorović 1977), the clay axes from Ostrovu Mare in Romania (Chicideanu 1995) or the boat from Darda in Croatia (Kiss 2007). Others occur in numbers. For instance, eighty-nine clay wagons are currently known from the Carpathian Basin, of which more than sixty date to the Bronze Age (Bondár 2012). There are dozens of clay birds from throughout the region (Guba and Szeverényi 2007; Maričević and Sofaer 2012; Bulatovic 2013), while there are more than 100 human figurines from sites primarily along the River Danube (Jovanović 2011). Plastic modelling also sometimes formed an integral part of ceramic vessels in ways that literally turned the whole vessel into a human, bird or animal through the manner of vessel formation. These include, for example, vessels with human feet such as that from Iváncsa in Hungary (Tompa 1935), a range of different kinds of bird-shaped vessels such as from Vatin in Serbia (Milleker 1905; Kovács 1972a) or Bökénymindszent in Hungary (Kovács 1977), askoi such as those from Zók-Várhegy (Tompa 1935) or Tiszafüred (Kovács 1977) in Hungary, as well as vessels that were turned into birds through the addition of bird head protomes, such as from Feudvar in Serbia (Reich 2005) or Žuto Brdo-Gârla Mare cups from Romania (Şandor-Chicideanu 2003). Clay modelling forms part of a regional tradition that can be traced back to the Neolithic and Copper Age (Bailey 2005; Bondár and Székely 2011), and that also extended into the Late Bronze Age (Kalicz-Schreiber 2010). The diversity of three-dimensional modelling and thus the use of clay as a medium for creativity, however, is particularly striking in the Early and Middle Bronze Age.

Ceramic models have been found in both settlement and cemetery contexts, although there are trends linking particular types of models with specific kinds of setting. For example, the Early to Middle Bronze Age animal figures of the Hatvan and Mad'arovce cultures in the north of Hungary and south-west Slovakia have been found on settlement sites (Kovács 1977; Tárnoki 2003), whereas the Middle Bronze Age elaborately decorated human figurines of the Žuto Brdo-Gârla Mare culture in the lower Danube region have been found primarily (although by no means exclusively) in cemeteries (Şandor-Chicideanu and Chicideanu 1990). There may also be geographical distinctions in the deposition of models. For example, bird-shaped rattles have been found in settlements in the north and east of the Carpathian Basin and in graves in the west (Guba and Szeverényi 2007). In the south and south-east they are found in both (Vukmanović and Popović 1996). There are also several stray finds or objects that entered museum collections through the work of antiquarians or private collectors for which context is uncertain.

Given their relative rarity compared to ceramic vessels, often visually striking appearance, and potential to lend insights into Bronze Age life because of their representational nature, clay models have been the focus of substantial archaeological attention. By far the most common understanding of ceramic models is that they had a ritual or cultic role, in the sense that they materialised belief systems or assisted in practices connected with these (Harding 2000). Perhaps some of the clearest possibilities for ritual use can be identified in models of birds, not least because bird symbolism was widespread in the European Late Bronze Age (Jockenhövel 1997; Wirth 2006; Guba and Szeverényi 2007). On the basis of their broad bills, many of the clay models appear to be of water birds, the only animal able to move between air, land and water (Vasić and Vasić 2000). Human-bird figures such as on the large and small clay chariots from Dupljaja, Serbia, bird-shaped representations standing on human feet such as the rattle from Királyszentistvan, Hungary, or the human face on the bird-shaped *askos* from Tizafüred, as well as rarer bird–animal combinations expressed as birds with horns or human–animal combinations, have been suggested to express mythical creatures (Kovács 1977, 1981; Reich 2005; Guba and Szeverényi 2007; Neagoe 2011; Palincaş 2012). A specific group of bird-shaped clay objects are rattles.

Their use to make noise has been considered part of shamanic or magical practices (Krstić 1985, 2003; Guba and Szeverényi 2007). More recently, analysis of an *askos* from Alsóvadász-Várdomb, Hungary, revealed the presence of animal proteins and high iron levels suggestive of blood, and it has been proposed that the vessel was used in some form of libation ceremony (Szathmári 2003a; Guba and Szeverényi 2007).

On the basis that some objects are scaled down or miniature versions of larger originals, ceramic models, in particular those of 'everyday' objects such as boats, ovens or carts, have also been regarded as toys (Šimić 2000; Kiss 2003, 2011; Medović 2006; Bondár and Székely 2011; Balen and Rendić Miočević 2012). A relatively small number of mortuary studies in which associations have been identified between ceramic models and young individuals have augmented this interpretation. For example, in burials of the north Transdanubian Encrusted Pottery group at the sites of Mosonszentmiklós in Hungary and Malá nad Hronom in Slovakia, young children were in some cases buried together with miniature objects and distinct grave goods (Kiss 2007). At the Žuto Brdo-Gârla Mare cemetery of Cârna in Romania, female figurines were found in some of the most well-furnished graves which were also those of children, leading to suggestions of inherited status as well as the idea that the figurines were placed there in order to protect the young and vulnerable deceased (Dumitrescu 1961; Şandor-Chicideanu and Chicideanu 1990). Miniatures are, however, also found on settlement sites, such as a clay oven and miniature vessels from the Middle Bronze Age Vatya tell settlement at Százhalombatta, Hungary. In these settings no such associations can be derived, and miniatures may have been made and used by a range of different people. Recent work on ceramic models in Neolithic and Bronze Age Aegean contexts has opened up other interpretative possibilities that might yet be considered in relation to the Early and Middle Bronze Age miniatures from the Carpathian Basin. These have theorised the extent to which scaled-down objects faithfully reproduce full-scale originals (Bailey 2005; Knappett 2012). A distinction has been drawn between those that retain the detail of the original and those that are less detailed, more abstract representations (Bailey 2005). The significance of this distinction, however, has been questioned on the grounds that by definition models or miniatures do not retain the function of the original object and that all models therefore represent an abstraction of sorts (Knappett 2012). It has been argued that miniatures form points in a semiotic network that exists within assemblages, and that miniatures have potential to intensify or distill meaning (Hagen 2002; Knappett 2012).

Some types of ceramic models, in particular those of bird-shaped vessels
and human figurines, show striking patterns of distribution along major
waterways, especially along the River Danube (Letica 1973; Majnarić-
Pandžić 1982; Guba and Szeverényi 2007; Biehl 2008). The Danube has
long been recognised as playing a significant role as artery for prehistoric
communication and exchange (Childe 1929; Letica 1973; Szentmiklosi 2006;
Biehl 2008; Kiss 2011). On this basis, and on the basis of geographical
differences in style, the figurines in particular have been used to explore
questions of inter- and intra-regional contact in the Bronze Age, although
scholars sometimes seem to assume somewhat contradictory positions.
Female figurines with a bell-shaped skirt have been divided into three
geographical groups. These correspond to a western group, including sites
from Baranja and Syrmia-Slavonia; the middle group, including sites from
Eastern Slavonia, Baóka, and mid-Banat; and the east/south-east group,
including the south-east Banat, the Serbian part of the Danube region,
Romania, and Bulgaria (Letica 1973). Based on stylistic analysis these three
groups are said to express chronological development from an older western,
more naturalistically depicted group, with a gradual increase in abstraction
over time, such that the south-eastern group has reduced highly stylised head
and facial features (Letica 1973). By contrast, the same suite of objects have
been used to describe systems of contact and communication between the
lower Danube region and Mycenae in Greece (Biehl 2008). In this interpretation the figurines are local imitations of Mycenaean figural representations, albeit ones that did not follow the same manner of creation, meaning
or function of the Mycenaeans, either because they did not know them or did
not wish to. Instead the figurines were part of a transfer of new symbols and
ideas linked to the Myceneaean acquisition of raw materials, in particular
copper ore, as a result of which the people of the lower Danube sought to
ideationally and symbolically connect themselves to mighty Mycenae and to
differentiate themselves from the neighbouring regions (Biehl 2008).

The figurines have also been used to reflect upon costume and gendered
social identity (Kovács 1972b, 1977; Matthäus 1985; Blischke 2002; Palincaş
2010, 2013; Bondár and Székely 2011; Grömer, Rösel-Mautendorfer and
Schumacher-Jovanović 2011; Bender Jørgensen 2013). There are a variety
of different kinds of figurines including simple highly stylised more plank-
like objects such as the Early Bronze Age Zók figurine from Velemszentvid
in Hungary (Kalicz 1968), solid figurines that seem to be wearing very
clearly defined jewellery such as the Middle Bronze Age so-called Dalj
idol from Croatia (Hoffiller 1928), highly elaborate and detailed figurines
with bell-shaped skirts that are more sculptural in nature such as the famous

Middle Bronze Age Žuto Brdo-Gârla Mare figurine from Kličevac in Serbia (Letica 1973), as well as much more abstract variants of such bell-shaped skirt figurines with highly elaborate decoration suggesting costume such as from Cârna in Romania (Dumitrescu 1961). The figurines from the lower Danube region are richly decorated with incised and white inlayed decoration. They appear to be wearing very elaborate necklaces and other jewellery, decorated skirts and also possibly make up and tattoos, although the latter two are debated (Harding 2000; Jovanović 2011). Even figurines that are quite simple in form such as the Early Bronze Age Hatvan torso from Szurdokpüspoki (Kovács 1977 plate 8-9) or Early Bronze Age Makó head of a figurine from Kőérberek (Horváth et al. 2005) in Hungary may have quite complex and detailed decoration. In the case of the former the decoration resembles embroidery. In the latter the figure seems to be wearing a semicircular headdress and perhaps earrings.

Ceramic models have also been used to trace Bronze Age technological and social developments. This is particularly so for wagons and boats, both of which have been considered as evidence for the role of transport in trade and exchange (Kiss 2007, 2011; Bondár and Székely 2011). Furthermore, wagons have been used as evidence for the secondary products revolution in terms of animal traction as well as the types of wagons used in the Bronze Age (Sherratt 1983; Bondár and Székely 2011).

The Act of Modelling

Irrespective of meaning, each model is the outcome of a series of creative acts of the hands within the modelling process. No two models are identical, even if the form is part of a genre (cf Bondár and Székely 2011). Furthermore, although some kinds of models are made in similar ways, typological classifications of others are not closely tied to the methods of modelling which give rise to form. Thus, for example, human figurines which appear to have different formal typological characteristics (Trbuhović 1956–57; Garašanin 1983; Şandor-Chicideanu and Chicideanu 1990) share similar forming principles and techniques, while the typological classification of bird representations (Guba and Szeverényi 2007) does not always accord with making practices.

Forming techniques used in making models frequently differ from those employed in the production of ceramic vessels, reflecting a different series of decisions faced by potters and different movements of the hands to those routinely used in the bulk of their work (Maričević and Sofaer 2012). In particular, the coiling and slab-building methods seen in the vessels of many Early and Middle Bronze Age groups in the Carpathian Basin, as well as the less common paddle and anvil technique (Kreiter, Budden and Sofaer 2006; Sofaer 2006; Sofaer and Budden 2009), were rarely used for clay models. Instead, many of the models were made by thumbing out, pinching, rolling out and folding clay shapes, or combinations of these.

These different kinds of manipulations, along with the hand movements and grips required in order to make objects using these techniques, can be traced in the archaeological record, as can the use of tools in forming and decorating. Clay is a plastic additive medium (Budden 2008), and the properties of clay are constant and predictable. It is therefore possible to explore embodied creativity by reconstructing the making sequence, combinations and complexity of hand actions that express the embodied knowledge of the potter. In the Bronze Age in the Carpathian Basin these can be related to two different categories of models: first, those that were made from a single piece of clay, and second, those that are additive forms made from two or more pieces joined together. These in turn can be subdivided into objects that are solid, those that are hollow but sealed, and those that have some kind of open void.

Objects Made from One Piece of Clay (Singular Forms)

Solid objects made from a single piece of clay are the simplest kinds of models in terms of the range of hand actions required in order to create them. Most often the clay was held in one hand (either cradled or, if a more secure hold was desired, using a cupping grip) and the clay was pinched out with the other hand. In the case of the small animal figures of sheep and pig from the Hatvan settlement of Piliny (Kovács 1977) and some from the Hatvan level at Jászdózsa-Kápolnahalom (Tárnoki 2003) such pinching movements were used to create the legs and head (Figure 1.1). In the case of a Vatin bird (Milleker 1905) the head and tail feather have been pinched out of the clay body of the bird (Figure 1.2). This model has a solid body but may have been supported on a stick during the modelling process (or designed to fit on a pole and therefore impressed by a stick) resulting in a somewhat finger-puppet-like appearance.

Other objects made from one piece of clay were thumbed out to create a void. These too are rather simple. Here the clay was likely held in a cupping grip in one hand and the tip or side of the thumb was used to work the clay up and out. In other words it was the forming of the void that lent the object shape and meaning (cf Heidegger 1971). In this sense this technique can be considered the opposite of pinching as it creates an object as a result of the construction of negative space (the void) rather than a positive pinching out. Examples of such objects include rather schematic models of ovens and miniature vessels (Figure 1.3).

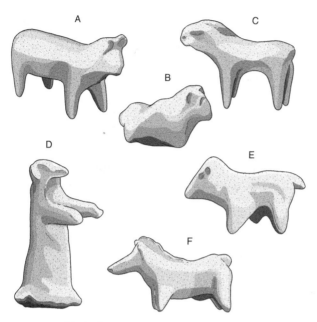

FIGURE 1.1 Pinched out animal figures: A–C) from Jászdózsa-Kápolnahalom, D) from Szihalom, E–F) from Piliny (redrawn after Kovács 1977).

Objects Made from Two or More Pieces of Clay (Additive Forms)

Although additive forms are more complex to make, as they may potentially involve several different kinds of actions in the making process, they are by far more common than those made from a single piece of clay. Manipulating clay in a range of ways through several kinds of hand actions offers scope for the production of a wider variety of objects and thus for creative expression.

Models made as solid additive forms include wagons, chairs and chariots. These were made by assembling several preformed clay pieces that had been made by pinching, rolling, flattening or cutting the clay into the desired shape. In order to join the different pieces together, elements of the model were probably held one in each hand using pinching or cupping grips and pressure was applied from both hands to push the pieces of clay together and to get them to stick. The join between the two pieces was smoothed out with finger or thumb movements, thereby also reinforcing the connection between the pieces. Where it was desired that more than two pieces should be joined, then the hand movements were repeated. For example, in the case of the so-called altar from Darda (Kovács 1977; Kiss 2007) the object is currently composed of five distinct pieces (a flat round and four legs), so the actions would have been

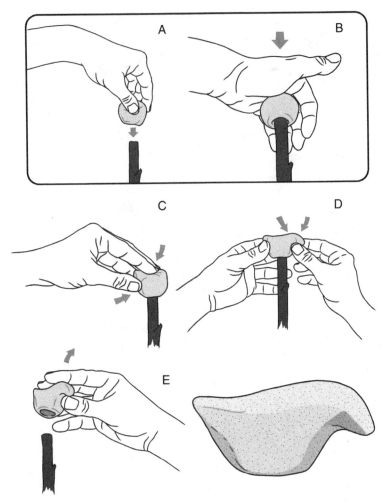

FIGURE 1.2 Actions involved in making a singular pinched out object: pinching out a bird from Vatin.

repeated four times (once for each leg) (Figure 1.4). It has been suggested that the object may at some stage also have had a back and therefore have been a chair (Kiss 2007), in which case at least one additional piece of clay would have been attached to the upper surface.

Hollow objects are a distinct group of additive forms and are primarily bird-shaped rattles. The body of the bird may be made out of two thumbed-out ovals joined together so as to form its belly and back, as is probably the case for a figurine from Mala Vrbica in north-east Serbia and a rattle from

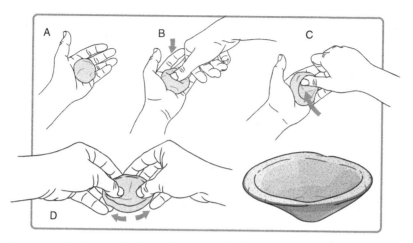

FIGURE 1.3 Actions involved in making a singular object with a void: thumbing out a miniature vessel from Százhalombatta.

Vatin (Garašanin 1972; Vukmanović and Popović 1996) (Figure 1.5). In many cases, however, rattles seem to have been constructed using precut sheets of clay such as in the rattles from Százhalombatta or Királyszentistván in Hungary (Thomas and Szentléleky 1959) (Figure 1.6). The sheets are of even thickness, suggesting that they may have been rolled out with a tool. A round or oval sheet was placed over a similarly shaped bottom sheet enclosing small pebbles. The two sheets were then pressed together around the margin in a series of pinching movements in a manner akin to crimping pastry along the edge of a pie that was later smoothed out. This method of making requires that the clay be neither too wet nor too dry so that the clay sheet neither sags nor cracks. Given the somewhat careful grip required to hold the rattle so as not to indent the clay and break the hollow bird shape of the object, for both these methods of constructing the body it is possible that the solid legs of the bird had been joined to its belly prior to the construction of the hollow body in order to avoid damaging the shape through the application of pressure while affixing the legs. The solid head was probably attached last, its shape being pinched out and then applied and the join smoothed out. In some cases, as for example the rattle from Vatin, this join appears to have been deliberately 'disguised' through decoration around the neck of the bird. The small eyes were most frequently impressed and feathers incised using tools with sharp narrow points, perhaps bones or sticks. Some bird rattles are smoothed and burnished and would therefore have been rubbed, possibly with leather or a pebble.

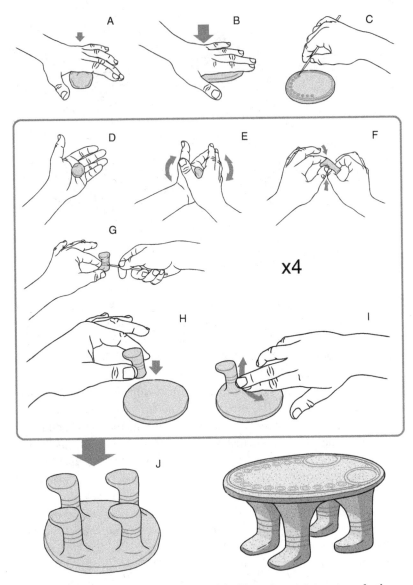

FIGURE 1.4 Actions involved in making a solid additive form: joining pieces for the 'altar' from Darda.

Additive forms with a void include vessels where the void acted as the body of an animal or bird. These objects were made using several sets of combinations of clay manipulation techniques and thus hand movements. Zoomorphic vessels such as the boar and sheep from Vatin-Bela

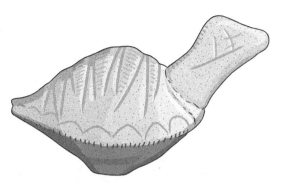

FIGURE 1.5 Thumbed-out ovals joined together to make a rattle from Vatin (redrawn after Garašanin 1972).

Bara in Serbia (Milleker 1905; Medović 2006) (Figure 1.7), many bird-shaped vessels and some *askoi* were made by an initial thumbing out of the clay to create the void during which the object was not gripped in a static manner but was probably rotated in order to achieve an even shape and wall thickness. Patches of clay were added to the thumbed out shape by squeezing in order to build up the thin walls of the object and to create a symmetrical shape. To attach the legs and head (if required), one hand was probably placed inside the void to apply counter-pressure as each of the legs was attached. Likewise, one hand probably gripped the object from the inside as finally the pinched out head or other anatomical features were attached. An alternative technique used to make some objects with a void, in particular bird vessels, combined thumbing out of the breast of the bird and the use of sheets of clay for its back in which a hole was located in order to provide access to the vessel, as in a bird vessel from Vatin (Milleker 1905; Kovács 1972a) (Figure 1.8). Like the rattles, many of these objects were smoothed and burnished, and embellished with incised and impressed decoration for which tools with sharp and rounded ends were used.

The making of vessels with bird-head protomes, widespread throughout the Žuto Brdo-Gârla Mare group, seems to have relied more upon estab-lished methods for making ceramic vessels. Although some vessel bodies were made through a combination of pinching and patching, others were produced by coiling thin rolls of clay. The bird head was almost always pinched out and attached to the rim of the vessel by pressing and smoothing around the join (Figure 1.9). These objects were smoothed and burnished and then elaborately decorated with incised, impressed and inlayed motifs.

A particularly distinctive suite of actions was used in the making of human figurines. The Žuto Brdo-Gârla Mare figurines with bell-shaped skirts from the lower Danube region (e.g. Dumitrescu 1961; Şandor-Chicideanu 2003)

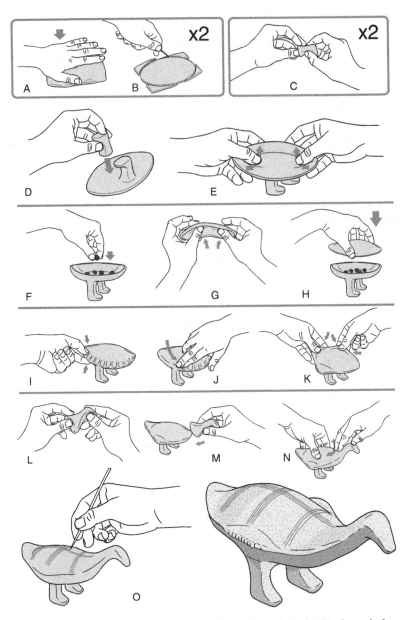

FIGURE 1.6 Actions involved in making a hollow additive form: bird rattle made from sheets of clay from Királyszentistván.

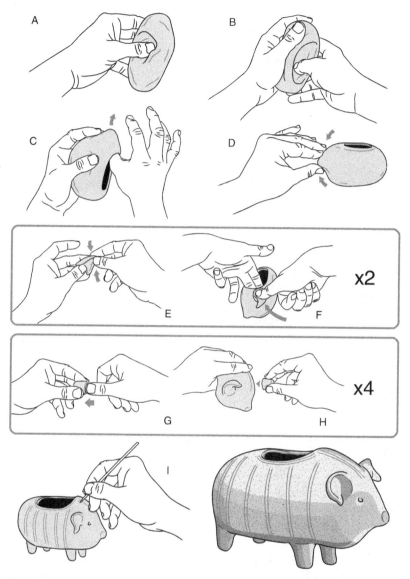

FIGURE 1.7 Actions involved in making an additive form with a void by thumbing out, patching and adding clay pieces: zoomorphic vessel in the shape of a boar from Vatin-Bela Bara.

were made in two sections. As their name suggests, the lower skirt section is frequently an inverted V- or U-shape. The form was created by taking a sheet of clay rolled to an even thickness and folding it in a similar manner to folding a napkin, such that the 'bell shape' was created (Figure 1.10). The edge of the

FIGURE 1.8 Bird vessel from Vatin with the body made from a combination of thumbing out and sheets of clay.

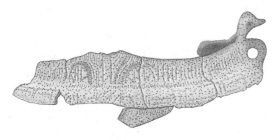

FIGURE 1.9 Vessel with bird-head protome from Vajuga-Pesak (redrawn after Premk et al. 1984).

fold was then pressed together and smoothed out. The body was made by folding over a sheet of clay to create the torso. This was then cut, pulled or squeezed into the desired body shape, and features such as the head or arms were pinched out or applied. The torso was then attached to the skirt. In some highly stylised variants the skirt of the figurine is more box-like, or the trapezoidal profile of the body may be replaced by a gentle wavy profile in which the flexibility of clay was exploited. Six headless figurines have a vertically pierced or partially perforated torso to which it has been suggested that an organic head might have been attached (Palincaş 2010). The figurines are frequently broken or cracked at the join between the torso and the skirt. This indicates that the fixing of the torso to the skirt was not always effective. Bronze Age potters also seem to have had concerns about disguising the join as they frequently concealed it with incised belts.

Modelling the World

The different ways of making clay models using the hands are expressions of embodied thought. They manifest a series of different principles and

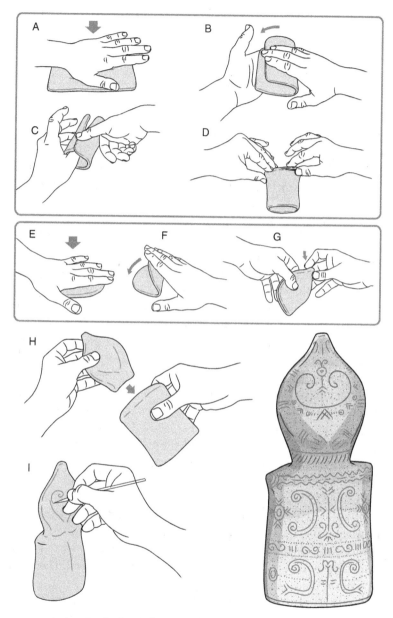

FIGURE 1.10 Actions involved in making an additive form by folding and adding: human figurine from Cârna.

practices in which the potential and challenge of clay as a plastic material was exploited and responded to in different ways to create a wide variety of forms. This creativity of the hands also extended to differing degrees of naturalism in modelling (Maričević and Sofaer 2012). For example, while some ceramic birds have been identified as belonging to specific species (Vasić and Vasić 2000), many others, while recognisable as birds, either lack features such as a head or wings or, as in the bird vessel from Dunaújváros and rattle from Füzesabony in Hungary, have extra features such as four legs (Kovács 1972a; Szathmári 2003b). It has been suggested that those on four legs are actually sitting on an altar (Kovács 1977), but the notable abstraction of other bird models and the relative body proportions of other clearly bird-like objects suggest that representation was not necessarily always intended to be realistic, allowing for creative expression (Maričević and Sofaer 2012). Likewise, a spectrum from realism to high abstraction in the human figurines defined in various typological schemes (Trbuhović 1956–57; Letica 1973; Garašanin 1983; Şandor-Chicideanu and Chicideanu 1990) suggests a creative engagement with understandings of the human form that was played out in clay (cf Palincaş 2010).

Such creative responses both to material and to the subjects that were modelled were, however, set within culturally and locally distinct traditions within the Carpathian Basin. While the general subjects that were chosen for modelling (objects, animals, birds, and humans) were fairly widespread throughout the region, their form and decoration were integrated into local practices. For example, the solid rather schematic Hatvan animal figurines in the north of the region contrast with the way that the decorated bodies of Vatin animals in the south-east were made as voids so that the animal became a vessel. Throughout the region birds were formed in a variety of ways, but they were decorated nonetheless in a manner that accorded with local styles of pottery decoration (Maričević and Sofaer 2012). Human figurines were made as solid objects in Hungary and Croatia, but in Serbia and Romania they have solid bodies attached to skirts made as voids. These too are decorated according to local traditions (Letica 1973; Şandor-Chicideanu 2003).

The deliberate integration of clay models into local traditions suggests the existence of communities of practice within which there were shared ideas that people learnt regarding 'how to do things' (cf Kohring 2013). With regard to the human figurines in the lower Danube region, it has been suggested that the making of figurines was based on a system understood by makers in which body shape, position, specific body parts, and

FIGURE 1.11 Cross section of figurine from Ravno Selo showing a folding-over making technique (photograph: D. Maričević).

gestures all held meaning (Biel 2006, 2008). Potters therefore were not entirely at liberty to create as they wished, but operated within a framework of rule-bound creativity where local decorative traditions and individual variation of a series of well-known design motifs offered a degree of freedom (Biehl 2006).

It is striking that many of the human figurines from throughout the region, both solid and those with bell-shaped skirts, seem to have been made using a shared technique to form the torso. Many figurines were broken at the waist, either deliberately or accidently, although they have subsequently been reconstructed for purposes of museum display. Nonetheless, this pattern of breakage means that forming techniques are sometimes visible. Where this is the case, the torsos appear to have been made in a similar manner to the Žuto Brdo-Gârla Mare figurines by folding a sheet of clay over on itself and subsequently shaping features such as arms or legs. For instance, a figurine from Ravno Selo in Serbia displays the same folding over technique as is found further south (Figure 1.11). Thus, there appears to have been a widespread understanding of how to form the human body that transcended both local communities of practice and any semiotic meanings attached to the configuration of the finished figurines. Given the range of gestures used to form other kinds of models, this method of making the human body was by no means the only technical solution available to Bronze Age potters, nor does it necessarily appear to modern eyes to be the most obvious one. It was a learnt technique that united several local groups within a larger regional community of practice.

It is tempting to interpret the folding over of clay to form the torso in terms of a widespread Bronze Age understanding of the fundamental nature of the human body itself. In other words, the common use of folded clay to form the body in a manner that went beyond other obvious local typological and decorative distinctions may have been linked to Bronze Age conceptions of the body as a folded entity. Recent research on the Žuto Brdo-Gârla Mare figurines has explored the ways that their iconography might reflect the world-view of the people who produced and used them, in particular the relationship between the human body and cosmological understandings (Palincaş 2010). Similarly, ethnographic and historical studies have revealed a wide variety of understandings of the human body expressed in material culture more generally, often linked to principles of cosmogony and human creation myths (e.g. Blier 1987; Barley 1994; Parker Pearson and Richards 1994). It is therefore possible that in the Bronze Age of the Carpathian Basin, a period and region rich in myths and cosmology, that the creativity involved in making the figurines might be understood as mirroring a wider cultural understanding of the creation of the living human body. If so, the hand actions of potters may have held meaning that was part of a shared belief system, such that the act of making evoked and echoed human creation itself.

The creativity of the hands, therefore, may have been a matter of working through and creating ones place in the world. This understanding can be applied not only to the human figurines but also to the clay birds, as well as to human-object and human-bird combinations that formed part of Bronze Age cosmological notions. Perhaps these objects were 'portholes through which to contemplate the cosmos' (Bâ 1976: 383), and maybe even a means of making physical contact with it through clay. The act of making was therefore a creative expression of experience and knowledge of the world. The creativity of the hands was an embodied understanding of self.

Encountering Creativity through the Hands: A Note

This exploration of creativity through the miniatures and figurines has itself required an encounter through the hands. It is largely by feeling examples – and to a lesser extent my own somewhat crude attempts at modelling – that it has been possible to understand the processes involved in their making. Objects mediate an experience of the processes by which they were made. In a way they 'invite the viewer/user to touch the hand of the maker' (Pallasmaa 2009: 104). Holding a handmade object is an intimate encounter where one touches what others have made and, in doing so, glimpses their embodied creative experience. When, quite understandably, these objects are put out of reach behind museum glass they tantalise and tease; the encounter is incomplete. As the architect Juhani Pallasmaa put it, 'The surface of an old object, polished to perfection by the tool of the craftsman and the assiduous hands of its users, seduces the stroking of the hand . . . . The tactile sense connects us with time and tradition: through impressions of touch we shake the hands of countless generations' (Pallasmaa 2005: 56).

CHAPTER 2

Recycling

The Reuse of Materials and Objects

In the twenty-first century, voices of gloom speak of economic and ecological crises. We are urged to cut back on consumption and to use fewer resources. In the words of a recent British environmental campaign to, 'reduce, reuse and recycle'. So-called sustainable innovation is seen as emerging as an important force for change in business and society in which products and services are developed with the aim of reducing environmental and resource impacts, and of improving efficiency (Larson 2000; Roy 2000). Yet at the same time in modern Europe we live, in the words of sociologist Zygmunt Bauman (2005), in a 'liquid society' where the well-being of its members hangs on the swiftness with which products are consigned to waste. 'In that society nothing may claim exemption from the universal rule of disposability, and nothing may outstay its welcome. The steadfastness, stickiness, viscosity of things inanimate and animate alike are the most sinister and terminal of dangers, sources of the most frightening of fears and the targets of the most violent of assaults' (Bauman 2005: 3).

Recycling, and its counterpart destruction, both offer possibilities for the creation of the new in which objects and materials have to be rethought. It is this creativity in reshaping and rethinking the possibilities of things that I wish to address in this essay. My case study is the Bronze Age tell site of Százhalombatta, Hungary. Here people lived surrounded by clay, yet they made striking, deliberate decisions about the recycling of ceramics. They also made decisions about when to end the lives of things in what might be termed a 'creative destruction' (Schumpeter 1942; Bauman 2005) which enabled them to start making things anew.

Recycling and Rethinking Objects and Materials

Things can be recycled as wholes, in parts, or as materials. In my local playground an old tyre has been converted into a swing. My neighbour cuts plastic bottles in half and uses them as cloches to protect his plants from winter frost. Cars and electrical products are stripped to recycle the metals within them. In all cases recycling involves an ability to create relationships and effect transformations.

In the case of whole and part objects, recycling redefines the original artefact. An object is removed from its original context and used for another purpose, yet this simultaneously recognises that its value resides as an already made thing. In this sense the very decontextualisation of the object can become part of a creative act, generating novelty and moving away from the expected (Guerra and Zuccoli 2012). For example, a modern potter may reuse a fork as a tool to decorate pots. At its extreme, radical decontexualisation can provoke surprise and shock as, for example, in the work of the artist Marcel Duchamp, who famously and controversially submitted *Fountain* – a urinal – to the Society of Independent Artists exhibition in 1917. Yet the movement of an object from one field to another can also become acceptable over time as people get used to it. In 2004 *Fountain* was voted the most influential artwork of the twentieth century (Jury 2004).

The redefinition of whole and part objects also takes place through the possibilities that recycling offers for the reshuffling and recombination of things. Thus the swing in the park is made by combining an old truck tyre with rope and a wooden gantry from which it hangs. Here creativity resides in recreation: the making of something from something (cf Liep 2001; Pope 2005: 41). Of course, things can be combined serendipitously or by accident (Ingold 1986; Leach 2004). So a precondition for creativity is that this process of combination is deliberately directed and that it results in novelty of form or outcome (Leach 2004; see also 'Margins', this volume). In the recycling of an object, this process of recombination adds another chapter to the object's life cycle.

With respect to the recycling of materials, creativity lies in the reincorporation of the material and the construction of the new as if from scratch. Here perceived value lies not in the object but in the material from which it is made; the form of the original object is not important. This is a familiar concept in Bronze Age studies in terms of the recycling of metal as scrap to create new items (Harding 2000). The recycling of materials necessarily involves the destruction of an original object in order to move on to the making of a new one. This creative destruction is the 'darker' side of the

creative process, connecting it with concepts of loss (Jeanes 2006). It highlights a relationship between creativity and control over resources, such that
creativity can also be employed in projects of seduction, control and
domination (Liep 2001: 5). Creativity thus involves a tension between the
old and the new that involves making judgments about where the perceived
value of things lies and what constitutes value, be that economic, social,
historical, emotional or a combination of these.

The creative reimagining of both objects and materials requires an
understanding of their potentials and possibilities based on knowledge of
their characteristics or affordances (cf Knappett 2005) – in other words,
their properties, form and suitability for a new function. This has been
described in terms of 'listening to objects' (Gandini 2005) and the development of an 'alphabet of materials' (Piazza 1997) in which the creation of a
language takes place through the development of gestures, tools and
experience of materials. Learning this language takes place through interacting with objects and developing a familiarity with them. It is not simply a
matter of abstract intellectual thought but of physical experience (cf Leach
2004). Thus objects and materials can suggest and inspire ideas, but it is
only through working with them that their properties and potentials
become clear. It is during the construction of a relationship with materials
(the interaction between people and things) that possibilities of modification, transformation and structuring present themselves (Piazza 1997). This
process of discovery includes the acquisition of a wide spectrum of knowledge including, for example, texture, shape, form, colour, and weight. As
different objects and materials have different qualities, this means that each
has its own alphabet which can be combined with other materials in order
to create something new.

Understanding the qualities of an object or material is partly a matter of
getting to grips with its physical characteristics; a water jug that is made of a
permeable material is not going to be practical. Yet objects and materials
also have culturally or even subject-specific emotional logics described
through the feelings that their use evokes or recalls (Guerra and Zuccoli
2012). For example, the allure of silk underwear lies in its sexy or romantic
connotations, while fleece or wool used to make a teddy bear appeal to a
desire for softness and cuddliness. Similarly, materials may have social or
symbolic references, such as in the modern British notion of ruby and
diamond wedding anniversaries, or a Bronze Age association between gold
and the sun (Springer and Grebe 2003). In this sense, working with
materials and knowing what something is 'good for' is an interweaving of
cognitive and imaginative ways of knowing. The Cornwall-based potter

Helen Marton has talked about this in terms of the 'resonance' of materials in which physical qualities, symbolic and emotional dimensions, and cultural and historical associations are linked together in the choices she makes in creating a new object (Marton 2012). Thus she is drawn to using local Gabbroic clay because of its tremendous plasticity, versatility and aesthetic qualities, which appeal to her need to form and fire. Equally important, however, is her emotional connection with the material, arising from the associations it has with where she lives and its long history of use by potters, which stretches back to the Bronze Age (Marton 2012). A familiarity with the qualities of objects and materials on one hand may open up new horizons, but on the other may have deeply rooted social, symbolic, and emotional associations. Listening to materials simultaneously makes traces of their identity emerge while bringing out our own experiences (Gandini and Kaminsky 2005).

Creativity, therefore, is based on a knowledge of objects and materials and their possibilities for use (Guerra and Zuccoli 2012). The question remains, however, as to why recycle? In other words, what are the conditions for this kind of creativity? The imperative for rethinking objects is not necessarily always self-evident and depends upon social attitudes to their integrity. In this sense the creativity expressed in recycling is socially and culturally specific. On one hand, people may be pushed into recycling in a 'needs must' scenario in which the scarcity of resources forces them to seek radical new ways of responding to daily needs. Such responses are visible in shanty towns around the world (Neuwirth 2006), although the 'unregulated zone of creativity' arising from the precariousness and deprivation of such places runs the risk of romanticisation (Savage 2010: 493). In an archaeological setting, it has been suggested that at the Late Bronze Age site of Tiryns in Greece, a scarcity of resources may have stimulated creativity within the workshops through the recycling of materials such as metal, plaster for lime and sherds used as gaming pieces (Brysbaert and Vetters 2012).

On the other hand, recycling can also take place under conditions of abundance, in which case it is a matter of attitudes towards waste and to the objects and materials to be disposed of. In modern European and American societies, often characterised in terms of wastefulness, this may sometimes be a question of social conscience linked to an awareness of the consequences of not recycling, as evident in the drive to recycle glass in order to reduce the pressure on landfill sites. It may also arise, however, from more intangible social attitudes that can be described in terms of thrift – in other words, a desire to conserve resources before reaching a moment of crisis, thereby pre-empting the possibility of scarcity. This may involve modifying or mending existing objects rather than throwing them away in order to renew them because of, or in order to maintain, their value. It also implies an attachment to, or a requirement for, an object to a degree that makes its repair worthwhile.

Under conditions of both scarcity and abundance the reuse and recycling of materials is a matter of problem-solving or smoothing out 'kinks' between design and reality (Ingold and Hallam 2007: 4) that sit in the everyday (Brysbaert and Vetters 2012). The creativity implicated in this rethinking of objects and materials may involve either premeditation or on-the-spot improvisation, but both can only take place in the context of accumulated knowledge and understandings. The new thus takes shape thanks to the ability to effect relationships and transformations based on knowledge and the perceived social, economic, ethical, symbolic, and emotional needs that people have (Guerra and Zuccoli 2012).

Creativity and Recycling: The Case of Százhalombatta

The site of Százhalombatta is situated on the right bank of the Danube, 30 km south of Budapest in Hungary (Figure 2.1). It is one of the largest and best preserved Bronze Age temperate tell settlements in central Europe. The site today is 200 m by 100 m in area, although it is estimated that up to one-third of the original area may have been destroyed during clay extraction by a local brick factory and erosion by the River Danube (Poroszlai 2000). The site was first occupied at the end of the Early Bronze Age (the classic Nagyrév [Szigetszentmiklós] to late Nagyrév [Kulcs] transition). It was continuously inhabited through the Middle Bronze Age Vatya period and Vatya-Koszider horizon at the end of the Middle Bronze Age, to the start of the Late Bronze Age. There followed a hiatus in occupation until the Urnfield phase of the Late Bronze Age, during which the site was again in use into the Iron Age. Occupation layers at the site are up to 6 m deep, and the majority of these date to the Early–Middle Bronze Age (2000–1500/1400 BC).

The site has been the subject of three excavation campaigns: the first in 1963 (Kovács 1969), the second in 1989–1993 (Poroszlai 1996, 2000), and an ongoing international excavation that started in 1998 (Vicze and Poroszlai 2004; Earle and Kristiansen 2010; Sofaer, Sørensen, and Vicze 2012; Sofaer, Vicze, and Sørensen forthcoming). The settlement was built on a bluff with valleys to the north and south and the River Danube to the east. It was fortified with a rampart and ditch to the west, a feature common to other

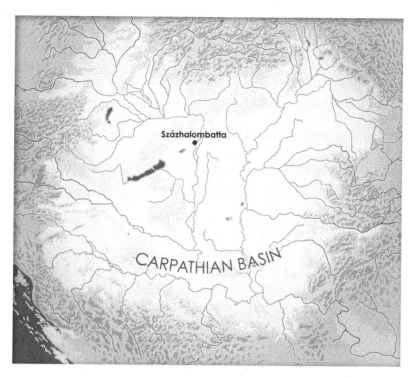

FIGURE 2.1 Map of the Carpathian Basin showing the location of Százhalombatta.

Vatya tells (Poroszlai 2000, 2003). Positioned at the end of the Benta valley, it controlled access to the tells and other settlements within the valley, as well as access to the River Danube. Current excavations focus on domestic contexts and are producing detailed new data revealing a picture of settlement structure, architecture and life inside Bronze Age houses (Vicze 2005; Sofaer 2010; Sørensen 2010; Sofaer 2011).

The settlement at Százhalombatta was densely packed. Houses were built and rebuilt on top of each other, separated by narrow, trampled earth streets or arranged around open areas (Vicze 1992; Sørensen 2010). In some cases they were so close together that the roofs may have touched at their base. There seems to have been a consistent use of house plots, suggesting a kind of community orderliness, control and agreement (Vicze 1992; Sørensen 2010; Sofaer 2011). The houses have a rather similar size and layout. They are rectangular with rounded corners, with a pitched roof and a single south-facing porched entrance off one of the streets. They fall into two size categories: the larger are two-room houses approximately

5 m by 10–11 m in size; the smaller are one-room houses approximately 5 m by 8–9 m (Poroszlai 2003; Sørensen 2010). In most cases, the larger houses seem to have been built by extending the one-room houses to the north in order to create additional space (Sørensen 2010). The size and configuration of dwellings suggest occupancy by single families (Sørensen 2010). The similarity in house sizes suggests the existence of rules regarding the equitable division of space on the tell, the notion of the household, and how much space individual households required (Sofaer 2011).

Finds from the site include pottery, metalwork, moulds, loom weights, phytoliths, worked wood, bone and stone, faunal and human remains. Of these, pottery is the most abundant, with almost two tonnes recovered since 1998, including many complete or partially complete vessels. From the Early Bronze Age through to the end of the Middle Bronze Age there is a wide range of vessels forming an exceptionally rich assemblage. Basic types such as cups, bowls, jugs, cooking vessels and storage vessels are present throughout and form the core of the assemblage, but the range and elaboration of vessels within each of these categories changes, resulting in complex typological variation (Budden 2007; Budden and Sofaer 2009; Vicze 2011). There are also miniature forms that replicate the assemblage as a whole. The transition from the Early to the Middle Bronze Age sees an increase in the range of forms within individual vessel types as well as the introduction of new types (Budden and Sofaer 2009), traditionally understood as a result of the conjunction of shifting cultural traditions of the Nagyrév and the influence of contemporary Kisapostag communities that gave rise to the emergence of the Vatya tradition (Bóna 1975; Poroszlai 2000). In the Vatya-Koszider phase at the end of the Middle Bronze Age, the range of vessel forms decreases, but there is noticeable elaboration and exaggeration of existing forms (Sofaer 2006; Budden 2007; Vicze 2011).

The assemblage is extremely rule-bound, and each vessel type has specific forms of decoration, fabrics, wall thickness and size ranges, although they do not fall easily into traditional categorisations of coarse and fine wares (Sofaer, Vicze, and Sørensen forthcoming). The Vatya and Vatya-Koszider ceramics from Százhalombatta have a distinct quality and style, notably in the tablewares (Budden 2007), while recent petrological and geochemical work has demonstrated that the overwhelming majority of the pottery at the site is locally made (Kreiter et al. 2007). In contrast, the Urnfield pottery represents a much more restricted range of vessel types with a clear distinction between coarse and fine wares. Fine wares include almost heart-shaped cups with high strap handles, straight-sided bowls, so-called turban rim bowls with inverted fluted rims and fluted (channeled) storage vessels. The coarse wares include cooking pots and large storage vessels.

Ceramics were not the only use of clay at Százhalombatta. The site is situated on a substantial local clay deposit, and there is an abundance of the material at the site. It was used for sun-dried loom weights, large weights that may have been used for weighing down roofs, and spindle whorls. In particular, clay was an important resource for building houses. The houses are exceptionally well-preserved through burning. This means that it is possible to gain detailed insights into the use of materials, revealing that the use and control over clay, and its combination with other materials, were vital to everyday life. Walls were made of wattle and daub, floors were made of clay or beaten earth that was usually layered with clean yellow clay and covered with matting (Kovács 2008; Sofaer 2010). Internal features of the house were made of clay, including built-in storage vessels and clay bins attached to the walls. Hearths, ovens and additional small grill-like hearths, with associated clean platform-like work surfaces, were also made of clay (Sørensen 2010). Life on the tell deployed a complex and sophisticated use of local building materials that were deliberately combined in specific ways to create particular architectural elements with different mixes and tempers (Kovács 2008; Sofaer 2010). The overwhelming use of local clay, while clearly practical and expedient, may also have bound people to the site through a close relationship between place and material expression, and control over desirable local resources. It also involved the recycling of both objects and materials.

Recycling Objects (Parts and Wholes) at Százhalombatta

At the end of the Vatya-Koszider horizon, the people living on the tell at Százhalombatta deliberately buried a series of pottery deposits in pits (Poroszlai 1996, 2000). One of the most remarkable of these was excavated during the 1989–1991 excavation season. Level II Pit 2 contained thirty-one complete or almost complete vessels, including a number of elaborately decorated Vatya-Koszider jugs, jars, bowls of different kinds (both thin-walled tableware and more chunky domestic vessels), cups, a storage vessel, a cooking pot, and an unusual two-handled anthropomorphic storage vessel with plastic representation of two human hands and breasts (Kreiter 2005; Poroszlai 2000). It has been suggested that the later was particularly sym-bolically charged, representing a deity or linked to fertility (Kreiter 2005). In addition, there were several diagnostic rim sherds and body sherds belong-ing to these vessel types. Most of the body sherds were elaborately decorated black burnished wares with incised, and occasionally applied, decoration (Kreiter 2005). Given the visually striking and highly diagnostic nature of these sherds, alongside the way that they reiterate the forms of the complete vessels found within the pit, it is possible that they were selected to stand for complete vessels. The fill of the pit contained large amounts of ash and charcoal, as well as charred seeds (Poroszlai 2000). All in all, the large size of the deposit, the elaborate and symbolically charged ceramics deliberately placed within the pit, along with the deposition of seeds, suggest some kind of votive deposit rather than simply a cache to which the inhabitants of the tell someday hoped to return.

Although it is possible that some of the vessels within the pit were produced especially for deposition, the evidence suggests that most were probably not. All the vessels found in the pit, apart from the female anthropomorphic vessel, have parallels in domestic settings elsewhere on the tell. Furthermore, the complete cooking pot and a deep domestic bowl show traces of use wear. It is likely, therefore, that the majority of the vessels were deliberately moved from the domestic arena into the ritual context of the pit. In particular, the somewhat ordinary and mundane cooking pot, sherds from other cooking vessels and a deep domestic bowl used for food preparation were clearly and deliberately moved from their original context and juxtaposed with elaborate and complex tablewares used for serving of food. Thus they were manipulated both in terms of context and in association. Pit 2, therefore, represents a recycling of objects in which vessels with different qualities and functions were deliberately selected and combined to produce a single new entity: a votive deposit. Implicit in the idea of such a deposit is the notion that it will have some sort of effect upon the future, for example, in terms of a desire for a successful harvest or protection of the settlement. While the reasons for such a deposition may remain opaque, it nonetheless expresses a creativity in bringing these objects together to place them in a new context in a way that would otherwise not have taken place, and in the imagination required to anticipate the effects of this conjunction.

At Százhalombatta, ceramics were also recycled and refashioned for use as tools. There are a small number of sherds with a single highly abraded convex or straight edge that may have been used for scraping, smoothing or polishing. Elsewhere similar objects have been widely reported as pottery-making tools used for smoothing out coil joins or for burnishing (e.g. Van Gijn and Hofman 2008; Douglass and Heckman 2012; Skibo 2013). At Százhalombatta, such tools were found in household settings and in an open area between the houses that was, at some points, used as a working

FIGURE 2.2 Recycled vessel from Százhalombatta used as a token (photograph: J. Sofaer).

area. They are not associated, however, with clear evidence for pottery manufacturing and may potentially have been used for a variety of tasks. In the Middle Bronze Age ceramics were also recycled for use as counters or tokens, perhaps for gaming, and for spindle whorls (Figure 2.2). For both counters and spindle whorls it appears that particular kinds of storage vessels with a standard wall thickness of 7–10 mm were most frequently selected. The counters are round, generally undecorated, and typically 25–30 mm in diameter. Some have clipped edges, indicating that they have been cut from larger sherds. In only a few cases are the edges abraded. The spindle whorls are larger and discoid in shape with a hole drilled in the centre and were occasionally made from decorated sherds. They weigh between 12 and 125 g, within the weight range for purpose-made discoid clay spindle whorls at the site, suggesting that a particularly wide range of yarns were produced at Százhalombatta (Bergerbrant forthcoming). In these cases objects were converted into other objects with very different uses to the original. Creativity lies in the vision to reshape and make them into something else.

In addition to the recycling of ceramic vessels to make new objects, there is also evidence of alterations and modifications to existing vessels (Figure 2.3). The handle of a Vatya storage vessel was clipped in order to narrow and exaggerate its shape. It appears that the vessel had been curated and was modified simply in order to change its appearance, perhaps to make it more fashionable. In another case, an elaborately shaped Vatya-Koszider bowl with scalloped rim may have had its original handle broken

FIGURE 2.3 Alterations made to ceramic vessels at Százhalombatta: A) modified handle of a storage vessel, B) Vatya-Koszider bowl into which holes have been drilled (photographs: J. Sofaer and Matrica Museum).

and the point of attachment had been filed down so as to create a smooth surface. Two holes had then been drilled into the vessel wall in order to allow it to be suspended by a cord. The positioning of the holes some distance below the rim suggests that the bowl had been used for display purposes. While the elaborate shape of the vessel suggests that this may also have been an element of its original purpose, the alteration to the object removed any original potential for holding wet food or liquid; the position-ing of the suspension holes meant that this would no longer have been practical as liquid would have run out of the vessel unless only a very small amount was placed in the base of the bowl.

Such modifications suggest that the people living on the tell explicitly understood objects as having value. Notions of value were not confined to ceramics as stone and bone tools were also sharpened, reused, and modified. Some ceramic vessels, however, may have been particularly prized. The elaborate black burnished tableware bowls and jugs, for example, were not only complex angular shapes that required skilled potting (Budden 2008; Budden and Sofaer 2009), but the extremely fine fabrics of some vessels must also have required substantial investment of time in order to wedge and levigate the clay (Budden 2007). In modern contexts, the high value attached to clays laid down, in some cases over many years, has been pointed out (Budden 2007). A concern with value may also have extended to the resources used to fire ceramics, as it has been suggested that the relatively low firing of vessels placed in Vatya cemeteries may have been partly due to a desire to conserve fuel in cases where pots did not need to fulfil the same functions as in domestic situations (Budden 2007). Furthermore, in Vatya cemeteries ceramic vessels were the most frequent objects deposited with the deceased, and it has been suggested that pots may have been the primary means of displaying status (Vicze 2011).

Recycling Materials at Százhalombatta

At Százhalombatta, ceramics were also recycled as a material in such a way that the form of the vessel was not important. Broken pottery of all kinds was used in the construction of architecture, although the manner of its use was extremely variable even within a single house. For example, there were several different methods for fixing posts in postholes. In some cases, posts were inserted into precut holes and then packed with stones, clay or domestic refuse including broken ceramics, around the post; in others, postholes that were cut into cultural layers were left unpacked, perhaps because they were sufficiently stable as a result of existing house material beneath (Sofaer 2010). Although the basic architectural form of houses was quite prescribed, and general building methods were common among houses, this variability in the method of execution suggests a degree of expediency and flexibility in attitudes, perhaps arising out of a need to adapt construction to slightly unpredictable situations found on a tell surface (Sofaer 2010).

Within the houses, hearths were sometimes made by placing a layer of sherds onto an ashy charcoal substrate (Figure 2.4). The latter may have acted as a bed in order to hold the sherds in place and ensure that they were flat. The sherds were then plastered over so as to provide an even surface.

FIGURE 2.4 Hearth from Százhalombatta using recycled ceramics (photograph: J. Sofaer).

This recycling of broken ceramics exploited their thermal dynamic properties, ensuring an even distribution of heat over the surface of the hearth. The evidence from both the postholes and the hearths suggest that in dwelling on the tell the people living at Százhalombatta were alert to problem-solving and able to improvise creatively by drawing on their knowledge about the properties of materials and how to deploy and combine them. In any given situation they thought through what solutions might work, anticipated the consequences of their actions, and recycled material accordingly.

Broken pots, therefore, were viewed as a resource that could be recycled along with other domestic rubbish from household rubbish dumps. Recent excavations at Százhalombatta have revealed that the narrow alleys between the houses were used for domestic waste disposal (Sørensen 2010), providing both a convenient means of simultaneously discarding and of curating materials. Places for the disposal of waste in the settlement seem to have been regulated since waste was concentrated in particular kinds of locations. This may have been especially necessary given the densely packed living conditions on the tell, which encouraged the development of social rules regarding the use of space (Sofaer 2011). The recycling of ceramics may also have been advantageous in reducing the accumulation of waste on the tell.

In addition, ceramics were recycled in the manufacture of new vessels. Middle Bronze Age tablewares were lightly tempered with grog or fine sand. Storage vessels, including both biconical and globular vessels of large and medium size, are characterised by a restricted range of fabrics which most often include small amounts of grog temper, with or without other additions such as limestone or quartz; 82 per cent of such vessels had 1–7 per cent grog deliberately added to the clay matrix (Kreiter 2007). The grog exhibits remarkably similar composition (type, firing, size, and mineralogy) to the surrounding clay matrix, suggesting that potters may have used their own broken vessels as temper in potting recipes (Kreiter 2007). Such a practice would imply the deliberate accumulation by potters of a stash of vessels that could be ground up for grog when required. Whether potters sought out their own vessels or whether users returned them to their makers when vessels were no longer required is an open question. In either of these scenarios such a system of recycling would require social engagement in order for it to take place. A third possibility is that potters may have recycled wasters, vessels that they were unable to exchange, or that they may even have made deliberately to crush into grog.

The complexity and consistency in the manufacture of large storage vessels suggests that they were made by experienced potters. Indeed, it has been posited that a system of apprenticeship was in place for potters learning their craft on the tell (Budden 2008). The rather low percentage of grog in the fabrics of the storage vessels would not have substantially affected the thermal dynamic of the vessel (Rice 1984) and was not, therefore, primarily a matter of its functionality. Although it may have had some use as a filler, the inclusion of the grog may have been part of a culturally defined practice in which old pots were used to symbolically give birth to new vessels and to materially express cultural continuity (Kreiter 2007). Grog was also used as an ingredient in the clay mix for domed ovens, although here it was combined with organic matter. It is possible to suggest that its use in ovens may have referred back to its use in hearths and pots and a possible symbolic relationship to heat and fire (Sofaer 2010). In this sense, for both vessels and ovens, the 'resonance' of the material (Marton 2012) was critical to the use of grog.

While the use of broken vessels in architecture may simply have involved a somewhat expedient recycling of vessels that had been accidentally broken during their use along with other domestic rubbish, by contrast, the selective recycling of pots for grog represents a mindful act of creative destruction. In other words, the making of grog requires the deliberate crushing of existing vessels that necessarily destroys the old in order to make way for the new. At Százhalombatta, creative destruction was not confined to ceramic vessels, but may be understood as part of a wider socio-cultural ethos.

The houses on the tell had distinct life cycles which were shaped by two contrasting kinds of events (Sørensen 2010). On one hand, houses were carefully maintained with regular replastering of internal walls and floors, external patching of wattle and daub walls, and the modification and extension of houses according to needs or abilities. On the other hand, despite this change and adaptation, individual houses were periodically abandoned and appear to have been deliberately burnt (Sørensen 2010). A new house was then built in the same location, with the debris of the old being used as the foundation for the new. In this way, 'the previous house was literally recycled' (Sørensen 2010: 153), generating a physical continuity and link with previous occupants of the settlement.

Creativity, Recycling and Social Attitudes at Százhalombatta

The recycling of ceramics at Százhalombatta took several different forms and took place in the context of different aspects of life on the tell. It included the recycling and reuse of complete vessels and sherds in ways that emphasised the importance of their form and function through placement in ritual deposits, their reconfiguration as tools, and in the modification of valued decorative objects. It also extended to the recycling of ceramic as a material used in building and as grog in the manufacture of new ceramics. In each case, recycling demanded an understanding of the potentials and possibilities afforded by objects and materials. With this knowledge in hand, it also required creativity to think beyond existing items and to consider other possibilities for their use in making something new by placing them into a different context or by reshaping them in some way.

Recycling – both as vessels and as a material – was in part a response to the exigencies of living on a tell with its attendant ritual needs, issues of space and the requirement to improvise in modifying the construction of houses to account for the unpredictability of building on a variable tell surface. While recycling may have been a practical option, it was not always a necessary one since clay, as a raw resource, was in abundant supply. Recycling, therefore, was not a creative response to scarcity stimulated by the absence of objects or materials. Instead it was a matter of thrift. In other words, recycling had to do with recognising the perceived economic, social and symbolic value of objects and materials, and perhaps also the safeguarding of these. At Százhalombatta, recycling was promoted by social attitudes rather than by necessity. This provoked a creativity driven by cultural mores and choices.

These social attitudes embraced creative destruction as a means of generating endings and beginnings; of simultaneously finishing the life cycle of things and moving forward into the next. This was not, however, the creative destruction of modernity that fears the 'stickiness' of things and consequently seeks to sweep away the past without leaving a trace (Bauman 2005). Rather, it was a destruction that was sensitive to long-term ties to place and to tradition that encouraged making of the new while deliberately retaining and articulating material ties to the past.

CHAPTER 3

Design

The Expression of Ideas and the Construction of User Experience

Creativity and design are often said to go hand in hand. Indeed it has been suggested that design is what links creativity and innovation inasmuch as it shapes ideas to become practical and attractive propositions for users (Cox 2005). Yet design is also frequently seen as an essentially modern notion linked to industrial production (Cardoso 2010). It has influentially been defined as what 'can be conveyed in words or by drawing' (Pye 1968: 17): the conceiving of a plan or instruction as the first part of a two-stage process with the intent that the object it describes be made by another person or, more likely, mass-produced by a machine (Risatti 2007). Such an understanding of design stands in opposition to contemporary notions of the craftsman or artisan producing handmade, unique or bespoke products in which value lies in the skill and understanding of materials required to make them (Risatti 2007; Cardoso 2010). It also implies that design did not exist prior to the industrial revolution of the nineteenth century, let alone in prehistory.

It is impossible, however, to imagine a world where objects are not intentionally configured but somehow emerge fully functioning in a serendipitous manner. Everything that is man-made has been designed, whether consciously or not (Cox 2005). Design is an inherent quality of all well-made things rather than a 'self-conscious characteristic' (Wildenhain 1957). The design of objects, whether something as everyday as a cooking pot or as complex as a supercomputer, provides a solution to human needs (Norman 2004). From an archaeological point of view, an understanding of objects as having been deliberately configured is fundamental to the investigation of human behaviour in the past. The notion that ideas become tangible through material culture is thus axiomatic to archaeology just as it is to design. This means that archaeology and design have the potential to share analytical axis (Knappett 2005).

The problem-solving and pre-planning implicit in design is evident for the European Bronze Age in a range of materials. For instance, the manufacture of bronze objects required the bringing together of copper and tin over long distances with the use of specific alloys for particular object types, and the development of the lost wax process enabled the creation of ever more complex shapes (Kuijpers 2012; Sørensen and Appleby forthcoming). In the *chaîne opératoire* of textiles it was evident in the breeding of sheep with white wools that could be dyed, the selective use of wool of particular qualities, and the collection of specific plants to produce particular colours, as well as in the setting up of the warp and weft on the loom, which defined the pattern in the fabric (Rast-Eicher and Bender Jøgensen 2013). In woodworking, the specific example of the staircase from the salt mine in Hallstatt is particularly ingenious. In order to accommodate different shaft inclinations as salt was extracted, the staircase had a demountable modular construction and was adjustable; the treads of the staircase were slotted into grooved side rails in a manner that allowed the pitch of the steps to be altered or for steps to be replaced without changing the whole staircase (Reschreiter and Kowarik 2009). Changes in access to the mine over time had clearly been anticipated, as had the need for upkeep, and the staircase was deliberately designed to accommodate these. As I hope to show later in this essay, notions of design also applied to ceramics.

Many Bronze Age objects were produced in multiples (although not mass produced in the machine sense). In particular, the well-known extent of Late Bronze Age bronze production might be described as taking place on an almost 'industrial scale', although such bronze objects were made by hand. The notion of a pattern that is copied and reproduced is also a familiar one in the Bronze Age, as demonstrated by the large quantities produced of single object types such as socketed axes. The distinction between the handmade as relating to a singular object and the modern designed object as something of which multiples are made (Risatti 2007) falls apart in the Bronze Age.

One might ask whether an important difference between past and present lies in the fact that prehistoric designers may well also have been the makers of the objects they conceived, whereas modern designers turn over their designs to others to make. Yet even in modern design contexts, making is interwoven throughout the creative process. Before a design concept takes expression as a finished object, models must be made, tools and dies designed and prepared, standards of quality established and production procedures worked out (Wallance 1956). Although the dichotomy between making and designing remains powerful within contemporary design and craft theory, some researchers are beginning to question this divide, identifying them as complementary aspects of the same ongoing process of shaping experience through the relationship between people and things (Cardoso 2010). At the same time, a parallel contemporary dichotomy between industrial production as the work of more than one person and the handmade object as the work of a single individual has also been subject to scrutiny (Cardoso 2010). Contemporary design is increasingly understood in terms of responses to community as well as individual needs, while the handmade object may involve the input of more than one person. Such arguments have also recently been made within archaeological contexts as objects are seen to respond to wider social imperatives and may be the product of different people working together through different parts of the production process to create the finished object (Crown 2007; Sofaer and Budden 2012).

The more one scrutinises the supposed differences between past and present, the more the notion of design as a purely contemporary phenomenon falls apart. However, what does differentiate design in prehistory from contemporary notions of design is that the designers of prehistoric objects are anonymous. In this sense, what may well need to be distinguished is the notion of design from more recent understandings of a singular professional named designer. One might also suggest that tradition was a more important factor in the production of objects and that this resulted in a less conscious concern with design in the Bronze Age than in today's society with its constant search for the new. In this sense the persistence of particular forms, decoration, or established ways of doing things fed into the making of objects. This means that time, measured in decades and centuries, was an integral part of the design process (Wallance 1956). The timescales of design were thus potentially different to the immediacy of change to which we are used in the present day.

Aspects of Design

The question, therefore, is not whether design existed in the Bronze Age but how design was articulated. Modern design theory frequently suggests that good design revolves around the usability, practicality and aesthetics of an object (Norman 1988). It also increasingly focuses upon the frontier between making and using in terms of the ways that objects may be designed for interaction or experience, or to elicit emotional responses (Norman 2004; Cardoso 2010).

The usability and practicality of an object can be understood in terms of its affordances: the qualities of an object that allow a person to perform an action (Gibson 1979; Norman 1988; Knappett 2005). For example, flat plates on doors afford pushing them open, while rounded handles on doors afford pulling them closed (Norman 1988). The concept of affordances is familiar to archaeology as a way of understanding the potentials of objects (Knappett 2005). Design theory, however, stresses that the affordances of objects critically depend upon the perceptions of users – in other words, the way that any given object relates to a user's goals, plans, values, beliefs, and previous experiences. All these will affect the ways in which people are able to conceive of an object's use (Norman 1988).

Understanding the aesthetics of an object is not about making a judgment about whether something can be considered universally 'beautiful' or 'ugly' since such notions are notoriously culturally specific. It is rather about identifying whether a particular Bronze Age aesthetic existed at a given place and point in time through identification of repeated form, colour, and decoration. It is therefore to do with consideration of the shape, line, and curve of objects. For decorated items it includes what design elements were used (e.g. circles, triangles, dots, or lines) as well as negative spaces (the spaces outside of any decorative elements) and the principles of their use. The latter refers to how elements were composed together and deployed on the object in terms of their balance (symmetry or asymmetry), rhythmic variation (the repetition or alternation of elements that establishes pattern and texture), proportion (the difference in scale between different elements), dominance (the visual weight of a design that establishes where the eye goes first in looking at a design), and unity. The latter concept stems from Gestalt theories of visual perception that consider the relationship between individual parts and the whole of a composition (Wallance 1956; Behrens 1998). Although the investigation of aesthetics shares some similarities with traditional archaeological analyses of style (cf Hegmon 1992), it is a somewhat broader notion that considers the composition as a whole, including the relationship between shape and decoration.

The ways that objects are designed to shape experience through the interaction between people and things are understood by contemporary designers in terms of interfaces (Cardoso 2010). The design of interfaces is known as interaction design, design for experience or emotional design (Cardoso 2010). It may be more critical to a product's success than its practical elements and is interwoven throughout it (Norman 2004). The emotional aspects of design have been characterised as having several components (Norman 2004). The first has been termed 'visceral design' and is concerned with appearances: whether we like how something looks and if it is visually appealing. The second is 'reflective design', which considers the rationalisation and intellectualisation of a product, in other words, what kind of meaning is attached to it. For example, can I tell a story about it? Does it appeal to my self-image or to my pride? The third is 'behavioural design', which is about the pleasure and effectiveness of use.

Although these different but complementary aspects of design are firmly situated within the contemporary world, they may nonetheless be useful in understanding Bronze Age material culture. I now want to explore them through one particular type of Bronze Age ceramics – the evocatively named Swedish helmet bowls.

Creativity and Design: The Case of Swedish Helmet Bowls

Swedish helmet bowls are large fine ware vessels characteristic of the later phases of the Middle Bronze Age in the central Carpathian Basin (1800/ 1700 BC–1500/1400 BC), now modern Hungary (Figure 3.1). They are found in settlements and cemeteries of the Vatya culture, such as at the sites of Százhalombatta, Dunaújváros and Kelebia (Bóna 1975; Poroszlai and Vicze 2004). Variants of this vessel type are also known from other contemporary cultural groups including the Gyulavarsánd and Encrusted Pottery cultures (Bóna 1975; Görsdorf et al. 2004). Named for their similarity with the shape of World War I helmets worn by Swedish soldiers (M. Vicze, personal communication 29 March 2012), they are frequently shallow with broad sweeping everted rims that are almost flat to the horizontal plane. A single disproportionately small handle loops from the rim to a strong carination that, in a Vatya-Koszider variant of the vessel, may be elaborated with pointed bosses at the quarter points. Vessel interiors are burnished but undecorated, whereas the exteriors are both burnished and decorated on the base (Figure 3.2). All in all, the affordances of these vessels clearly indicate that not only were they open containers (as by definition of a bowl), but that they were designed to hang on a wall and be displayed, their flat rims fitting snugly against the surface with their bases visible to see (Sofaer 2011). Füzesabony fine ware vessels may have inverted or inward sloping rims, but they too have elaborate compositions on their bases. In all cases, the form of these fine ware bowls was designed to facilitate the display of decoration upon their large bases. Indeed a key

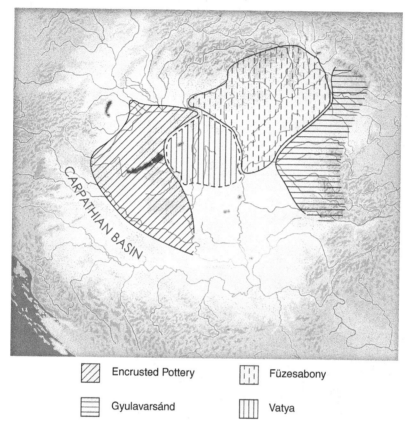

Encrusted Pottery   Füzesabony

Gyulavarsánd   Vatya

FIGURE 3.1 Map of the Carpathian Basin showing Middle Bronze Age cultural groups in the central Carpathian Basin with elaborately decorated bowls.

function of the vessel might be said to have been the display of the motif (Sofaer 2013).

The range of decorative elements and their composition into motifs on the base of fine ware bowls is remarkably restricted. The most frequent elements are concentric circles incised around the base. Sometimes there may be a single circle, but most often there are two or three, and in some cases up to five circles. This may be augmented by the addition of four further concentric circles or half circles at the quarter points of the vessel, smaller impressed dots, or small circles depending on cultural affiliation. In some Gyulavarsánd, and occasional Vatya and Encrusted Pottery examples, circles may be drawn round an

omphalos base, the dimple acting as an integral part of the motif. Such motifs can be understood as representing the sun, a key concern of Bronze Age cosmology, and an image that appears on a range of other contemporary ceramic and metal objects in the region and throughout Europe in this period (Kristiansen and Larsson 2005; Sofaer 2013). On Gyulavarsánd and Füzesabony bowls, five or more incised semi-circles or swags were sometimes linked around the base of the vessel to form a central star-shaped negative space with a circle or concentric circles in

FIGURE 3.2 Swedish helmet bowl from Százhalombatta (photograph: J. Sofaer).

the centre of the star. The star motif has also been understood as representing the sun (cf Kristiansen and Larson 2005; Sofaer 2013) (Figure 3.3).

Circles may also be combined with straight lines. The latter were used to divide the circular vessel base into quarters to form a wheel motif. The four spokes of the wheel radiate from a central circle that may either be incised or an omphalos base. On some vessels, this central circle may double both as a wheel axle and as a sun through the use of concentric circles or repeated small incised dashes around the circle. The spokes of the wheel may also terminate in concentric half circles. In such cases, the decoration can be read as a combination of wheel and sun motifs. More rarely, this doubling up of motifs can be seen in the division of the central circle into quarters, turning the concentric circles of the sun into a wheel-cross. The wheel is particularly common as a motif in the Vatya and Encrusted Pottery cultures. At first glance it seems less frequent on Gyulavarsánd vessels, where decorative traditions focus upon curvaceous rather than linear motifs. Nonetheless, here too the wheel is strongly present. On some Gyulavarsánd Swedish helmet bowls, rather than 'drawing' the motif on the vessel, concentric circles at the centre of the base act as a sun/wheel axle, while the undecorated space between pointed bosses emerging from semi-circles placed at the quarter points of the vessel act as wheel spokes. In such cases the whole bowl is turned into a wheel, the rim of the vessel acting as its margin (Figure 3.4). These vessels, therefore, can be read in two ways: through the positive addition of decorative elements and the negative space between these. Like the sun, the wheel was a key cosmological theme in Bronze Age iconography, appearing on a range of other contemporary objects, particularly metalwork (Bóna 1975; Kaul 2004; Kristiansen and Larsson 2005).

The ways in which decorative elements were composed to form both sun and wheel motifs deployed the same design principles of radial symmetry, regular rhythm and nesting of elements of different proportion (concentricity), with no element appearing more dominant than any other (there is no use of perspective). Together, these help to promote the unity of the design since patterns of similar size, shape and colour tend to be grouped together by the viewer, as do items in close proximity or aligned with one another (Stafford 2007; Wells 2012). Unity is particularly important in making meaning out of an abstract representation. Important here too is the relationship between the shape of the vessel and its decoration. The round shape of the vessel and its base are used as an integral part of these motifs. In other words, the vessel doesn't just facilitate the motif in the way that a flat surface might facilitate incised decoration, or frame it in

FIGURE 3.3 Sun motifs on Swedish helmet bowls: A) Vatya bowl from Cegléd-Öreghegy, B) Füzesabony bowl from Megyaszó, and C) Füzesabony bowl from Gelej-Kanálisdűlő (redrawn after Bóna 1975).

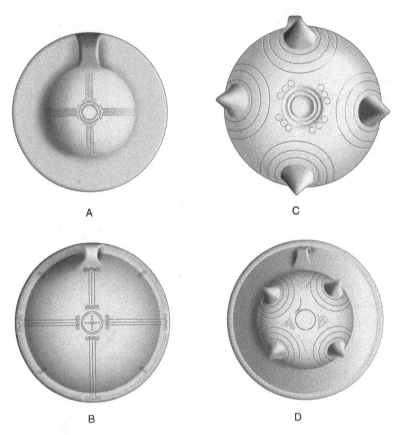

FIGURE 3.4 Wheel motifs on Swedish helmet bowls. Left: Motif created through 'drawing' it on the vessel in Vatya and Encrusted Pottery cultures: A) Vatya bowl from Kelebia, and B) Encrusted Pottery bowl from Királyszentistván. Right: The motif created through the undecorated space between bosses on Füzesabony and Gyulavarsánd vessels: C) Füzesabony bowl from Golop, and D) Gyulavarsánd bowl from Gyulavarsánd-Laposhalom (redrawn after Bóna 1975).

the way that a picture frame might surround a painting. Rather the three-dimensionality of the bowl shape is actively used to form part of the motif.

In the Vatya culture Swedish helmet bowls are frequently oxidised. Their lighter colours often stand out from the rest of the predominantly black fine wares. This does not always hold for other cultural groups where the bowls are black or, as in the case of encrusted vessels, make use of colour contrasts with white inlay tracing the decoration on a black vessel. In all cases, however, the surface of the vessel is burnished and therefore shiny. Not only do the surfaces and decorative motifs on the vessel draw the eye, but the sometimes rather baroque additions also produce distinct and sometimes colliding sensory effects when touched, such as simultaneous sharpness of the points of bosses and smoothness of surface. In combination, the limited motifs and repeated shape, colour and surface of the bowls result in a distinctive aesthetic. Indeed, one might suggest the archaeological response to this aesthetic is, at least in part, one aspect of how we recognise them today as belonging to the Bronze Age.

The bowls were thus designed to appeal to the senses and were deliberately made to be visual and tactile. Their disproportionately small handles reinforce the idea that they were designed for visual appeal with the decorated base turned towards the viewer. The decoration on the vessels reiterates geographically and chronologically widespread motifs that are found in several different contemporary media and contexts, suggesting that they express cornerstone myths and beliefs prevalent throughout the European Bronze Age. On this basis it is possible to argue that the motifs on pots would have been familiar to Bronze Age people and that they stood for broader cosmological notions. In particular, the iconography of the sun and the wheel has been widely discussed in terms of a complex Bronze Age mythology of the sun and its daily voyage through different spheres of the cosmos (Kaul 1998, 2005). In a pre-literate society it is therefore possible to imagine that the bowls may have had a role in reminding people of these myths in much the same way as stained glass windows in medieval churches were used to convey biblical stories to people who could not read. On this level it is plausible that Bronze Age people had an affective response to the bowls through their reflective or intellectual appeal.

It is also possible to suggest that an additional aspect of the reflective design of the bowls lay in their appeal as status symbols (Sofaer forthcoming). These technically complex vessels display high levels of skill in their production and decoration, representing an investment of material as well as skill in their manufacture beyond that of regular household wares (Budden 2008). Furthermore, although prestige has traditionally been ascribed to metalwork of this period, much of the metal comes from hoards. The quantity of metalwork from cemeteries and settlements in the Carpathian Basin is relatively small and in both these contexts pottery is by far the most abundant material. For Middle Bronze Age cemeteries in particular, the relative quantities of metalwork and pottery has led to the suggestion that pots may be the primary means of displaying status (Vicze 2011). This may also be the case for settlements (Sofaer 2013).

Yet the bowl is also a functional form. The Swedish helmet bowls were more than pretty prehistoric wall decorations; if the latter had been required then Bronze Age people might as well have directly elaborated the wall, as in fact they did at the Early Bronze Age site of Tiszaug-Kéménytető (Csányi 2003) and later at the Vatya settlement at Százhalombatta. There was indeed a distinct choice made in the making of bowls as forms that could be used. They were not autonomous or self-standing in the sense of a work of art that is not meant to be touched and is an object of purely visual contemplation (Adamson 2007: 4). Significantly, the motif would only have been visible when the bowl was either turned upside down or deliberately displayed by hanging it on a wall. Thus, while the vessel was in use the motif would have been concealed, literally making the sun or wheel disappear, as in the myths about the daily cycle of the sun. The users of these vessels, therefore, could have replayed cosmological myths through the act of using the vessels (to make the motif disappear) or by turning them upside down (to make it reappear). In other words, the bowls allowed their users to tell and retell stories. The wide flat rims of the vessels not only enable the vessel to lie flush against a vertical surface but also facilitated a swivelling of the vessel when the palms of the hands were placed under the rim to support it. The vessel may thus have had an aesthetic optical appeal, but it was through touching and using the objects that users were able to fully appreciate their design (cf Adamson 2007: 5).

The Role of Design

In his essay 'The Storyteller', the German cultural theorist Walter Benjamin explored the historical and practical relationship between story-telling and craft (Benjamin 1968; Leslie 1998). For Benjamin, artisans were master story-tellers for whom the making of objects 'combined the lore of faraway places, such as a much travelled man brings home, with the lore of the past, as it best reveals itself to residents of a place' (Benjamin 1968: 85). Just as the story-teller takes what he tells from his own experience and that of others and makes it the experience of those hearing the tale, so does the craftsman (Leslie 1998). For Benjamin, making pottery was a model and metaphor for the transmission of experience and wisdom through story-telling (Leslie 1998). He says, 'It sinks the thing into the life of the storyteller, in order to bring it out of him again. Thus traces of the storyteller cling to the story the way the handprint [Spur] of the potter clings to the clay vessel' (Benjamin 1968: 91).

Such an understanding of the relationship between story-telling and potting gives a clue as to the role of design in expressing the ideas that sat within the making of the Bronze Age Swedish helmet bowls. The bowls combined a cosmological tradition that was deeply embedded within

Bronze Age society throughout the continent with a local Carpathian present in which the currency of the myth of the sun, along with stories of long-distance travel to and from other realms, played an important role. In a similar way that modern religious symbols such as the crucifix may be hung in homes today, the Swedish helmet bowls were material mnemonics for the story of the sun's journey. They brought cosmology into the houses in a clear and highly visible manner, presenting an image of the universe that continually reminded inhabitants of their place in the cosmos. In this sense, the bowls not only enabled story-telling, but they also became the story; stories were literally sunk into these things.

If the pots can be understood in terms of stories, what then of the story-tellers? I have suggested that by interacting with the vessels users had the potential to become story-tellers – in other words, the vessels were designed to enable the creative act of story-telling. To continue with Benjamin, his model also proposes that the potters may themselves have been story-tellers. Given the widespread nature of sun and wheel symbolism during the Middle Bronze Age and thus the pervasiveness of the myths with which they were associated, it is difficult to argue that potters would not have been aware of the significance of the vessel form and motifs. Thus, although they worked within a tradition that directed them towards particular ways of articulating these, in making the vessels they too engaged in a story-telling in which the bowls were both 'material facts and imaginative acts' (Pope 2005: 17). While the Swedish helmet bowls each contain the same design elements, follow the same principles and aim for the same affects, each vessel is more or less subtly different to another. This, of course, is the outcome of the handmade, but it is also the story-telling of individual potters which, just like in oral story-telling, was slightly different every time. Yet despite the uniqueness of each vessel, not every potter was a designer (cf Pye 1968). While the variation in the vessels implies a degree of creativity in decision-making, this is at a level similar to using a dress pattern and changing the fabric or slightly altering the cut without impacting on the final shape of the garment. Potters clearly shared understandings of the design principles deployed in the manufacture of the vessels. Where then does the creativity in the design of the bowls lie? To understand this we need to take a look at what kind of vessels came before them.

Creativity and the Design of Swedish Helmet Bowls

The Middle Bronze Age Vatya culture was preceded by the Nagyrév culture of the Early Bronze Age (2500–1800/1700 BC), the former

TABLE 3.1 *Differences in affordance, aesthetics, and user interactions for bowls from the Early and Middle Bronze Age in the central Carpathian Basin*

	Early Bronze Age Nagyrév Bowls	Middle Bronze Age Vatya Swedish Helmet Bowls
Affordance	To be used on a horizontal surface	To be hung from a vertical surface or placed on a horizontal surface
Aesthetics	Wide range of elements	Restricted range of elements
	Elements assembled in variety of combinations with a loose range of motifs and schematic anthropomorphic representations	Elements assembled in strict combinations to form defined motifs
	Narrative decoration	Abstract decoration
	Horizontal and vertical bands, or free decoration	Radial symmetry
	2D use of vessel as surface to inscribe	3D use of vessel with integration of motif into vessel form
	Motifs not specific to vessel type	Motifs specific to vessel type
User interactions	Motif cannot generally be hidden by turning or rotating vessel	Motif can be hidden by turning vessel over
	Stories told on the pot	Stories told with the pot

identified as emerging directly from the latter both geographically and culturally (Poroszlai 2003). Yet Swedish helmet bowls were novel and innovative in both concept and design compared to their Nagyrév predecessors. Swedish helmet bowls represent a number of creative developments in affordance, aesthetics and user interactions with the objects (Table 3.1).

The sweeping curves of Swedish helmet bowls were quite different in shape to the more conical Nagyrév fine ware bowls. The Early Bronze Age bowls sometimes have a small pedestal and lack a handle; they were vessels designed to be placed on a horizontal surface, not displayed on a wall. The move to decorate the base of Swedish helmet bowls also represented a shift since the decoration on Nagyrév vessels is on the exterior surface of the vessel wall or on splayed rims (Figure 3.5). Early

A   B

FIGURE 3.5 Nagyrév vessels with incised surface decoration: A) Vessel from Százhalombatta B) Vessel from Budapest XI. District, Pannonhalmi street

Bronze Age vessels were meant to be viewed from the side or from the top, rather than the base. The highly codified, restricted, decorative schemes of the Middle Bronze Age bowls also marked a departure from the varied range of elements loosely used to construct motifs in the Early Bronze Age. Early Bronze Age elements were most frequently geometric and included crosses, zigzags, dots, triangles, vertical and horizontal lines, L-shapes, and step-like motifs. They appear on other media including house wall decorations, worked bone and boar tusk, and probably extended to dress and body ornamentation (Vicze 2009). There are also occasional, rather schematic, human representations with apparently upraised arms or sometimes with comb-figure motifs, as well as a so-called house motif (Csányi 1982–83; Vicze 2009). Some vessels have applied plastic ribbed decoration, although this is relatively infrequent (Csányi 1982–83; Vicze 2009).

In the Early Bronze Age, decorative elements could be used rather simply or in quite complex combinations; the structure and organisation of the patterns are quite diverse. Nonetheless Vicze (2009) has described three main ways in which they are deployed. Most commonly, motifs and their individual elements are used to create symmetrical or strictly geometrical compositions such that elements are used repeatedly in bands or ribbons. The second way in which they are used involves the complex arrangement of a combination of selected motifs in horizontal and vertical arrangements. Incised motifs are either placed in bands or in vertical fields around the vessel, or alternatively cover the whole of the vessel exterior. The third way of deploying the motifs is through the elaborate and not necessarily symmetrical division of the vessel into sections with complex motifs within some of these. This latter category includes the vessels with the human figures and house motif. These are not common, but they nonetheless constitute a distinct class of finds rather than just a 'one off' (Vicze 2009). The decoration on these vessels constitutes a narrative told round the pot and has been widely interpreted as cosmological or quasi-religious in nature, such that the pots depict creation myths (Girić 1971; Tasić 1972; Schreiber 1984; Vicze 2009).

Although the decoration on both Early and Middle Bronze Age vessels was linked to cosmological notions, the ways in which this was articulated was substantially different. The Middle Bronze Age link between specific motifs and particular vessel forms, in which the motif was integrated within the three-dimensionality of vessel shape, marked a conceptual shift from earlier understandings of vessels. In the Early Bronze Age, motifs were applied to a range of different vessel types and the vessel was treated as a two-dimensional surface on which to inscribe. Furthermore the cosmological motifs on the Swedish helmet bowls were fully abstract, marking a departure from the representational and narrative style motifs that preceded them. In these abstract compositions negative space was an important element that was used to create and define the design, in a similar way that Heidegger (1950) argued that it is not just the positive shape of a vessel that defines it but also the void within it that produces the idea of what kind of thing something is. These diachronic changes in decoration can be seen as creative acts that condensed the meaning of motifs. They required users to reconsider and distil their perceptual experiences (Nichol 1997; Bohm 1996).

The design of Swedish helmet bowls facilitated interaction in new ways. Manipulating the vessel allowed users to make the motif appear or disappear, but the motifs on Nagyrév bowls could not be similarly concealed. Whereas Nagyrév vessels told stories that were meant to be read, the Swedish helmet bowls were meant to be handled and may have formed part of the act of recounting stories. One can liken this to the difference between reading a book and playing with a model. Even if the story is the same, the bodily involvement in the latter is a more active kind of experience. Playing with a model also has the potential to be shared with others, whereas reading is a more solitary, internalised, imaginative experience. In common with other, perhaps more well-known Bronze Age objects, such as the Trundholm sun chariot or the Dupljaja model, the Swedish helmet bowls were designed to be interactive things. From the point of view of their behavioural design, they were innovative interfaces.

Why Design?

In the twenty-first century a desire for individual experience, along with ever more sophisticated machines and flexible models of industrial production, the pressing question is not what to design, but why (Cardoso 2010). For Bronze Age potters the answer to this question was clear. In a world pervaded by cosmology and myth, design offered a way of expressing these and was intimately linked to, and inspired by, them.

Swedish helmet bowls appear to have had a swift uptake and were used and made by a number of cultural groups in the central Carpathian Basin, each of which employed the same design concepts but configured them in culturally specific ways. They were in use for only a few hundred years, a relatively short time in prehistoric terms. Yet many of the design concepts, including vessels as a medium for display on walls, abstract sun and wheel motifs, radial symmetry, three-dimensional incorporation of the motif into the vessel form, and the development of vessels in terms of a user interface, persisted (albeit in modified form) into the Late Bronze Age (Sofaer forthcoming).

In this sense, the design of Swedish helmet bowls must be considered successful and, as with all successful designs, the bowls were embedded within, and interrelated with, wider cultural notions (Petroski 1997). Their design was the product of the conditions and social conditioning which rendered them possible (Bourdieu 1968), and this familiarity facilitated uptake of the objects by users (cf Sofaer Derevenski and Sørensen 2002). Thus, despite the creativity expressed in these vessels, they also accepted and promoted the established social order, while the high value attached to the vessels meant that the social order in turn legitimised the design, creating a system that denied a critical look into the system itself (van Toorn 1994). The creativity at work here, therefore, was not the kind of innovation that actively seeks to disrupt, resist or to transcend boundaries, as is presently expressed at the limits of contemporary craft design (Adamson 2007). It was, rather, about finding ways to establish and reaffirm existing understandings of the world. In doing so, immaterial beliefs were made material – ideas were literally shaped into objects – and the design of vessels recast makers and users as creative agents.

CHAPTER 4

Margins

Locations for Creativity

The philosopher Ludwig Wittgenstein once declared that the best place in which to resolve philosophical problems is a railway station, leaving one to wonder how he would have fared in twenty-first century airports! What Wittgenstein was referring to, of course, is the importance of place as an arena in which creative processes can unfold (Törnqvist 2011). Since creativity is a characteristic of people, it is difficult to argue that a place or setting can be creative in and of itself any more than it can be happy, angry or curious (Törnqvist 2011: 25). Places, however, can offer conditions under which creativity can flourish.

In recent years cultural geographers and sociologists have become increasingly interested in the relationship between creativity and place (Scott 2000; Florida 2002). Within the context of contemporary Western urban life, this work has frequently described how creative people and industries tend to form clusters of activity in city neighbourhoods. It has been argued that the close proximity of like-minded people with a variety of relevant skills leads to interrelationships and generates positive feedback leading to new expressions and ideas (Scott 1999). Pierre Bourdieu (1993) called this a 'creative field', as in the dot-com boom of the 1980s in Silicon Valley in the United States (Koepp 2002) or Renaissance Florence (Törnqvist 2011). Research has often been policy-driven by way of an interest in how to cultivate creativity and stimulate economic growth through city planning. More recently, however, researchers have argued that the focus on urban environments has led to assumptions about where creativity is located that need to be challenged (Gibson 2010). They have looked elsewhere, finding that creativity is also manifest in small, suburban, rural and remote places with small populations, and that it is implicated in a range of social, economic and technical transformations peculiar to those localities (Gibson and Connell 2004; Gibson 2010). The conditions for creativity, therefore, are potentially more complex, variable and subtle.

In this essay, I want to explore the relationship between place and creativity by looking at one particular kind of location – the geographical margin of cultural phenomena. Margins offer particular possibilities for encounters between people as well as potential freedom from constraints and conservatism felt at the centre. Marginal environments can lead, therefore, to creative developments. My case study is drawn from the Csepel group of Beaker sites in Hungary that lie on the southern edge of the Europe-wide distribution of the Early Bronze Age Beaker culture.

Margins and the Conditions of Creativity

Margins are both physical and metaphorical locations. The notion of the margin can refer to physical distance, but it can also refer to a social understanding of one's own and others' place in the world or in relation to a group. Associated with these twin concepts of margins are a series of tensions and contradictions. On one hand the notion of the margin has a negative connotation implying inferiority, deficiency, disadvantage and outsider status, including lack of productivity or lack of knowledge. For instance, we talk about 'fringe' ideas or behaviour, people being marginalised in the sense of exclusion, or unproductive marginal land. This notion of the margin is closely linked to geographic and economic models of core and periphery and is strongly embedded within archaeology, including the study of the Bronze Age. Thus interactions between core and periphery have been understood in terms of unequal economic exchange in which peripheries were dominated by centres (Kristiansen 1998). Likewise, distance from a core is understood to 'deform' (Mikołajczak and Szczodrowski 2012: 181) or to 'diminish' and 'fade' (Potrebica 2008: 202) the original context or conceptual values associated with objects.

On the other hand, the notion of the margin has been used to refer to the place where existing boundaries are pushed and which is in the vanguard of new developments (Dogan 1999). In this case margins are understood as frontiers and the crossing of boundaries is identified as a productive activity. Similarly the transgression of boundaries allows insights into the lives of others and to 'spy out human invention and ingenuity behind the stony and solemn facades of seemingly timeless and indomitable creeds' (Bauman 2004: 14). For example, the philosopher Jacques Derrida lived in exile and built his philosophical home on a 'cultural crossroads' (Bauman 2004). Being on the margin of a society or group may also make it easier to resist dominant forces. Recent analysis of the so-called Arab Spring has suggested that people on the margins of economic and power structures do not acquiesce to their fate but find ways to exercise agency in dealing with their situations (Bush and Ayeb 2012). Thus margins can be creative locations.

Research in the history of science shows that pioneers of new fields frequently generate breakthroughs at the edges of disciplines (Lindholm-Romantschuk 1998). In academic contexts the concept of 'creative marginality' (Dogan and Pahre 1990) has been used to describe the process by which researchers move away from the mainstream and interact across disciplinary boundaries in a way that promotes intellectual cross-fertilisation. It has been suggested that the margins of research are less densely populated and therefore provide more room for ideas to grow, in contrast to the density and overcrowding of more conservative cores; in an area that is over-populated with scholars it is difficult to add something new (Dogan 1999). The combination of material and ideas from two or more fields allows greater scope for creativity (Dogan and Pahre 1990). The cross-fertilisation of theories and practices between the fields promises not only the possibility of innovation at the site at which their margins overlap, but also the possibility of producing a new subfield. For example, developmental psychology, in attempting to fill in the gap between psychological development and biological development, has become an important field in its own right (Dogan and Pahre 1990). Being on the edge of something, therefore, allows a degree of freedom and imagination to create something new that has its own integrity.

In this sense creativity resides in re-creation: the deliberate making of something from something (cf Pope 2005; see also 'Recycling' this volume). It involves the recognition of novel relationships or connections between previously unrelated things or ideas (Koestler 1964). This recombinatory view of creativity is not limited to the study of innovation within academia, but is also deeply embedded elsewhere. As Tim Ingold (2007: 46) points out, it underlies Claude Lévi-Strauss's (1966) notion of the creative mind as a *bricoleur* that engages in the novel assembly of structures of thought out of bits and pieces of old ones. It also sits within Noam Chomsky's notion of 'rule-governed creativity' as the capacity to build an infinite range of expressions from a finite repertoire of lexical items (Chomsky 1964). Importantly, in this recombinatory view of creativity, it is only possible to identify creativity through understanding how the new relates to pre-existing elements, and thus how they have been reconfigured. An individual idea or object cannot be recognised as creative in isolation.

Yet, just because margins exist and have the potential to be locations for creativity, either through being crossed or because of their permeability, this does not necessarily mean that creativity will take place. For example, in medieval Al-Andalus a reinforcement of existing social behaviours in Islamic groups may have occurred as a result of the perceived threat by Christians from the other side of the boundary (Inskip 2013). Creativity, therefore, is not inevitable, and contextual factors are key to understanding creativity (Perry-Smith and Shalley 2003). Furthermore, even where exchange and mobility take place across boundaries, cultural differences between groups still exist (Barth 1969). The question, then, is not just about how creativity occurs but why culture does not become more and more integrated over time (Liep 2001). In part this may be a matter of access to resources and of existing power structures. Yet, it also calls for an understanding of the ways that creativity may itself give rise to cultural contrast and heterogenisation (Liep 2001: 8).

In the context of cross-cultural relations and the interface between two or more cultural influences, this process of recreation leading to cultural contrast has been described in terms of 'creolization' (Hannerz 1987, 1992; Archetti 2001; Eriksen 2003). Here newness is seen as a result of recontextualisation, mixing, and the ongoing merger of formerly discrete symbolic realms (Hannerz 1992). It has been particularly powerful as a means of understanding post-colonial encounters. For example, in modern Argentina (a country with immigrants from many nations), national discourses of class and race have been explained in terms of cultural strategies where 'creoleness' is used in an explicit way (Archetti 2001). Similarly, in historical archaeology the concept of creolisation has been used to explore the interactions between African American slaves with Europeans and indigenous peoples in the Caribbean and in the South of the United States (Ferguson 1992; Dawdy 2000). In modern contexts, rather than seeing cultural globalisation as a euphemism for cultural imperialism, cultural flattening, collapse and blatant commercialisation, it has more optimistically been identified as a two-way process entailing a democratisation of symbolic power that leads to encounters between different symbolic universes. These creative confrontations stimulate exchanges and innovative 'glocalization' (Robertson 1992; Eriksen 2003).

Nonetheless, the extent to which recombination creates something that is entirely distinct from its 'parent' cultures or whether it instead bridges the two deserves scrutiny. The former refers to a creole identity which distinguishes itself in that it does not recognise the existence of pure, discrete cultures – for example, people who identify as Muslims, but at the same time eat pork and drink beer (Eriksen 2003). The latter explicitly recognises the existence of two discrete bounded categories but attempts to straddle them as, for instance, people in modern European society who may refer to themselves as British-Pakistani or Turkish-German. Such hyphenated identities combine inputs from both cultural universes but presuppose that there are clear boundaries between the groups in question and thus require conscious or unconscious switching between the two (Eriksen 2003: 233). In this case people may have grown up in another country and have distinctive customs, but at the same time have adapted to a new country. The British politician Norman Tebbit infamously reduced such notions of identity to a 'cricket test' saying that people's national loyalties could be indicated by which team they supported in international sports matches (Banks 1996). Creolisation and hyphenated identities reflect different kinds of social realities, but both involve reassembly and therefore creativity (Eriksen 2003). The deceptively simple question 'Where do you come from?' therefore belies the complexity of the potential answer (Sofaer 2012). Similarly, the restricted options available on modern ethnicity monitoring questionnaires may bear little relation to people's self-perception, forcing the questionee to agonise over 'who they are' and to resort to ticking the 'other' box.

The notion of creolisation has frequently been used to describe the creation of new social orders in terms of the recombination of often large-scale intangible symbolic structures that impact upon the identities of people. Equally, however, the combination of symbolic systems to create new cultural forms cannot exist without people making it happen. Psychologist Mihaly Csikszentmihalyi (1988) has argued that creativity has to be understood in terms of a three-way relationship between the domain (symbolic system or culture), the field (social system) and individual person. Creativity, therefore, is a matter of the actions of people in relation to the social and cultural contexts in which they are situated. In terms of material culture, the ways that people act upon their environment defines them through their ability to enrol objects and the wider material world in relation to abstract thought (Leach 2004: 162). In other words, although objects will inevitably pre-exist action, thereby lending structure and meaning to thought (Renfrew 2001), new ideas must also take a physical form if they are to be realised; the creativity of the subject is expressed in objects. Thus, if new cultural forms are made up of unique combinations, the same might be said of the people who generated them (Leach 2004) since creativity must always and ultimately be traced back to people.

In the Melanesian context similar arguments have been used to propose a model of personhood and subjectivity that is distributed in objects (Leach 2004). This allows for an understanding of a distributed and public creativity in the making of the material world that is contingent upon the combination and recombination of subjectivity depending on an individual's shifting position in relation to others. Understanding the link between creativity, people and things further opens up the possibility of describing the process of recombination through the notion of the hybrid and process of hybridization in the sense articulated by Bruno Latour (1993). He argued that the boundaries between people and things – in other words between nature and culture, subject and object – break down as they are mutually implicated in complex actor-networks (Latour 1993). Hybrids are made up of changing associations and dissociations between people and the material world (Latour 1993). Hybrids can be anything from climate change and genetically modified food (Blok and Jensen 2012) to seriously ill bodies maintained through medical technologies (Place 2000), but in all cases they involve the combination of human and non-human entities. While such hybridity is not without limits (Strathern 1996), creativity is implicit in the notion of hybrids and the process of hybridization in terms of the creation of the new through the different ways in which people and things are combined. Of course, hybrids are not confined to cultural or geographical boundaries – the notion of the hybrid forms part of a more general statement of what occurs during the creative process – but because of the particular potentials of margins for creativity, it is possible that the conditions for the creation of new hybrid forms might be heightened there. The challenge is to distinguish between different forms of hybrids in specific contexts (Van der Ploeg 2004; Sofaer 2006), how people and objects work together as part of dynamic creative processes at the local level (Price 1999), and how these are integrated in a meaningful and credible way into an existing milieu (cf Hirsch 2004).

Creativity and Margins: The Case of the Csepel Group

The Csepel group is situated in the Budapest region in Hungary. More than sixty sites are known to belong to the group, which is named after the large complex of settlement and cemetery sites on Csepel Island in the River Danube. The remainder of the sites are located on the right bank of the Danube with only a few scattered finds known further away (Endrődi 2012). The sites occupy a narrow strip of about 40 km from the bend of the River Danube north of Budapest to the southern outskirts of the city

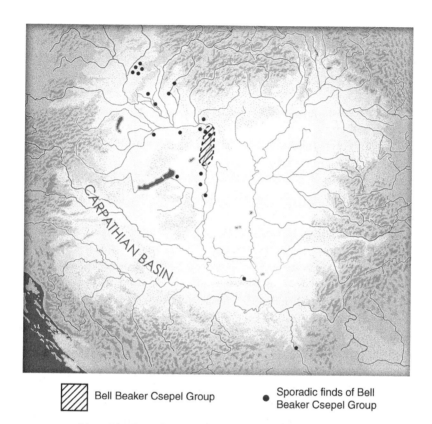

⧄ Bell Beaker Csepel Group   ● Sporadic finds of Bell
Beaker Csepel Group

FIGURE 4.1 Map of the Carpathian Basin showing the distribution of the Csepel group
(redrawn after Endrődi 2013).

(Machnik 2001; Endrődi 2012) (Figure 4.1). The Csepel group dates to the
Early Bronze Age, 2500–2200 BC (Forenbaher 1993; Patay 2013). It forms
part of the widespread Bell Beaker phenomenon characterised by distinctive shared elements of material culture, in particular the presence of an
inverted bell-shaped pottery vessel – the eponymous bell beaker – along
with other objects forming part of the so-called Beaker package found
primarily within mortuary assemblages (Thomas 1991). The Beaker culture
is found in 'hot spots' throughout much of Europe from Denmark in the
north, to Sicily and north Africa in the south, to Britain and Ireland in the
west, to Slovakia and Hungary in the east (Heyd 2005; Vander Linden 2007;
Turek 2012). The Csepel group forms the most south-easterly of these 'hot
spots', although occasional sherds of bell beaker pottery have been found
further to the south-east in Serbia (Koledin 2008). The Csepel group,

therefore, can be said to fall on the margin of the European Beaker distribution, although in a regional context it has itself been considered a core area that may have influenced neighbouring regions leading to Beaker–inspired objects further afield in Romania, Dalmatia, and Greece (Heyd 2005). The marked similarities in Beaker material culture and its widespread yet irregular distribution across Europe have long led to debate about whether migration and colonisation, or networks of trade and exchange among indigenous elites, resulted in the spread of Beaker objects and ideas (Harrison 1980; Brodie 1997; Price et al. 2004; Heyd 2005). Recent research suggests that both mobility of people and of ideas took place, contributing to these shared material expressions (Price et al. 2004; Zoffmann 2006; Desideri 2011).

The Csepel group, however, was only one of many contemporary early Bronze Age groups in the centre of the Carpathian Basin. It formed an island of culture linked to the north and west of the continent (Patay 2013), but was surrounded by groups that drew upon local Carpathian and Balkan traditions. To the north and east of the Csepel group, the material culture of the late Makó-Kosihy-Čaka and the Nyírség groups appear to have drawn upon pre-existing local Carpathian Copper Age traditions, while to the south lay the proto-Nagyrév group and the widespread Somogyvár-Vinkovci group which drew upon elements from the central and southern Balkans (Kulcsár 2003, 2009; Endrődi 2012).

The large Csepel group settlements were situated at strategic points along the River Danube (Endrődi 2013). Excavations have revealed the remains of 'boat-shaped' houses on average 14 m by 5 m in size, with timber frames and curved walls made of wattle and daub such as from the sites of Szigetszentmiklós-Üdülősor (Endrődi 2013), Albertfalva (Endrődi 2005), and Bucsu-Hosszú Aszúdűlő (Ilon 2005). Such extensive settlements and this type of house have not been found elsewhere in Beaker or in contemporary groups in the Carpathian Basin and are specific to the Csepel group (Endrődi 2013). Domestic ceramic assemblages include plates, cups, storage vessels, clay spoons, and ember covers as well as sherds from bell beakers. In addition, there is evidence of agricultural and production activities. Other objects include bone tools, metal awls, wire, and cinder indicating copper production (Choyke and Bartosiewicz 2005; Endrődi 2003; Endrődi, Gyulai, and Reményi 2008).

The cemeteries were located close to the settlements on the side of the settlement away from the River Danube (Endrődi 2012). Whereas across most of Europe, Beaker cemeteries vary in size from single figures to many tens of burials (Hájek 1968; Dvořák 1992; Heyd 1998; Turek 1998), the cemeteries of the Csepel group contain many hundreds of burials. The cemetery at Budakalász–Csajerszke contained 1,070 burials and is the largest Beaker cemetery in Europe (Czene 2008). The cemeteries are strung out like beads on a string parallel to the settlements over several kilometres, rather than being clearly bounded (Kalicz-Schreiber 1997). At the sites of Tököl and Békásmegyer, the graves extended over approximately 1 km (Schreiber 1975; Kalicz-Schreiber 1984) with 50–100 m between small groups of graves. Individual graves were sometimes closely spaced with only 50 cm between them, but they may also be more dispersed with several metres between graves (Machnik 1991).

The Csepel group also differs markedly from other parts of the Beaker distribution in the variability of its modes of burial and the widespread use of cremation to dispose of the dead. Three types of burial rite have been distinguished: inhumation graves, unurned cremation graves where the remains were placed directly in the grave without a vessel, and urn burials where the cremated remains were placed inside a vessel. In addition, so-called cenotaph or 'symbolic' graves have also been identified in which objects (predominantly ceramics) were deposited apparently without a body (Schreiber-Kalicz 1984; Machnik 1991; Czene 2008; Endrődi 2012; Patay 2013). Some of the unurned cremation graves were surrounded by ring ditches with openings on the eastern side as at Szigetszentmiklós-Üdülősor (Endrődi 2012), Szigetszentmiklós–Felső-Ürgehegyi-dűlő (Patay 2008), and Budakalász-Csajerszke (Czene 2008). Rarely more than one grave was included within the ring ditch, these also occasionally being 'symbolic' graves (Endrődi 2012). Cremation was the most common method of disposal of the body – 62–80 per cent of graves, depending on the cemetery (Machnik 1991; Endrődi 2012; Patay 2013) – with urn burial usually the most prevalent rite (Kalicz-Schreiber 1997). Inhumation burial was comparatively rare. In some cemeteries only 2 per cent of burials were inhumations (Kalicz-Schreiber 1997; Endrődi 2012). An exception to this is the cemetery at Szigetszentmiklós where 47 per cent were inhumations, a higher proportion than any other contemporary Beaker cemetery in the Carpathian Basin (Patay 2013). There does not appear to have been any clear spatial separation between particular types of graves, although the different kinds of graves are not always evenly distributed within cemeteries. For example, at Békásmegyer, inhumation graves were more prevalent in the northern part of the cemetery than in the denser southern part (Kalicz-Schreiber 1984), while the eastern part of Csepel Island was dominated by urn graves (Kalicz-Schreiber 1997).

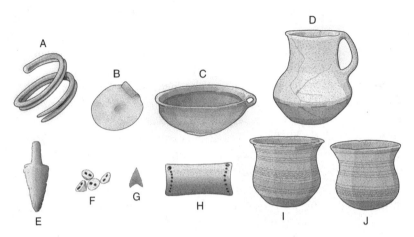

FIGURE 4.2 Examples of Beaker objects from the Csepel group: A) spiral ornament, B) disc ornament, C) bowl, D) jug, E) dagger, F) perforated buttons, G) arrowhead, H) wristguard, I) beaker, and J) beaker (redrawn after Czene 2008 and Patay 2008).

The mortuary assemblages include objects belonging to the Beaker 'package' (Figure 4.2). The form of these objects is very similar to those found in the eastern Bell Beaker group. Like bell beakers found in Bohemia and Moravia, those of the Csepel group may be without handles or have a single handle (Kalicz-Schreiber 1997; Heyd, Husty, and Kreiner 2004). There are both decorated and undecorated examples. When decorated, this is with zones of impressed, stamped or incised decoration, or by means of rouletting. Motifs include zigzags, circles, lines of dots, herringbone patterns, and criss-cross patterns that may imitate textiles. Frequently this decoration covers the entire exterior surface of the vessel. Some of the bell beakers were highly burnished prior to decoration resulting in an exaggerated relief and contrast between the red, shiny, flat bands of the vessel or interstices of decoration, and the matt decoration itself. Sometimes the motifs were inlaid with a white paste. There is a range of kinds of daggers, stone wristguards, arrowheads, copper awls, V-perforated buttons, hair-rings, and pins with a rolled head used with clothing (Machnik 1991; Czene 2008; Patay 2008, 2013). Bone and limestone beads, blades possibly for sickles, and miniature axes with a narrow head have been found (Kalicz-Schreiber 1984; Machnik 1991; Patay 2008). There are also other objects characteristic of the eastern group of the Bell Beaker, in particular, crescent-shaped bone pendants decorated with groups of diagonal lines (Patay 2013). In rare cases silver, electron, gold, and copper ornaments have been found (Endrődi, Gyulai, and Reményi 2008; Patay 2008). Some of the most spectacular have been reconstructed as a headdress from the site of Szigetszentmiklós-Üdülősor (Endrődi 2012).

Although the non-ceramic objects are largely those associated with the Beaker tradition, the majority of objects in the graves are local Carpathian ceramic forms. Analysis of the chemical composition of both bell beakers and local ceramic forms in Bohemia and Hungary indicates that Beaker and local pottery were similar in composition, suggesting that both were made locally (Rehman, Robinson, and Shennan 1992; Toth 2002 in Endrődi, Gyulai, and Reményi 2008). Different kinds of mugs and jugs are the most common forms, but there is a wide range of pottery that includes several different types of deep and shallow bowls with and without feet, perforated clay 'lids', and cooking and storage vessels. The latter, sometimes termed 'amphorae' with two handles placed below the rim, have been considered particularly characteristic of the Csepel group (Kalicz-Schreiber 1984; Machnik 1991), but many of the ceramics have been associated with other regional groups.

The relationship between Beaker elements and local Carpathian cultural forms has frequently been discussed in culture-historical terms (e.g. Kalicz-Schreiber 1984; Kalicz-Schreiber and Kalicz 1998/2000, 2001; Heyd, Husty, and Kreiner 2004; Endrődi 2013). What is striking about the Csepel group is the way that objects from different traditions were dynamically combined. These combinations can be explored at three scales analogous to those proposed by Csikszentmihalyi (1988) in his psychological analysis of creative processes: culture (the symbolic system), assemblages (the social system), and in relation to the body (the individual).

Creativity and the Cultural Combination of Objects

In addition to the Beaker tradition, the pottery of the Csepel group has been related to three other contemporary groups that surrounded it geographically: the proto-Nagyrév, late Makó-Kosihy-Čaka and younger Somogyvár-Vinkovci (Kalicz-Schreiber 1981, 1984; Kalicz-Schreiber and Kalicz 1999; Endrődi 2013) (Figure 4.3). Ceramics from these groups are widespread throughout Csepel sites. For example, at the cemetery site of Budatétény biconical jugs with comparatively tall necks and strap handles are characteristic of the proto-Nagyrév group (Kalicz-Schreiber 1984; Machnik 1991; Endrődi 2013). Decorated bowls and bowls with straight sides and a knob on the rim have been linked to the Makó-Kosihy-Čaka group (Kalicz-Schreiber 1984; Machnik 1991), while radiocarbon dates associated with

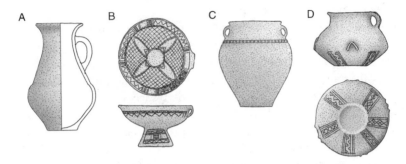

FIGURE 4.3 Examples of ceramics found in the Csepel group: A) proto-Nagyrév biconical jug, B) late Makó-Kosihy-Čaka bowl, C) Beaker amphora, and D) Somogyvár-Vinkovci vessel (redrawn after Machnik 1991, Kalicz-Schreiber 1997, Endrődi 2013).

the first appearance of type 34/35 jugs with rounded bellies, found throughout much of the Balkans and Beaker groups in Eastern Europe, suggest their first appearance in the Makó-Kosihy-Čaka (Piguet and Besse 2009). At the site of Békásmegyer a large proportion of non-Beaker ceramics, including various storage vessels, bowls and jugs, have been attributed to the younger Somogyvár-Vinkovci horizon (Kalicz-Schreiber 1997). Combinations of Beaker and Carpathian forms are also found in settlement assemblages. For example, at Albertfalva, storage vessels have been identified as reflecting Somogyvár–Vinkovci influence and jugs that of the Nagyrév (Endrődi 2013).

Most of the ceramics are undecorated although there are a number of more elaborate vessels. Some decorated vessels belong to regional decorative traditions while others show mixing of local ceramic traditions with Beaker decoration. The former include mugs with a bulging rounded belly and handle springing from the rim that are decorated with applied ribs on the belly; some of the ribs may be arranged in triangles or crescents, or as tendrils flowing from the base of the handle. The form of these vessels is similar to vessels of the Makó-Kosihy-Čaka group, and on a small number, additional decoration on the lower half of the vessel belly consists of incised slanted vertical lines composed so as to form a zigzag motif typical of the Nyirség-Zatin group (Kalicz-Schreiber 1984; Machnik 1991). There are also pedestalled bowls decorated on the interior of the vessel with a star-like motif around a central circle and with zigzags and/or triangles on the exterior of the vessel below the rim sometimes inlaid with white paste.

These have been understood as local versions of Makó-Kosihy-Čaka bowls (Machnik 1991). Vessels mixing local and Beaker decoration include inverted rim four-footed bowls decorated on the rim with motifs similar to those on bell beakers, and a small number of mugs ornamented with zigzags and lines on the upper part of the belly using a typical bell beaker technique (Machnik 1991). A particularly elaborate one-handled beaker with an asymmetric handle found at Szigetszentmiklós-Üdülősor combines Beaker decoration with a Nagyrév form (Endrődi 1992, 2013).

The ceramics of the Csepel group therefore combine Beaker and local traditions on two levels. The first is through the bringing together of culturally distinct objects. The second is through the combination of shapes and decorations on individual vessels. The integration of local ceramic forms into Beaker mortuary contexts is not unique. In some particularly well-furnished burials in the eastern zone of the Bell Beakers, in addition to one or more bell beakers there may also be a range of local ceramics known as *Begleitkeramik*. These can include plates and bowls depending upon the local context (Heyd, Husty, and Kreiner 2004). What is different in the case of the Csepel group is the type and extent of the use of local forms – in other words, the balance between bell beakers and local forms within assemblages since the former are by no means ubiquitous. In some cemeteries it has been estimated that only about 5 per cent of graves contain classic bell beakers or other richly decorated vessels typical of the wider Bell Beaker phenomenon (Machnik 1991). They are therefore relatively rare within the assemblage as a whole. This means that when bell beakers do occur they are rather striking, especially when, as on occasion, more than one such vessel is found in a single grave (see Endrődi 2012). This observation also raises the question as to what emphasis should placed on these particular vessels in interpretations of the cultural constitution of the Csepel group, or whether the more widespread combination of vessels of different local cultural traditions within the assemblage as a whole might be more significant. What is also unusual in the Csepel group compared to other Beaker contexts is the cross-fertilisation between local forms and bell beaker decoration, although compared to the overall number of ceramics such vessels appear to be relatively rare.

The ceramic repertoire of the Csepel group was a complex 'melting pot' in which objects from at least four different traditions were brought together at the single relatively small geographical meeting point of the Budapest region. Here the borders of the cultural units met, creating a cultural crossroads and the conditions for creativity. Rather than resisting 'the other', the people who lived here embraced this diversity by combining objects in a creative process of *bricolage* to create a new repertoire distinguished by its very variability.

This combination of objects can also be understood as bringing together different understandings of the world, ideologies and beliefs. Elsewhere in Europe the relative homogeneity of the Beaker material repertoire has been described in terms of a coherent ideological system in which the promotion of emerging social hierarchy and values linked to martiality, marksmanship, and a warrior ethos were expressed (Vandkilde 2007; Fokkens, Achterkamp, and Kuipers 2008). At the margin of the Beaker distribution, a process of blending took place in which different culturally specific ideas co-existed and combined in new ways (cf Turek 2012). This is vividly expressed not only in the range of burial rites co-existing within single cemeteries but may also have found expression in the articulation of beliefs, in particular an interest in the sun and celestial movements (Endrődi and Pásztor 2006; Endrődi, Gyulai, and Reményi 2008; Pásztor 2009). This, perhaps, can be understood in similar terms to the creation of a new 'interdisciplinary' field of knowledge formed through the combination of ideas at the margins. As in the development of any new field, however, this was not without potential tensions. Thus, while there are conspicuous differences between the objects placed in graves and in the elaboration of grave contexts themselves which have been related to hierarchy expressed in mortuary contexts (Kalicz-Schreiber and Kalicz 1998/2000; Endrődi 2012), such social differentiation does not seem to have been expressed in domestic settings. The houses in the large settlements at Szigetszentmiklós-Üdülősor and Albertfalva are extremely consistent in size and architecture (Endrődi 2012).

Creativity and the Combination of Objects in Assemblages

The recombination of objects and ideas evident at the broad cultural level was played out in different ways in the social categories expressed within mortuary contexts. In the Budapest region there are graves in which only Beaker objects were deposited, graves with both Beaker and Carpathian objects, and graves with only Carpathian objects. Within each of these categories there also appear to be complex combinations of different kinds of ceramics and personal objects. Given that objects reflect the social context of the people with whom they were deposited, the deliberate combination of objects in different ways thus created potential for the creation of different kinds of social presentations, which included the mixing, as well as the maintenance, of Beaker and local identities.

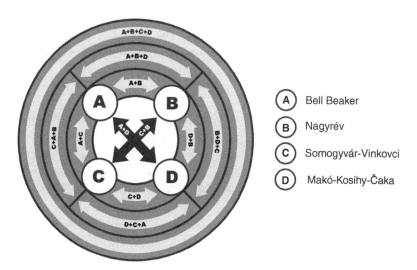

FIGURE 4.4 Range of identity categories that could potentially be created through the combination of objects in a Csepel group cemetery. A total of 15 potential categories of identity can be constructed, ranging from singular Beaker, Nagyrév, Somogyvár or Makó-Kosihy-Čaka to a combination of all of these.

In light of the wide range of ceramic and other objects available for combination, the variety of potential identities that could be created through this process was extremely complex (Figure 4.4). It not only included the combination of Beaker and Carpathian objects to create novel assemblages but the combination of objects to make assemblages composed of objects from more than one Carpathian tradition. Nonetheless, although there was a wide range of different combinations of objects, there are hints that these combinations were subject to a degree of social regulation in a manner that is reminiscent of Noam Chomsky's (1964) notion of rule-bound creativity. It was not a 'pick n' mix' society.

This regulation acted to maintain a distinction between people receiving different modes of burial. Beaker pottery and its combination with Carpathian forms is found most frequently in the unurned cremations as well as in inhumations (Kalicz-Schreiber 1997; Endrődi 2012; Patay 2013). It is less frequent in urn burials, which are primarily composed of local pottery types (Kalicz-Schreiber 1997). It therefore appears that within individual grave assemblages, the recombination of objects was carried out with an awareness of differences between people: in particular, those with Beaker affinities and those with distinctly Carpathian associations. Thus, while there are assemblages which bring together different material traditions there seems to have been an awareness of different cultural universes co-existing as well as blending. The Csepel group was not a completely creole society in which everyone shared a unique composite identity. Rather, individual assemblages combining objects from two or more otherwise distinct cultural systems may suggest the articulation of a sliding scale of cultural identification. Given that there was a social aware-ness of difference between Beaker and Carpathian objects, it is possible that their combination also expressed a bridging between different identities. The Csepel group may therefore represent a more subtle and complex mélange in which different kinds of combinatory identities – both creole (Beaker + Carpathian) and hyphenated (Beaker-Carpathian) – as well as singular identities (Beaker, Nagyrév, Somogyvár-Vinkovci, Makó-Kosihy-Čaka) co-existed. What appears to have been going on was an active creative renegotiation of what it meant to be both Beaker on one hand and linked to Carpathian traditions on the other.

Such renegotiation is also hinted at in graves containing objects belong-ing to the Beaker package through the ways that they were combined in order to express other aspects of individual identities. Elsewhere in Europe, the rather restricted range of objects forming the Beaker package is deployed in specific gender- and age-related combinations in a hierarchical manner; the deposition of particular objects in individual graves is linked to each other and to the presence of a bell beaker vessel (Thomas 1991). In general, based on associations between anthropologically sexed bodies and the objects placed within them, the assemblage in adult male graves may include a bell beaker, dagger, archery equipment and V-perforated bone buttons. Female graves may have a beaker, awl, beads of various materials that are arranged in different compositions, small metal ornaments includ-ing various metal discs and rings for attachments, and personal jewellery (Thomas 1991; Sofaer 2002; Vander Linden 2006).

For the Csepel group, although there is currently relatively little osteo-logical data available and some large recently excavated sites await full publication, the picture appears to be more complex than elsewhere on the continent. Although it shares similarities with burial practices in regions west of the Carpathian Basin, in terms of the structured deployment of objects with particular social categories, the Csepel group seems to have treated Beaker conventions as somewhat elastic. Thus, as in Central Europe, inhumations were placed in gender-specific positions (women on their right side and men on the left) with heads to the east (Patay 2013). There are also familiar associations such as between bell beakers, daggers and wristguards, or bell beakers, wristguards and arrowheads in grave assemblages (see, e.g., Kalicz-Schreiber 1976; Endrődi 2012). Other kinds of combinations, however, are notable. For instance, bell beakers have been found with a dagger, awl, ornament, and Carpathian bowl (Kalicz-Schreiber 1976: fig. 19), combining objects associated with men and women as well as Beaker and local traditions. Occasionally, lone elements of the Beaker package such as V-perforated buttons have been found in urn graves with local pottery (Kalicz-Schreiber 1976: fig. 22), although elsewhere in Europe these would likely be found together with other objects forming part of the Beaker package. It is possible, therefore, to tentatively suggest a bending of Beaker rules that were strongly enforced elsewhere. In the Csepel group the strict hierarchy of objects, and their alignment with social categories expressed in the graves of other Beaker communities in Europe, does not seem so clearly defined. This implies that in the Csepel group it may be useful to understand the 'Beaker package' slightly differently. Whereas elsewhere on the continent it refers to a specific combination of objects found in hierarchical association within a single grave assemblage, in the Csepel group it was expressed in terms of a cultural package from which elements could be extracted. This made it possible for just a single Beaker object to be deposited in a grave without being associated with a bell beaker vessel.

Creativity and Combination with the Body

In the Csepel group, creativity through recombination did not only apply to objects. It also took place through the recombination of objects with bodies in new ways, and in the variety of those combinations. Although the so-called symbolic graves do not, by definition, include human remains, the very absence of the body within these contexts acts to reinforce the impor-tance of body-object configurations within the cemeteries of the Csepel group. The intimate associations between bodies and objects in graves can be understood as creating something new – hybrids between nature and culture (Sofaer 2006) – and took a number of different forms (Figure 4.5).

In inhumation graves the body was placed in a crouched position on its right or left side most frequently in an oval or rectangular grave (Czene 2008; Patay 2013), although round graves have also been documented (Endrődi 2013). As previously discussed, this positioning resembles the principles employed for Beaker burials elsewhere in Europe where men were buried on their left side and women on the right (Mikołajczak and Szczodrowski 2012). As elsewhere, ceramics were placed in groups at specific points in relation to the body, such as at the feet, head, behind the pelvis, or in front of

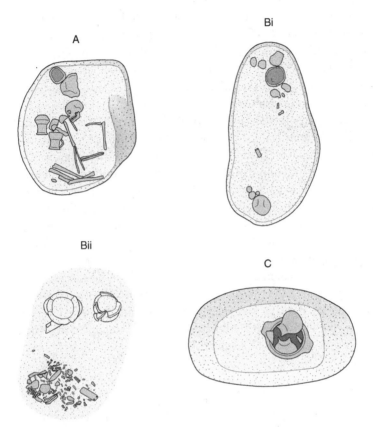

FIGURE 4.5 Forms of burial in the Csepel group: A) inhumation burial with objects placed on and around the body from Békásmegyer (redrawn after Kalicz-Schreiber 1976); B) unurned cremation burials: i) cremated remains scattered on the floor of the grave with objects placed around a 'ghost body' from Szigetszentmiklós-Üdülősor (redrawn after Endrődi 2012), and ii) cremated remains placed in a pile together with objects from Békásmegyer (redrawn after Kalicz-Schreiber 1976); C) urned cremation with objects, including ceramics, placed inside the vessel from Csepel-Vízmű (redrawn after Endrődi 2002).

the body (Kalicz-Schreiber 1976; Endrődi 1992; Czene 2008) (Figure 4.5A). Where other objects were deposited with the deceased, these were generally placed on the body in the position that they would have been used in life, such as the placement of a wristguard on the arm, bone pendant on the shoulder, or beads around the neck (Endrődi 2002; Patay 2008).

The unurned cremation graves resemble the inhumation graves in shape and size. Unurned cremations are also known from Moravia where they comprise up to 20 per cent of Beaker graves (Turek 2002), but in the Csepel group they are more common; at Békásmegyer 31 per cent of graves were scattered cremations (Kalicz-Schreiber 1997). In the Csepel group the bones in these graves were deposited in three distinct ways, creating different kinds of possibilities for associations with the body. In the first kind of unurned cremation the remains of the deceased were scattered over the floor of the grave. Here objects were sometimes placed around a 'ghost' body following a similar kind of choreography as in inhumation graves. For example, in grave 863 at Szigetszentmiklós-Üdülősor, a wristguard was placed in position as if it had been on an intact body, with pots at the 'head' and 'feet' of the grave (Endrődi 2012: fig. 3.1.2) (Figure 4.5B(i)). Vessels were also sometimes placed in a line along the centre of the grave as if marking out the long axis of a body (Kalicz-Schreiber 1984: table XLI; Endrődi 2013: fig. 2.3). The second kind of unurned cremation involved the placing of the cremated remains in a single pile (Figure 4.5B(ii)). In this case, where personal objects were deposited with the deceased, they appear to have been deposited together with the bones as they were excavated within the remains. Ceramics were placed in a group close to the pile of bones (Kalicz-Schreiber 1976). Objects were sometimes burnt on the pyre with the deceased and then placed with them in the grave (Kalicz-Schreiber 1976). In the third kind of unurned cremation, the ashes were not placed in a pit but simply strewn over the surface (Patay 2013).

The urn burials consist of an urn (usually an amphora) containing the ashes of the deceased, which was placed either in a small pit or inserted straight into the soil without a pit (Patay 2013). The cremated remains were placed within the urn, which was sometimes covered with a bowl and surrounded by a few other vessels (e.g. Endrődi 2002: fig. 6) (Figure 4.5C). Personal objects such as ornaments were placed within the urn together with the remains, but objects were sometimes also placed together with the accessory vessels. Bell beakers were only occasionally deposited with urned cremations (Patay 2013). Such urned cremation burials are not part of a Beaker burial tradition elsewhere on the continent. Instead they form part of a local Carpathian tradition seen particularly in the contemporary Somogyvár-Vinkovci group (Kulcsár 2009).

There are therefore several types of hybrids that coexisted simultaneously within the Csepel group. These included different kinds of body substances (skeletal or cremated bodies) and represent a spectrum in the presentation of the integrity of the human body from its full articulation in inhumation, through its reconstitution by means of the placement of objects, to its full reduction in scattered and urned cremations (cf Sørensen and Rebay-Salisbury

2008), and absence in the so-called symbolic graves. Ceramics and other objects were deliberately placed in relation to bodies both physically present and imagined. They were positioned in ways that created geographies of the body (Sørensen 2010), being placed around the body, containing it, or both. The variation in the range of distinctive and novel combinations of pottery and other objects with different types of bodies distinguishes the Csepel group both from other groups in the Carpathian Basin and from other Beaker groups on the continent. Inasmuch as hybrids are by definition creative expressions, it appears that at the margins the heightened potential for such creativity was fully embraced.

The creation of these hybrids was part of a dynamic process based on social connections between people in the melting pot environment of the Budapest region. In understanding how this creativity came about, it is important to note that each of the elements of these combinations – inhumed bodies and cremated bodies, ceramics of different forms, and personal objects – was familiar to at least one, and sometimes more, of the four groups that met in the central Carpathian Basin. Their creative combination within the mortuary domain was not, therefore, the result of a sudden innovation, but may instead have been made possible through a familiarity with the materiality of substance, if not of ideas. Thus, for example, a familiarity with cremation in the eastern Bell Beaker tradition, while not the dominant mode of disposal of the body, may have made it possible to embrace a wider Carpathian tradition of urned cremation, and vice versa. Each of the groups also used ceramics in mortuary depositions, even if this was differently expressed. In more recent contexts similar processes have been proposed, for example, for post-contact Mexico in the manner in which Christianity came to be seen as part of the Aztec divine through the selective combination of Indian and Christian iconographies, even if the systems of belief and ideologies of these two societies were quite different (Wake 2003). On one hand, such recognition involves the translation of practices into one's own cultural language (Mikołajczak and Szczodrowski 2012), but on the other it can only take place in the context of the development of new.

A Place for Creativity

Margins are places where people and ideas come together. In the Early Bronze Age, the Budapest region was one such place, and the people who inhabited it embraced the creative potential of this geography through dynamic interaction on a series of interrelated levels. On a cultural level, they brought together objects from at least four traditions, using them contemporaneously within a single social system. On a social level, these objects were recombined in a structured but also sometimes slightly eclectic manner to create a wide range of relational social identities. On an individual level, bodies and objects were combined as hybrids in a variety of ways that involved the creative reconfiguration and mixing of people and objects.

Embedded within the Csepel group was a distributed creativity in which relations between people were negotiated and expressed through the public combination and recombination of objects and different kinds of body materials. Here creativity was not the sole preserve of individual 'bright sparks'; it took place through the contextualised actions of people as part of dynamic and developing traditions. On one hand the extent of such recombination could be viewed as a dilution of Beaker ideology at the margin of the culture. On the other it can be seen as a positive, productive response to encounters with other groups. The dynamics between these different groups took place as an interchange of ideas and objects, even if this was not necessarily always an equal exchange, as the dominance of Nagyrév forms towards the end of the Csepel group might indicate. This creativity gave rise to difference and to the distinctiveness of the Csepel group through a multi-directional social dynamic. As the author Salman Rushdie put it, 'Mélange, hotchpotch, a bit of this and a bit of that is how newness enters the world' (1991: 393).

CHAPTER 5

Resistance

The Reappropriation of Objects, Actions, and Ideas

Anyone who has lived in Britain will be familiar with the phenomenon of the school uniform. Schools insist upon uniforms in order to generate a feeling of school community, create equality among students and to enforce a degree of discipline through the regulation of dressing behaviour. Students, however, constantly seek to modify and wear their uniform in different ways; boys deliberately wear their tie in a loose knot, while girls alter the length of school skirts. Such reactions to the requirement to wear a uniform are not simply fashion statements but can also be understood as deliberate attempts to resist regulation and authority by reconfiguring dress, albeit within established rules, in order to express a sense of individual identity.

Struggles to assert individual, group or local identities in ways that at once conform to, but at the same time also resist, dominant paradigms are widespread. They are particularly relevant in an increasingly globalised contemporary world culture in which individuals and communities continually create 'islands of identity' out of the ocean of culture flowing round them (Ó Crualaoich 2003). In this way, aspects of global culture are meaningfully interpreted and recreated in a local communal context; international trends are reinterpreted for oneself (de Cléir 2011). Research has sought to analyse responses to domination and the ways in which people resist oppression in everyday life. This perspective has seen expression in archaeology where material aspects of resistance have recently been a focus of investigation (e.g. Frazer 1999; Wilkie 2000; Leone 2005).

The identification of such responses to domination, or 'discipline' as Foucault (1977) calls it, raises the question as to what lies beneath such responses. In other words, by what means do people simultaneously act as part of society yet at the same time resist being reduced to mutely acquiescing machines? How do people manipulate the mechanisms of discipline and conform to them only to evade them? What ways of operating form the counterpart (on the dominee's side) of the establishment of socioeconomic order? (de Certeau 1984). The ways in which people manipulate dominant cultural forces by reappropriating objects, actions and ideas in order to conform to, but at the same time also reconfigure or resist, dominant paradigms can be understood as 'the procedures of everyday creativity' (de Certeau 1984: xiv). In this essay, I want to explore these issues through the distinctive ceramic assemblages found in the Late Bronze Age cemeteries of Velika Gorica and Dobova in Croatia and Slovenia.

Resistance and Everyday Creativity

In his book *The Practice of Everyday Life* (1984), Michel de Certeau argues that people employ 'tactics' of reappropriation. Such tactics relate to a notion of practice (or practical action) through which people exercise their creativity by manipulating or reconfiguring the ideologies, objects, or images that they consume. The creativity of which de Certeau speaks lies in cultural consumers resisting or reconfiguring ideas and objects by doing things in ways that are novel or different to those expected by dominant producers; de Certeau (1984: 24) calls this the 'art of practice'. Such 'tricks' are a way of coping or making do with a system that does not fit one's needs, resources, expectations, or aspirations. For example, de Certeau (1984: 30) discusses how a North African immigrant living in a low-income housing development in Paris and speaking the French language insinuates into the system imposed on him ways of 'dwelling' (in a house or a language) that are specific to his native Kabylia. The immigrant thus resists becoming entirely French by superimposing and combining ways of living in a manner that establishes a degree of plurality and creativity. Similarly, de Certeau (1984: 31) points to the ways that the Spanish conquest of the Americas was diverted from its intended aims by the use that indigenous Indian culture made of it. The indigenous people made the laws, practices and representations that were imposed on them 'function in another register' (de Certeau 1984: 32) by employing them to ends other than those of their conquerors. They thus remained 'other' within the system through procedures of consumption that maintained their difference, even in the spaces that the colonisers organised.

The culture of everyday life is thus a mixture of creativity and constraint (Fiske 1992) in which people use elements of cultural repertoire to carry out operations of their own. It is also contextually dependent and has its own historicity. Such notions are akin to Barthes' (1967) notion of the 'death of the author' inasmuch as they hand over creativity to the reader or user, recognising that people do new and potentially unexpected things with knowledge, ideas or materials. They, however, differ from Barthes in identifying not just the consequences of such reconfigurations but in analysing exactly how and what people *do* with these in the process of reconfiguration. Furthermore, in contrast to Barthes (1967), de Certeau (1984) argues that the intentions of dominant groups (or original authors) can be detected. By framing his exploration as resistance and reconfiguration in the practice of everyday life, de Certeau attributes both agency and a political dimension to the responses of consumers. As he points out, the extent and nature of creativity can only be understood by examining it in relation to the power structures and expectations of producers (de Certeau 1984). Since the practitioners of these reconfigurations or ruses (the workers, peasants, or lower classes – the 'popular' of popular culture as opposed to the elites) have less socioeconomic or ideological power than those who dominate, their resistance and independence in interpretation and use of the things they consume adds a political dimension to everyday practices. In this sense, analyses of creativity and resistance in everyday life are not simply a matter of description of behaviour but are about how people transform ideas, objects or images embedded in the dominant cultural economy in order to adapt them to their own interests and rules (de Certeau 1984).

This emphasis may be understood as a somewhat optimistic worldview inasmuch as it suggests that resistance and reappropriation are not only possible but also positive in nature. Nonetheless, the extent to which people can exercise creativity while remaining within the limits of cultural acceptability remains open to question. An emphasis on the 'creative consumer' may also be critiqued as belonging to a capitalist, market economy, although de Certeau suggests that tactics of reappropriation may go back into deep history (Buchanan 2000). Creativity is, in this sense, a fundamental part of the human condition and can be more widely understood as a response to unequal access to resources and to the imposition of dominant ideologies.

Importantly, such creative practices are not merely discursive but are expressed in tangible material ways. Since creativity is a way of thinking invested in a way of acting (de Certeau 1984), and acting involves relating and responding to the material world, investigation of the ways in which material culture is deployed is therefore key to understanding the creativity at play in specific settings. Objects offer to the analysis the *'imprints of acts'* (de Certeau 1984: 21 original emphasis) or 'museums of tactics' (de Certeau

1984: 23) that relate to ways of operating. The use or making of objects, and their roles in systems of representation, are not only normative frameworks but 'tools manipulated by users' (de Certeau 1984: 21 original emphasis). The material consequences of practice, therefore, are critical to recognising creativity. Furthermore, while the social order may constrain and oppress people, at the same time it offers them material resources to resist and reconfigure those constraints for their own purposes (Fiske 1992: 157). Analysis is thus about how to 'discern in these practices of appropriation indexes of the creativity that flourishes at the very point where practice ceases to have its own language' (de Certeau 1984: xvi–xvii).

To illustrate how this works it is useful to draw upon contemporary examples, including the work of Brett Williams (1988) on black American working class culture and Ondina Leal (Leal and Oliver 1988; Leal 1990) on first-generation urbanised Brazilian peasants. Williams (1988) describes how the poverty and material constraints of everyday life are compensated for by the 'texture' (the density and intensity of experiences, practices and objects) that is packed into the relatively small spaces of a neighbourhood or a single apartment. She argues that since people lack the resources to expand or transform their living spaces, they need to find ways to make it bearable. They do this by 'texturing' domestic spaces; weaving through them various sights, sounds and rhythms. To middle class taste the interior of an apartment might seem cluttered with knick-knacks and decorations, but this is part of a need to fill what otherwise appears to its inhabitants to be a glaringly empty space. It is a tactic to cope with apartment life. Producing texture is a creative use of the conditions of constraint (Fiske 1992: 156). It is making do with what people have (Fisk 1992: 158).

Leal's (1990) work describes how Brazilians moving to the city use objects to live meaningfully within the contradictions between urban and rural life. Here objects act as a symbolic system to 'conquer' the urban cultural space and indicate prestige to people from rural backgrounds, while still delimiting and differentiating the urban from the rural space that remains part of their identity. Leal (1990) describes objects placed around the TV set in one such Brazilian house: plastic flowers, a religious picture, a false gold vase, family photographs, a broken laboratory glass, and an old broken radio. In contrast to upper and middle class perceptions of plastic flowers as cheap, manufactured and ugly, to urbanised peasants plastic flowers were more beautiful than natural ones because they represented the manufactured and the new; since they cost money they brought with them legitimacy and prestige. They were part of an 'ethos of modernity' (Leal 1990: 25) and the new 'better' life people hoped to find by moving to the city. Natural flowers were part of the life they were fleeing. The meaning of the different kinds of flowers was thus reconfigured (Fiske 1992).

Such analyses speak strongly to established archaeological notions of domination and resistance (cf Miller, Rowlands, and Tilley 1989), while framing them within an understanding of the creative processes that underpin human responses. Furthermore, they suggest that the materiality of 'everyday creativity' (de Certeau 1984) lends itself to archaeological analysis. In particular, a focus on how and what people do with the material world speaks to archaeology inasmuch as it requires a description and narrative of objects in terms of their context, production, and use.

Creativity and Resistance: The Case of the Cemeteries at Velika Gorica and Dobova

The Late Bronze Age cemetery of Velika Gorica lies 10 km to the south of Zagreb, Croatia (Figure 5.1). It lends its name to the Velika Gorica group, a south Pannonian regional variant of the late phase of the Urnfield culture. The latter is found across the Carpathian Basin and, in turn, formed part of the broader European Urnfield phenomenon, the culturally dominant ideology of the Late Bronze Age in Europe. The Velika Gorica group also includes the cemetery sites of Krupače, Trešćerovac, Žamarija, Ozalj, and Zagreb-Horvati in continental Croatia (Vinski-Gasparini 1973; Karavanić 2009). In neighbouring Slovenia the cemetery at Dobova, as well as the first phase of the cemetery at Ljubljana, form part of the same cultural unit (Vinski-Gasparini 1973, 1983; Teržan 1999), although here it is known as the Dobova cultural group. A number of graves in the cemetery at Škocjan at Ponikve in Slovenia have also been suggested to have graves of 'Dobova type', but the mixture of traditions apparent at this site mean that it has been considered part of the so-called Karst cultural group (Teržan 1999). Similarly, the contemporary cemeteries of Ruše and Pobrežje in north-east Slovenia have been compared to those of Velika Gorica and Dobova in terms of both finds and social organisation (Teržan 1999) but are maintained as distinct cultural entities within the archaeological literature. All these cemeteries, however, form part of a similar set of burial traditions within southern Pannonia dating from the second half of the tenth century to the middle of the eighth century BC (Vinski-Gasparini 1983.).

Velika Gorica and Dobova are two of the best known late Urnfield cemeteries within the region. Velika Gorica was, however, excavated in a

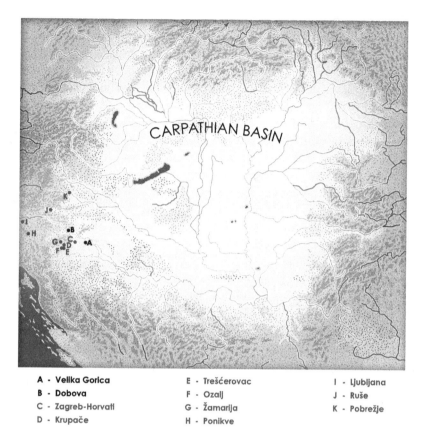

A - Velika Gorica	E - Trešćerovac	I - Ljubljana
B - Dobova	F - Ozalj	J - Ruše
C - Zagreb-Horvati	G - Žamarija	K - Pobrežje
D - Krupače	H - Ponikve	

FIGURE 5.1 Map of the Carpathian Basin showing the location of sites of the Velika Gorica and Dobova groups.

somewhat piecemeal manner at the start of the twentieth century (Hoffiller 1909, 1924; Staré 1957b). Several objects are mentioned in passing in excavation notes as having disintegrated upon lifting (Karavanić 2009). There is also a relatively large number of stray finds or finds from 'destroyed graves' (Karavanić 2009). Nonetheless, forty-one grave assemblages have been carefully reconstructed by Snježana Karavanić (2009). Dobova was excavated more systematically in the 1950s and early 1960s (Staré 1975). The number of burials known from the site is substantially larger than at Velika Gorica with 418 graves, suggesting frequent, regular use of the cemetery over the duration of its use. Velika Gorica and Dobova lie just 37 km away from each other on the natural pass from the upper to lower Sava valley that runs between the Medvednica and Žumberak-Samoborsko Gorje mountains (Karavanić 2013). The sites, therefore, were positioned on an important route from east to west and towards the northern Balkans (Karavanić 2000). Zagreb-Horvati lies between Velika Gorica and Dobova close to the river Sava. It was discovered in 1912, but unfortunately the finds from the site cannot be associated with individual graves (Karavanić 2009). Krupače, Trešćerovac, Ozalj, and Žamarije are on, or near to, the river Kupa, which flows into the Sava in the locality of Sisak. Krupače and Trešćerovac were discovered in the nineteenth century (Balen-Letunić 1981). The fragile objects did not always survive the excavation, and the contexts from which they derived are not always secure (Karavanić 2009). Ozalj and Žamarije were excavated in the 1970s, but only nine and one graves respectively are known from each of these cemeteries (Balen Letunić 1981). In addition to these cemeteries, there is a growing number of recently excavated contemporary settlements, including fortified sites in elevated positions (Vrdoljak 1996; Karavanić 2009, 2013;). The sites are also in a region with a history of earlier Bronze Age occupation (Dizdar, Tonc, and Ložnjak Dizdar 2011).

The Velika Gorica/Dobova burial rite conformed to the broader Urnfield tradition involving cremation of the body of the deceased. Most frequently, the cremated remains were deposited in an urn in a pit along with other ceramic vessels placed in a choreographed manner, sometimes together with bronze objects. However, within this general tradition the details of individual burials are somewhat varied both within and between cemeteries, a trend that is in line with recent observations regarding the complexity of Urnfield burials across the continent (Sørensen and Rebay 2008, 2009). In some cases, as at Krupače and Trešćerovac (Brunšmid 1898), smaller vessels containing the cremated bones were placed inside a larger vessel and a bowl placed upside down over the small and/or over the large vessel creating a nested or 'Russian doll' effect. Sometimes a cup or other small vessel was placed in the pit next to the larger vessel. More rarely, a suite of three or four vessels of different types were placed in a group next to each other, as for example in a number of graves at Dobova. At Velika Gorica smaller urns were generally used and were rarely covered by another vessel. Here, the cremated bones were not always inside the urn but placed near to it in the grave pit (Karavanić 2009). The number of vessels in any given grave is extremely variable (between one and nine), although large numbers of vessels are infrequent. Sometimes the cremated bones were placed directly in the pit without any vessel at all, as in several examples from Dobova (Staré 1975).

When metal objects were included in the grave, in some cemeteries, as at Dobova, these were most frequently placed inside a ceramic vessel (Staré 1975), although at Velika Gorica bronze objects were probably placed directly into the pit or possibly in an organic container such as a bag. Some objects, such as a bronze socketed axe from Velika Gorica seem to have been wrapped with textiles (Hoffiller 1909). Occasionally, as at Ozalj and Velika Gorica, other objects such as spindle whorls were also deposited in the grave (Balen-Lutenić 1981). The manner of construction of the grave is also very varied. Grave pits may be packed or lined with stones, as in a number of graves from Dobova and Ozalj (Staré 1975; Balen-Lutenić 1981). Ceramic fragments may also have sometimes been used as part of the packing (Staré 1975). At Trešćerovac, stone slabs were placed as if to seal the grave (Ljubić 1885), while in other cases the pit does not seem to have been elaborated in any way. All in all, excluding those graves which lack any grave goods, no two graves of the Velika Gorica and Dobova groups are identical either within a single cemetery or when compared with other burials in the group, suggesting a degree of freedom within burial practice.

Despite this variation in mode of burial, and the relatively modest nature of most of the burials in terms of the quantity and range of objects placed within them, the mortuary ritual was regulated in terms of the ways that particular combinations of objects were used to mark the age and sex of the deceased, as well as their status within the community (Trežan 1999). At Dobova the graves can be divided into three groups: burials without any grave goods, burials with only ceramic vessels, and burials with both ceramics and metal objects (Teržan 1999). At Dobova, the most frequent types of graves were those with only ceramic vessels (49 per cent), followed by those without any grave goods (29 per cent) and finally those with metal objects, primarily ornaments and jewellery as well as razors and tools (22 per cent) (Teržan 1999). The latter group could be further subdivided into five subgroups based on the types and combinations of metal objects, in particular those used to define different costumes, which Teržan (1999) relates to a single category of adult men and four differentiated categories of women.

At the other sites belonging to the Velika Gorica and Dobova groups the same material and social categories cannot be so easily identified. Many of the cemeteries have relatively small numbers of documented graves. Furthermore, because some were excavated in the nineteenth century or start of the twentieth century, graves without objects were not always recorded. Such graves undoubtedly existed, but the exact number is unclear (Karavanić 2009, 2011). Nonetheless, for Velika Gorica, while it is not possible to say how many individuals may have been buried without grave goods, Karavanić's (2000, 2009) work hints at the existence of different categories of person relating to interlocking status and gender categories (Karavanić 2009). At Velika Gorica fifteen graves contained only ceramic objects, nine contained only metal, and seventeen contained both ceramic and metal objects. Overall the cemetery contained 296 grave goods compared to 732 at Dobova. At Velika Gorica there seems to have been greater prominence given to metal objects, whereas at Dobova ceramics were emphasised (Karavanić 2009, 2011). At Velika Gorica there are three outstanding graves that contained a particularly rich and varied range of objects, including bronze tools, weapons and ornaments. One of these (grave 1/1911) has been identified as that of a warrior on the basis of the objects found within it (Karavanić 2009, 2011). Five other graves contained relatively large numbers of objects (between five and ten items), while some graves contained less than five objects (Karavanić 2009).

At both Velika Gorica and Dobova, analyses of objects placed with the deceased indicate that different social groups were expressed through material culture in the mortuary domain. Other cemeteries in southern Pannonia, for which similar analyses of graves goods have been carried out, in particular Pobrežje and Ruše, also reveal the articulation of such categories (Teržan 1999). As in the wider Urnfield world, differences in quantity and type of objects between graves can be understood in terms of the expression of hierarchy, gender relations and differential access to resources, in particular the ability of elites to access bronze, suggesting a need to demonstrate the 'place' of people within the social order.

Metalwork and Ceramics at Velika Gorica and Dobova

The metalwork repertoire in the graves at Velika Gorica and Dobova is very similar to that shared by other contemporary microregional groups in north-west Croatia and Slovenia (Vinski-Gasparini 1973: 198; Karavanić 2009). It demonstrates links eastwards to the wider Pannonian region, as well as north and westward towards the Alpine region, and contains generic classes of objects such as knives, fibulae, pins, ornaments and weapons that were common throughout the Urnfield world. Discussions of the parallels between specific objects in the cemeteries and elsewhere are extensive (Staré 1957a; Vinski-Gasparini 1973; Weber 1996; Karavanić 2009). To give some selected examples: At Velika Gorica knives of the Pfatten, Hadersdorf, Stillfried, and Seeboden types have parallels with sites in north-east Slovenia, Czech Republic, eastern Croatia (Eastern Slavonia), and the north-west Balkans (Glogović 2002). A knife from Dobova is similar to one in grave 125 in the cemetery at Budapest-Békásmegyer (Črešnar 2010). A so-called violin-bow fibula in grave 289 at Dobova is of a more widespread type that may have been made, or at least has relationships with, similar objects in the Posavina region of north Croatia (Pavišić 2003). Hairrings (*Noppenringe*) of different types including simple spiral coils, as well as more complex spirals with decorated or undecorated ends (usually assumed to be female ornaments), are found in both Velika Gorica and Dobova (Karavanić 2010); those from Velika Gorica are directly analogous to finds from Hungarian Transdanubia (Karavanić 2010). Pins of the so-called Velika Gorica type (found at both Velika Gorica and Dobova), have been connected to the Kvarner area of coastal north-west Croatia, while pins with a bulbous-shaped head, such as those found at Dobova, are from the south-eastern Alpine area to the Sava river basin (Blečić Kavur 2011). Finally, the spectacle fibulae (metal dress fasteners with a bow in the shape of a double spiral made of wire worn by women of high rank) have an extremely widespread distribution throughout the continent but are thought to have their centre of distribution in the Carpathian Basin (Alexander 1965; Pabst 2012).

Not just individual items but also combinations of objects further suggest relationships with the wider Urnfield world. For example, a rich female grave (3/1916) from Velika Gorica contained what may be a pair of small spectacle fibulae, a likely fragment of a harp fibula spiral, four bronze torcs, a possible fragment of a bronze sheet bracelet, a spiral ornament with pseudo-figure of eights and a knife. This reflects a combination of costume elements originating from the south-eastern Alpine and the central Danubian area (Ložnjak Dizdar 2009). Connections and influences from the south may also have existed. The large number of necklaces found in Velika Gorica (Karavanić 2009) speaks to links with the nearby Japodian tradition, as do the torcs found in Dobova (Ložnjak Dizdar 2009).

The material traditions of a wider region, therefore, were selectively embraced by communities in southern Pannonia as part of a 'nurturing of late Urnfield traditions' (Loznjak Dizdar 2009: 181). In this sense the elites of Velika Gorica and Dobova can be understood to have 'bought into' and to have conformed to the modalities of the dominant European Urnfield culture, and to have promoted these within their own communities.

The ceramics from Velika Gorica and Dobova emerged from the earlier Virovitica, Baierdorf-Velatice, and Zagreb Vrapče pottery traditions of south-west Pannonia (Vinski-Gasparini 1973, 1983) and are more regional in character than the metalwork. Nonetheless, as with the metalwork, many ceramic types are shared by the two sites (Karavanić 2009), just as they are shared by other sites and microregional groups in southern Pannonia (Vinski Gasparini 1983). For example, vessels with a conical neck, pronounced body and two handles on the shoulder (amphorae) are found at both sites and in almost all groups of the late Urnfield culture in the region (Karavanić 2009). Similarly, cups with a round body and a strap handle are found at both sites and are a widespread form characteristic of the late Urnfield cuture (Karavanić 2009). There are also bowls with flat bases and straight sides/rims, cooking vessels with everted rims, biconical vessels, bowls with inverted rims, slightly biconical cups, and bowls with an S-shaped profile. Decorative elements are also widespread throughout the region. For instance, similar forms of incised decoration (*pseudoschnur* decoration) may be seen on vessels from Velika Gorica, Ruše and Pobrežje (Karavanić 2009: 67). Even more widespread is the use of fluted decoration, which is present at Velika Gorica and Dobova on several different pottery shapes and is characteristic of Urnfield pottery throughout the continent. The so-called turban rim bowl – named for its twisted fluted decoration – of which there are examples at Dobova, is found throughout the Carpathian Basin. The ceramic choices made by the people of Velika Gorica and Dobova in their mortuary ritual were therefore integrated within a regional tradition of ceramic types and, as with the metalwork, point to wider Urnfield cultural references.

Yet, in addition to what one might term the standard cultural repertoire of Late Bronze Age cemeteries in southern Pannonia, there is also a highly distinctive form of urn that is found only at these sites and possibly one other – the cemetery of Tolmin in north-west Slovenia, although this site seems to have a different cultural affiliation (Svoljšak and Pogačnik 2001, 2002; Karavanić 2009). The vessels at Velika Gorica and Dobova can best be described as looking somewhat like cut-off prehistoric bowling balls (Figure 5.2). They have flat bases and rounded profiles. Many, although by no means all, have slightly inverted rims and the basic shape has several variants – some vessels are squat, others narrower and taller – while a small number are more bowl-like, being wide at the rim (Karavanić 2009). They range from 8.2 to 19 cm in height and have wall thicknesses of 0.5 to 1 cm (Karavanić 2009). Such variation suggests that they may have been made by several different potters. Nonetheless, a key shared feature is the presence of a round or slightly oval hole in the vessel wall, or less frequently (and only at Dobova) a hole or semicircle-like 'bite' at the rim. These holes were made as part of the manufacturing process prior to firing. The poor quality of the urns has frequently been remarked upon (Hoffiller 1924; Karavanić 2013).

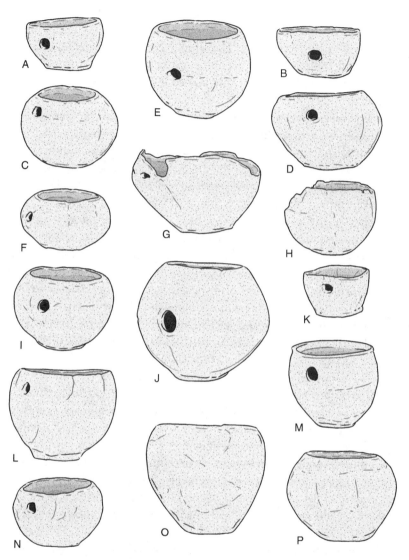

FIGURE 5.2 Urns from Velika Gorica (redrawn after Hoffiller 1924).

Many have been low fired, the fire-clouding suggestive of bonfire firing, and as a measure of their low quality, in contrast to other contemporary vessels, many have had to be heavily consolidated in order to conserve them. Both exterior and interior surfaces of the vessels frequently look rather lumpy, a feature which results from an undisguised simple thumbed out manufacturing technique and clay patching that is distinct from the predominantly coiled and smoothed manufacturing techniques of other vessels within the cemeteries. The simple forms, unstandardised vessel shapes, and distinctive manufacturing methods give the impression of production by people who were not trained in the making of ceramics, in contrast to other more complex vessels from the sites. Indeed, one might go as far as to suggest that the urns are 'homemade'. Certainly, they represent a completely different aesthetic to other contemporary vessels.

Viktor Hoffiller, the excavator of Velika Gorica, suggested that the urns with holes were local versions of the more elaborate house urns of the Late Bronze Age and Early Iron Age in Italy and Germany; he called them 'shrunken urns in the shape of a house' (Hoffiller 1924; Karavanić 2009: 66). The Velika Gorica and Dobova urns, however, lack any recognisable architectural features. This does not in itself mean that they were not house urns but, given the variety of positions of the hole (including on the rim), the relatively small size of the holes compared to the vessel body, the open form of many of the urns and the lack of lids or covering with other vessels at Velika Gorica, Hoffiller's interpretation must be brought into question. It is possible that the holes had some cosmological significance (Staré 1975), as has been argued for the so-called soul-holes observed on the earlier urns of Middle Bronze Age groups such as the Vatya culture in Hungary (Vicze 2011). Equally, they could have been used for some form of libation or for feeding the dead, both of which appear to have been part of Urnfield mortuary practices in other regions. For example, many of the boot-shape vessels in the Urnfield cemetery at Budapest-Békásmegyer, Hungary (Kalicz-Schreiber 2010), have holes at the toe end, presumably to facilitate the pouring of liquid. At Vollmarshausen in Germany, holes were made in previously fired urns after the funeral to feed the dead (Bergmann 1982; Rebay-Salisbury 2012). Irrespective of the specific interpretation of the urns at Velika Gorica and Dobova, and the possibility of shared customs with other Urnfield groups, the holes in the urns clearly represent a distinctive concept.

The urns with the holes at Velika Gorica and Dobova thus stand apart from other contemporary vessels in southern Pannonia in form, manufacturing technique and concept. They were, nonetheless, also used in a manner conforming with the dominant Urnfield tradition as they were used to hold the ashes of the deceased, and were placed in grave pits. To explore this tension between nonconformity and conformity, it is useful to examine the grave contexts in which they were found.

Urns with holes are known from eleven out of a total of forty-one graves at Velika Gorica for which assemblages can be reconstructed (Table 5.1),

TABLE 5.1 *Frequency of graves containing urns with holes and other objects at Velika Gorica and Dobova*

	Total number of graves in cemetery	Total number of graves containing urns with holes	Number of graves with only urns with holes	Number of graves with urns with holes + other ceramic types	Number of graves with urns with holes + bronze	Number of graves with urns with holes + other ceramic types + bronze	Total number of graves containing bronze
Velika Gorica	41	11	5	0	6	0	26
Dobova	418	55	26	4 (+7 graves containing sherds that may have been part of grave fill)	7	8 (+3 graves containing sherds that may have been part of grave fill)	92

Source: Based on catalogues in Staré (1975) and Karavanić (2009).

although it is possible that the actual number of urns from the site is higher as there are a number of graves with fragmented, incomplete vessels of the right shape to be urns. Additionally, there are three urns with holes from destroyed graves that are lacking context. However, given the excavation history of the site and the lack of recording of graves that did not contain objects, it is difficult to estimate the overall proportion of graves containing urns with holes. At Dobova, fifty-five graves contained urns with holes out of a total of 418 Late Bronze Age graves at the site. Of the graves containing urns with holes, at both Velika Gorica and Dobova, approximately half are not associated with any other grave goods. A small number form part of a grave assemblage containing urns with holes along with other types of ceramic vessels (four graves at Dobova and none at Velika Gorica). At Velika Gorica, six graves that had urns with holes also contained metal. At Dobova the urns were associated with metal in a total of fifteen graves; eight of these also contained other types of ceramic vessels in addition to the metalwork. At Dobova ten graves with the urns contained sherds (as opposed to complete vessels) of other vessel types. These may have been deliberately smashed as part of a funeral ceremony and/or used as part of the grave fill.

It is important to note that where urns with holes are associated with bronze objects and other ceramic forms, these tend to place the urns with holes in the same chronological horizon as the other graves in the cemeteries (Karavanić 2009). Explanations for the urns with holes, therefore, are not a function of chronology but must lie in the social realm.

Hoffiller (1924) suggested that the urns with holes were used to bury the poor of society. Karavanić (2009: 66) rightly points out that this statement is too simplistic, pointing to the numerous rich graves. It is notable, however, that although urns with holes do occur together with bronze objects, they do not generally feature in the richest assemblages. At Velika Gorica only one out of the richest eight graves (those containing more than five objects) included such an urn, while at Dobova only one grave containing an urn with a hole is in Teržan's (1999) Group I, which she describes as the wealthiest graves.

In the context of an hierarchical society such as clearly existed in Velika Gorica and Dobova, just as it existed in the wider Urnfield world, it appears that, with some exceptions, urns with holes were not objects desired by most members of the socioeconomic elite who had access to the greatest range of metal items. On the whole, those who were able to access objects that were widely accepted across the region as conforming to the dominant Urnfield ideology did not want anything that stood out as 'different'. By contrast, it may be suggested that in response to the dominant ideology that swirled around them, those who had limited or no access to otherwise widely accepted Urnfield metal and ceramic objects did not attempt to imitate them in a more shoddy or less skilled fashion but instead created new local forms. Furthermore, despite the importance of gender within Urnfield society, it appears that these novel forms were given to both men and women and were not gender associated; urns with holes are found in graves with typically male objects such as razors, as well as in graves with typically female ornaments.

The Urns of Velika Gorica and Dobova: A Creative Response

The Velika Gorica and Dobova urns with a hole may thus be understood as creative responses in which less powerful members of society simultaneously resisted and reconfigured the rules of existing dominant Urnfield practices. While the elites were both able and willing to buy into a widespread regional acceptance of Urnfield ideology and to promote this in the mortuary ritual, those without access to such resources exercised their creativity by bending the rules to fit their own needs through a creative 'making do' with the resources at their disposal. In making the urns they did with the resources and skills available to them in a manner that took on and manipulated widespread Urnfield ideas but reinvented them as a local phenomenon.

The 'art of practice' (de Certeau 1984: 43) at Velika Gorica and Dobova, saw creativity expressed through the making of material culture that did not conform either to prevailing Late Bronze Age aesthetic notions or, indeed, to modern concepts of beauty. Like the plastic flowers enjoyed by the modern Brazilian peasants who moved to the city, particular members of Late Bronze Age communities at Velika Gorica and Dobova also sought to define themselves through a different aesthetic that complemented and added texture to the burial rite. Ludwig Wittgenstein pointed out that it is from the inside that it becomes possible to recognise an outside (Janik and Toulmin 1973). By using urns with holes in the burial rite, members of the Velika Gorica and Dobova communities engaged in an act of self-definition that conspicuously set them apart from others. Thus while they conformed to Urnfield rules through the rite of cremation and, where metal and occasionally other ceramic items were used, to established Urnfield material forms, they also asserted a local identity. Given the variety in the form of these urns and their distinctive manufacturing traits, it is possible that they may even have produced the vessels themselves, adding another dimension of deliberate action to the reconfiguration of Urnfield burial practice.

Such creativity was made possible by prevailing attitudes to burial practice. As no two Urnfield graves in southern Pannonia are identical, this variation in Urnfield burial practice meant that there was creative space available to manipulate and work through the Urnfield rules. In other words, there were gaps within the prevailing ideology that permitted creativity in burial practice to take place. This facilitated the creativity of the people within the communities at Velika Gorica and Dobova in making and using the distinctive forms of urns found at these cemeteries. They made Urnfield ideas 'function in another register' (de Certeau 1984: 32), retaining their local identity or 'otherness' in the face of the wider Urnfield ideology.

Such arguments have wider relevance to established archaeological understandings of the concept of status and social difference that are typically based on the assumption that distinct forms of material culture reflect different social groups. This is, of course, the premise that I have used in my analysis. Yet *why* such identities should be expressed is frequently taken for granted. Similarly, the processes of *how* they are maintained have rarely been interrogated. Analysing these within the frame of creativity offers a human understanding of the ways that people can play with material difference to define, reconfigure and maintain understandings of self in relation to others.

CHAPTER 6

Mimesis

The Relationship between Original and Reproduction

When my son Noah was seven years old, he did a show-and-tell project at school. This involved taking in a few of his favourite things and telling the class about them. Along with the Spiderman figure, family photo and book, the star attraction of his presentation was, as he put it 'a *real copy* of a sabre-toothed tiger tooth'. What did he mean by 'real copy'? He knew that it was not original, but in his imagination he saw it as real. It was as close to the tiger as he could get. By all accounts the class were most impressed by the tooth. I like to imagine the oohs and aahs as this most exotic of imitations was brought out of Noah's bag.

This anecdote is about mimesis – the relationship between original and reproduction – which has long been understood as fundamental to discussions of creativity. It provides a means of understanding the move from the existing to the new since creativity does not emerge in a vacuum but is based upon existing knowledge (Pope 2005). Only through understanding this relationship is it possible to identify novelty and what constitutes creativity. The concept of mimesis has a role in understanding visual art, aesthetics, literature, language, music and theatre and has more recently informed research in psychology, education, post-colonial studies, political theory, biology and anthropology (Potolsky 2006). In archaeology, however, mimesis has only relatively recently begun to be overtly explored, although it has long had an implicit role in understanding material culture.

In this essay, I want to look at a range of different approaches to mimesis and their implications for exploring creativity in archaeology. My case study focuses on ceramics from the Late Bronze Age/Early Iron Age site of Vukovar Lijeva Bara in east Croatia.

Mimesis, Materiality and Creativity

Plato first introduced the term 'mimesis' in the *Republic*, articulating it in terms of the physical representation or imitation of actions, words or forms. To Plato copies were inherently inferior to originals on the basis that an imitation can never be identical to (and therefore not as good as) an original (Edwards 1967; Potolsky 2006). He was particularly concerned with the way that mimesis raises questions of ontological uncertainty, epistemological issues of how to distinguish the genuine and the impostor, the morality of mimesis, and how to deal with optical illusions that epitomise the deceptiveness of the material world (Newbold 2010), since the deception inherent in mimesis affects the perception and behaviour of people. Yet deception and illusion are also important creative phenomena. For example, effects such as the trompe l'oeil, or image reversal, have long been identified as part of the creative process in Western visual art (Seckel 2004). To Plato, however, mimesis was threatening. The nature of mimesis is such that it highlights the shiftiness of the world. It thrusts before the perceivers the problematic relationship of original and copy and forces them to ask: What is reality? What is illusion? (Newbold 2010). Traditional archaeological culture-historical interests in describing origins and the relationships between objects based on typology are essentially Platonic concerns. Mimesis is fundamental to the replication of objects within a tradition and to their social acceptance.

In contrast to Plato's distrust of mimesis, his pupil Aristotle viewed imitation as a means of learning about nature that allows people to get closer to the 'real' (Potolsky 2006), an idea familiar to those of us who were taught that by drawing (rather than photographing) archaeological objects we would see them differently and thereby understand them better. Here mimesis is not a way of tricking the observer into thinking that the copy is a reality – the reproduction is understood to be a simulation – but stands embedded within the creative process. Reproductions do not mirror reality but are effective if they resonate with the beliefs of the observer (Potolsky 2006). This approach to mimesis can be seen as underpinning the production of skeuomorphs: the manufacture of an object in one material that imitates their production in another. Skeuomorphs are not simply metaphors for other artefacts (cf Hodder 1993) but are mimetic and as such have a range of culturally specific associations. For example, in his study of Minoan ceramics, Carl Knappett (2002) explored the way that ceramic skeuomorphs of silver cups were 'icons' of the group to which they referred but were consumed as emulations, rather than as originals, and were 'indexical' of elite status in their own right.

The Romantic movement of the eighteenth century expanded the relationship between original and copy by understanding mimesis as part of individual creativity in which representations could encompass internal, emotive and subjective images. Imitation was not limited to the physical or 'real' but could also be of the idealised and experienced (Kelly 1998), an idea that continues to influence understandings of art, music, film and theatrical performance today. Jean-Jacques Rousseau, however, also saw mimesis as dangerous and potentially corrupting (Potolsky 2006), arguing that the foundation for imitation comes from a desire not to learn or to improve but rather to 'make an impression on others' (Rousseau 1979: 104), thereby implicating it in social relations (Potolsky 2006). This idea resonates in widespread archaeological understandings of the production, replication and use of so-called high status objects.

Nineteenth and twentieth century psychoanalytical turns on the concept of mimesis were influenced by Aristotelian thought and its subsequent development (Dornisch 1989), notably in the work of Sigmund Freud (1899) and Paul Ricoeur (1984). Both developed the twin themes of experience and threat in the analysis of narratives, including stories and dreams and the ways that these relate to the original reality of experience. In particular, Ricoeur's focus on the relationship between narrative and time has had archaeological appeal (Hodder 1993). Ricoeur was concerned with the interweaving of fictional and historical narrative (Dornisch 1989) and suggested that mimesis has three modes: practical experience or the experience of being caught up with stories, emplotment or the way that events are pulled together to create a narrative, and the process of reading or the way that the story relates to the experience or actions of the reader. There is, therefore, an interplay between lived experience, including social relations, and the narratives that order such experiences (Hodder 1993). This is of direct relevance to archaeology since material culture is the result of practical experience and, in its representational, expressive and symbolic aspects, the result of telling stories about ourselves to ourselves (Hodder 1993: 270). In other words, the material record was produced within a narrative experience (Hodder 1993: 279). As Ricoeur (1975) pointed out, the construction of narrative – its language, rhetoric, metaphors, and imagination – is fundamentally creative.

In the nineteenth and early twentieth centuries, colonial engagement with 'the other' gave rise to anthropological accounts of premodern imitation and sympathetic magic as described by anthropologist Sir James Frazer in *The Golden Bough* (1890), and by Marcel Mauss and Henri Hubert in *General Theory of Magic* (1904) (Potolsky 2006). These continue to be highly influential in contemporary reflections, drawing upon the concept of mimesis. For example, in his essay 'Viscerality, Faith and Skepticism: Another Theory of Magic' (Taussig 2006), the writer and anthropologist Michael Taussig describes how the work of so-called shamans, witch doctors and sorcerers relies on a dialectic between belief and skepticism. On one hand shamans recognise the existence of the spirits and efficacy of their practice. On the other they understand that what they do is based on slight of hand, tricks and deception and they may express deep reservations regarding the putative powers of others who share their profession. Shamans thus pretend that they are what they refer to, but at the same time they recognise the artifice (Taussig 2006). This process is shared by those around them, inviting a kind of collusion in what Taussig (1992, 2006) calls the 'nervous system'. Recognising and revealing tricks is central to the creation and maintenance of this system through 'the skilled revelation of skilled concealment' (Taussig 2006: 123), since it is only through exposure that it becomes possible to sort out real magic from that which is deceit. Unveiling the trick is thus no less necessary to the magic of magic than its concealment (Taussig 2006: 129). But at the same time the deceit has power of its own. In such sympathetic magic at stake is the creativity of the shaman within the field of deception and revelation but also his or her creative agency in terms of an ability to effect change in the world.

In archaeology, it is this anthropological understanding of mimesis that has most frequently been deployed. Archaeologists have drawn upon Alfred Gell's *Art and Agency* (1998), in which (like Taussig) he discusses the role of objects in terms of mimetic or sympathetic magic (e.g. Kinahan 1999; Harrison 2003; Jones 2005; Nakamura 2005). Here, as in the eponymous 'voodoo doll', where the manipulation of the doll affects the person whom it represents thereby offering the possibility to effect change remotely, objects represent people or create concrete associations between disparate phenomena (Kinahan 1999). In other words, access to an object offers similar possibilities to having access to the body of the person themselves or to other things. The object is thus positioned as an agent which creates change through the mimetic process, be that for good or bad. This is what might be called 'mimetic magic' or 'contagious magic involving what appears to be a physical connection in order to effect, through rite, the substance connected' (Taussig 2006: ix–x). In this sense materiality is essential to mimesis (Nakamura 2005; Taussig 2006). The vital link between mimesis, materiality and creativity is implicit. It lies in the human creative imagination – the ability to make the leap from object to person. Creativity also demands agency: the ability to change the world through the medium of material objects (cf Harrison 2003).

The triangular relationship between mimesis, creativity and social relations was further developed by the writer and philosopher Walter Benjamin in his seminal essay 'On the Mimetic Faculty' (1933). Benjamin saw mimesis as an essential part of the human condition. He argued that mimesis is not a question of straightforward imitation but akin to a process of modelling which results in a constructive reinterpretation of an original, to the point where the representation may assume the character and power of the original (Taussig 1993). For example, a child's acquisition of language and social behaviour is based on modelling surrounding adults, but the child reconfigures these to make something entirely new (Benjamin 1933). The same principle sits beneath familiar twenty-first century concerns regarding the effects of violent computer games and advertising on the behaviour of children and young adults.

According to Benjamin, mimesis can be expressed not just between things that resemble each other but in similarities between things that are materially different, animate and inanimate, the microcosm and macrocosm, in what Benjamin (1933) called 'nonsensuous similarity' (Potolsky 2006: 127). To illustrate this concept he used the example of a child imitating a train or a windmill (Benjamin 1933). In his understanding of mimesis Benjamin was heavily influenced by anthropological accounts, pointing to 'magical correspondences and analogies that were familiar to ancient peoples' (Benjamin 1933), suggesting that material forms can mirror the structure of the cosmos (Stafford 2007: 81). Mimesis is thus a matter of evocation rather than of imitation. For instance, in music the expression of a place, feeling, weather or even animals as in Camille Saint-Saëns famous suite *Carnival of the Animals* (1886), recalls its point of inspiration but retains an identity as something distinctly new (cf Calderoni 2010).

Benjamin's primary concern in discussing mimesis was the nature of language and art as they pertain to social relations (Benjamin 1933). For Benjamin, language was the crucial means for the formation of nonsensuous similarities (Potolsky 2006). Thus, for example, the possibility of translation offers the opportunity for nonsensuous similarity between words, although they refer to a common concept, whereas reading produces nonsensuous correspondences between text and spoken word, and text and the world (Potolsky 2006: 127). Benjamin's focus on language and his apparently immaterial concerns may go some way to explaining why his thought has so far been little explored within archaeology, despite his profound influence elsewhere in the humanities. Yet in the *Arcades Project* and elsewhere (Benjamin 1999), he developed an interest in material culture and in what has been termed an 'archaeology of modernity' (Emden 2006: 101). He also reached for the object-centred discipline of archaeology as a means of exploring the literary and making it concrete (Réjouis 2009). Benjamin considered technology (which he saw together with the notion of art in its broadest sense) as part of the human facility for mimesis (Desideri 2005). Technology is mimetic since not only is its Promethean nature fundamentally transformative, but technological activities require premeditation as to how something should turn out, and this invites conscious mimesis (Desideri 2005). Mimesis is thus a social practice that constructs new realities and is in itself a creative act. Indeed, Benjamin saw mimesis as the original impulse of all creative activity (Leslie 2000); mimesis is essential to creativity in moving from the existing to the new.

It is important to realise here that Benjamin's approach to mimesis relies upon culturally specific understandings of conventions such that there is a match between the new and the expectations of its audience (Potolsky 2006: xv). In other words, Benjamin's mimesis only works within the orbit of a familiar context. Thus, as in Marcel Proust's famous account of the tea-soaked madeleine which the narrator brings to his lips in *In Search of Lost Time* (Proust 1992), the taste of the madeleine does not simply recall *to him* Combray but *is* Combray. This so-called Proustian effect (Sofaer and Sofaer 2008) is one of mimesis such that objects are the means by which scenarios and situations that are not present at the moment get conjured up in the mind's eye (Stafford 2007: 81), but if you or I were to eat that same madeleine, then the mimetic power of the object would not necessarily work for us. Nonetheless, mimesis can also promote shared experiences as in the shared evocations created by music or film. Similarly, posting photographs on Facebook may be seen as an attempt to provoke shared responses. This creates a further dimension to mimesis emphasised in modern psychology inasmuch as imitation is not just limited to replication of an object or to the intellectual comprehension of another person's intentions, but embraces the ability to intuit and feel along with what another person may be feeling at any given moment (Stafford 2007: 84). Such 'emotional contagion' (Jeannerod 2002) – the involuntary impulse to mimic, replay or stimulate someone else's waves of feeling within our own – can also be provoked by responses to material culture (Stafford 2007).

The relationship between copy and original persists as a key concern in explorations of creativity in postmodern society as witnessed, for example, in contemporary anxieties about the role and effects of rapid prototyping in contemporary art, virtual reality and the Internet. They have been particularly influenced by the work of philosopher Gilles Deleuze (1968) and his concept of the simulacrum – the image that is its own original and does not depend on an origin for its effect – and Jean Baudrillard's (1988) notion of hyper-reality. In the latter, people living in a society without boundaries never experience reality, but only simulations of reality – that is, mimetic reproductions or what he refers to as simulacra – through the television and the Internet. The media thus constructs the meanings of objects. Such concepts seem far from the more rule-bound situated materiality of prehistory in which the balance between tradition and novelty, belief and skepticism, were different to today, although the concept of the simulacrum has been explored within the context of the replication of objects in the Scandinavian Early Bronze Age (Flohr Sørensen 2013). In a provocative twist, it has been argued that postmodernity has returned to the premodern condition of sympathetic magic, where mimesis is inextricably woven into the fabric of reality itself (Potolsky 2006: 140).

Mimesis has several different layers. It is both process and thing. It may be either of oneself in relation to another person or object, or in making a reproduction of something else. Or it may occur as a third party engages with a reproduction, in which case it becomes a vehicle for identifying with the original act or thing. Mimesis, therefore, may be expressed both by the person who makes an object and by the person who experiences it. Mimesis can be an individual or a shared experience. In all cases, however, mimesis has a creative dimension, whether this lies in choosing materials, the act of making, imagining, using, perceiving, narrating, experiencing objects, or a combination of these. The link between mimesis, creativity, material culture and social life lends it particular analytical potency.

Rather than focus on one particular definition or understanding of mimesis, I want to explore these different layers of mimesis and the different kinds of creativity they engendered in the ceramics from the Late Bronze Age/Early Iron Age site of Vukovar Lijeva Bara.

Creativity and Mimesis: The Case of Vukovar Lijeva Bara

The cemetery of Vukovar Lijeva Bara lies in the region of western Syrmia close to the most eastern point of modern Croatia (Figure 6.1). It is located on the right bank of the River Danube at the transitional point from the alluvial plains of the lower Drava River to the elevated loess plateau of the River Danube (Vinski 1959; Demo 2009). Vukovar has a long history of prehistoric occupation dating back to at least the Early Neolithic (Demo

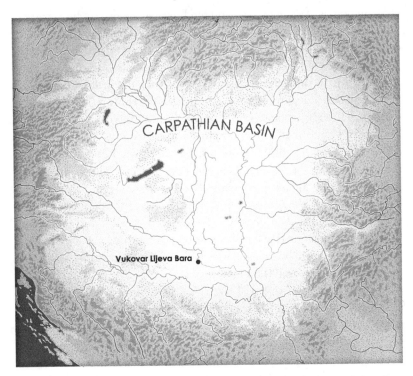

FIGURE 6.1 Map of the Carpathian Basin showing the location of Vukovar Lijeva Bara.

2003; Durman 2007) including Bronze Age settlements (Balen-Letunić 1996).

The site was investigated during rescue excavations from 1951 to 1953 and is multilayered. Overlying a substantial Late Bronze Age/Early Iron Age cemetery were a small number of isolated La Tene cremation burials and a large early medieval cemetery (Vinski 1959; Demo 2009). A total of 101 cremation graves were discovered from the Late Bronze Age/Early Iron Age phase belonging to the local Dalj group of the Urnfield culture (1000–550 BC) (Vinski 1955, 1959; Vinski-Gasparini 1973), along with nine contemporary prehistoric inhumation graves (Vinski 1959; Demo 1996, 2009; Metzner-Nebelsick 2002); the mode of burial and grave goods of the latter have been interpreted as evidence for foreign ethnic elements in the context of wider inter-regional communication and as showing the influence of the Bosut culture (Vinski 1959; Metzner-Nebelsick 2002; Durman 2007; Potrebica 2008). As a result of this palimpsest, the prehistoric grave contexts were sometimes disturbed (Vinski 1955, 1959; Metzner-Nebelsick

FIGURE 6.2 Graves from Vukovar Lijeva Bara (photographs: Archaeological Museum in Zagreb).

2002). The excavated area was 3,050 m² although it is possible that the actual area of the cemetery was larger (Demo 2009):

The Urnfield graves usually took the form of round pits up to 1.80 m in diameter (Vinski 1959; Metzner-Nebelsick 2002). Within the pit was placed an urn containing the ashes of the deceased that was occasionally covered with a bowl. Up to eleven other vessels were grouped around the urn (Balen-Letunić 1996; Metzner-Nebelsick 2002; Durman 2007; Karavanić 2009) (Figure 6.2). The number of vessels varies according to which of three chronological horizons the grave assemblage belongs (Metzner-Nebelsick 2002). Deposition of metal objects in the graves was rather rare. Only thirteen of the cremation graves contained bronze, and in these there were only one or two metal objects per grave (Vinski 1959; Metzner-Nebelsick 2002). They included earrings, fibulae, spiral hair ornaments, and buttons (Vinski 1959; Durman 2007). The male Bronze Age inhumations contained weapons, a whetstone and metal costume fittings whereas the female inhumations contained hair-rings, bracelets, and diadems (Vinski 1955, 1959; Durman 2007). As in other contemporary cemeteries, the metal objects were fire-damaged, suggesting that they had been burned together with the deceased (Metzner-Nebelsick 2002; Karavanić 2009). It is likely that cremation took place within the cemetery, as indicated by areas of burning also associated with faunal remains (Metzner-Nebelsick 2002). Stone structures within the cemetery hint that there may also have been graves in which the ashes of the deceased were placed directly in the ground without an urn (Metzner-Nebelsick 2002); there are thirteen graves without pottery (Karavanić 2009).

The Bronze Age ceramics from the site include those typical of the Dalj group, displaying similarities to vessels from the sites of Dalj, Batina, Šarengrad, and Doroslovo (Balen-Letunić 1996; Metzner-Nebelsick 2002). The assemblage includes a relatively restricted range of forms: large and small biconical vessels with everted rims and cylindrical necks (with or without small strap lugs), S-profile vessels, cups with high looped strap handles, so-called turban rim bowls with twisted inverted rims and variants of these with faceted rims, as well as inverted rim bowls with a pedestal and higher walled straight-rim bowls (Balen-Letunić 1996; Metzner-Nebelsick 2002). The distribution of the inverted rim bowls is particularly widespread, being found in contemporary settlements of the Karlovac region to the west, and further to the north in the centre of the Carpathian Basin in the Vál group of the Urnfield culture in Hungary (Tkalčec, Karavanić, and Kudelić 2011), as well as to the east in Vojvodina.

Mimesis and Illusion

Decoration on the Dalj group vessels is restricted and is linked in a strict way to particular vessel forms. For urns and turban rim bowls in particular, the relationship between vessel decoration and form creates striking visual optical effects.

Similar to other Urnfield pottery throughout the continent, the urns have fluted (sometimes called channelled) decoration. This fluting sits around the belly of the pot. The lines of the fluting tend to vertical orientation and may be relatively close together or wider apart depending on the width of the channel, suggesting that the pots were decorated by different hands. In all cases, the lines of fluting are evenly spaced, however the curved belly of the pot generates perspective. This means that when viewed from the side the lines appear closer together. The fluting draws the eye across the widest part of the pot and appears to elongate it. The bulging shape of the pot is thereby exaggerated, and the pot appears to be larger than it would be without the decoration. In Figure 6.3 the decoration on the right side of the

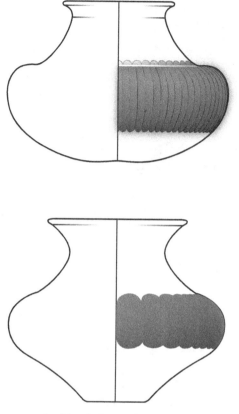

FIGURE 6.3 Vessels from Vukovar Lijeva Bara. The decoration on the right side of the drawing creates an optical illusion, making the vessel look larger than its undecorated mirror image on the left side.

vessel makes it look larger than its mirror image on the left minus the decoration.

The decoration on the turban rim bowls also creates an optical effect (Figure 6.4). Most of these vessels have either an omphalos base resulting in a circular raised bump in the centre of the interior of the vessel, or an applied boss in the centre of the interior of the bowl. These frequently have an incised groove around them that draws the eye to this point. The majority of turban rim bowls lack further elaboration and the bosses are mostly undecorated, although there is a range of motifs that divides the boss into four quarters, for example, incised triangles filled with slanting lines. When turban rim bowls are more extensively decorated, this follows one of

FIGURE 6.4 Turban rim bowl from Vukovar Lijeva Bara. The decoration draws the eye to the centre of the vessel while the twist of the rim appears as diagonal lines moving away from it. The effect is to create an optical illusion of depth (photograph: J. Sofaer).

two existing decorative schemes. The first and most common scheme is a series of incised concentric circles described around the central boss; it is arguable that even when there is a boss without further elaboration or a boss with a single incised groove around it that this may simply be a pared down version of the motif. The second involves a series of four, six or sometimes more incised or applied lines radiating from the central boss. In both cases, the circularity of the vessel shape is drawn into the motif. Looking into the bowl, the twist on the rim appears as diagonal lines moving away from the centre. When combined with the boss in the centre of the bowl, this twist and the elements of the motif (either the circles or radial lines) create an impression of depth, although the bowls themselves are rather shallow (circa 4–5 cm deep).

The decoration on the urns and turban rim bowls follows principles of visual perception that can be understood today in terms of optical illusions. The essence of illusion is to deceive the viewer by imitating something else. In other words, they are mimetic in a sense that echoes the Platonic concern with the constitution of reality.

Mimesis and the Imitation of Form

A notable feature of the assemblage is difference in the firing and surface finish of vessels even within a single vessel type. Some vessels are well fired and highly burnished. These tend to be those that are more elaborated. More frequent are rather low-fired vessels that are more lightly burnished and therefore have a more matt appearance. The latter would be much less efficient in holding food or liquid as they are rather porous. Therefore, it is possible to suggest that there are two classes of pottery in use at the site: vessels that were originally produced for use in households or settlements and those that were made specifically for deposition during the burial. While the quantity of Dalj pottery known from cemeteries far exceeds that from settlements, many of the forms seem to exist within both contexts (cf Vinski-Gasparini 1973, 1983; Metzner-Nebelsick 2002; Potrebica and Dizdar 2002; Tkalčec, Karavanić, and Kudelić 2011).

The phenomenon of cemetery pottery – pottery made specifically for the burial – is well known in the Carpathian Basin (e.g. Budden 2007). Low-firing of vessels conserves fuel resources during the firing process (Budden 2007). Likewise, lightly burnishing vessels reduces the time and effort of the potter when vessels do not need to be water resistant. Maintaining the socially recognised shape of the vessel, however, ensures that the ability to make an impression on observers is retained. The low-fired, lightly burnished pots, therefore, were not intended as straightforward one-to-one copies which Bronze Age potters could undoubtedly have produced had they so desired. They are more complex. Through mimesis they interweave a lived experience of material culture by way of their association with domestic contexts, with a fictional narrative in which they *look* like they could be used for utilitarian purposes, although a familiarity with domestic vessels (as one might expect for Bronze Age people) would make it clear that in fact they could not. The poignancy of this intertwining of different narratives is accentuated through the burial context where, as I shall suggest shortly, cosmological stories played an important role.

Mimesis and Assimilation (Revelation and Concealment)

Although a somewhat cursory inspection of some of the vessels would have exposed their lack of utilitarian promise to someone familiar with the requirements of domestic pottery, the mixing of 'original' and 'imitation' vessels within the cemetery acts to highlight the possibility that any given vessel *might* be 'real'. This play between original and imitation is further expressed at a more detailed level on some vessel types, in particular the turban rim bowls.

The turban rim bowls were designed to be displayed (Sofaer forthcoming). They commonly have a single small lug placed on the exterior of the vessel below the rim. On some bowls these lugs are fully pierced, in which case the vessel was clearly designed to be suspended from a cord strung

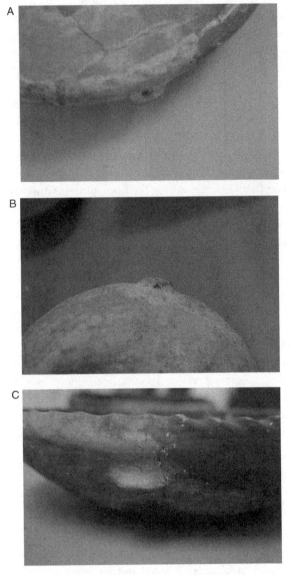

FIGURE 6.5 Lugs on turban rim bowls from Vukovar Lijeva Bara: A) pierced lug,
B) pseudo-pierced lug, and C) unpierced lug (photographs: J. Sofaer).

through the lug. On other bowls, however, the lugs are pseudo-pierced. In
other words, the hole does not go all the way through the lug. In a third
variant the lugs are completely unpierced (Figure 6.5). The well-fired and
more elaborately decorated bowls tend to have the fully pierced lugs. Less

well-fired and less elaborate vessels, such as those with a central boss but little else, often have either pseudo-pierced or unpierced lugs. These vessels, therefore, are made in such a way as to suggest to the casual observer that one *could* hang the vessel if one wanted to, although it is not in fact possible.

The bowls therefore demand that the viewer look to see whether they are real or fake, in much the same way that the tricks of the shaman demand close scrutiny. The deception provoked by the lugs is very subtle and is only apparent when one is up close. Indeed, with some of the pseudo-pierced lugs it is only perceptible when one physically tests the lug by trying to push something through, although of course more obvious differences in firing, finish, and decoration might offer an initial clue. As with shamanic practice, this constitutes the skilled revelation of skilled deception where 'faith not only coexists with skepticism but *demands* it, hence the interminable, mysterious, and complex movement back and forth between revelation and concealment' (Taussig 2006: 123 original emphasis). The inclusion of pots within the burial that *seem* to fulfil a range of functions (as containers and for display) but that, in fact, could not suggests that mourners believed that these vessels had the same efficacy for the deceased as the 'original' vessels. As in sympathetic magic, the tension between the original and the imitation is resolved through the physical connection between the original and the imitation (here expressed through a shared shape) and in the way that the latter assumes the power of the original through action upon it in the very act of deposition. The tension between the original and imitation is thus resolved through a mimetic process of assimilation or merging of the vessels with the objects that they imitate (Taussig 2006: 155).

Mimesis and Nonsensuous Similarity

The concentric circles and radial lines decorating the interior of turban rim bowls (Figure 6.6) echo decorative motifs on Bronze Age metalwork in the Carpathian Basin, including ornamented belt fittings, buttons, pendant-like or amuletic objects to be sewn onto clothes and pins (Hänsel 1968; Bóna 1975; Metzner-Nebelsick 2002: 304, 349), as well as more unusual or particularly high-status objects such as the 'drum' from Hasfalva (Kristiansen and Larsson 2005). The motifs are widely held to have cosmological significance. In particular, concentric circles are understood to represent the sun and the radial motif a wheel (Kristiansen and Larsson 2005; Sofaer 2013; see also 'Design' this volume). The myth of the journey of the sun was key to Bronze Age beliefs throughout the continent. Based on

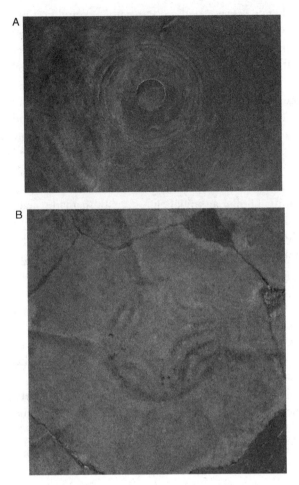

FIGURE 6.6 Decorative motifs on turban rim bowls from Vukovar Lijeva Bara: A) concentric circles representing the sun, and B) radial lines emerging from a central boss representing a wheel (photographs: J. Sofaer).

Scandinavian Bronze Age objects, Flemming Kaul (1998, 2005) has described a complex mythology of the sun and its voyage through different spheres of the cosmos assisted by different agents (the horse, snake, and fish) with day and night ships facilitating the sun's transport. The images on prehistoric rock art have been argued to signal some of the same ideas (Bradley 2006). Kristian Kristiansen and Thomas Larsson (2005) have described a shared Indo-European myth about the sun's journey in which the twin brothers and helpers of the sun maiden, the Divine or

Heavenly Twins, come to help her in the guise of ships and horses so that the sun can rise in the morning. The four-spoked wheel or wheel-cross motif has also been associated with the sun (Kaul 2004; Kristiansen and Larsson 2005). The wheel is important to the story of the sun's journey as it is part of the chariot of the sun pulled by a horse as in the Trundholm chariot from Denmark, or a chariot ridden by a bird-head figure as in the Dupljaja model from Serbia. The motifs on the turban rim bowls at Vukovar Lijeva Bara, therefore, reiterated geographically and chronologically widespread motifs that are found in several different contemporary media and contexts.

The bowls can thus be understood as materialising Bronze Age cosmology in a process of nonsensuous similarity. Excavation photographs from Vukovar Lijeva Bara show that the positioning of the bowls appears to have been carefully choreographed; they were placed on their bases in the grave so that the motif was visible. Looking down into the grave pit, the mourners would have been able to literally gaze into the cosmos. Furthermore, by filling vessels with food or liquid during the course of a burial ritual, one could potentially make the sun or wheel disappear and reappear, actively telling myths with the vessels (Sofaer forthcoming; see also 'Design' this volume). One might speculate that within the emotionally charged atmosphere of a funeral, the shared knowledge and understanding of the myths expressed in the bowls created a profound linkage between the cycle of life and the daily cycle of the sun (cf Kaul 1998: 270), and that this helped to develop empathy or emotional mimesis among mourners.

Mimesis and Simulacra

Vessel shape and decoration at Vukovar Lijeva Bara are in many respects highly standardised. There were clear ideals regarding what were the necessary elements for acceptable ceramic vessels. This similarity, however, also means that it is possible to compare vessels and to identify the making 'signatures' of different potters (cf Crown 2007; Sofaer and Budden 2012). For example, the technique used to make the twists on turban rim bowls, the length and breadth of facets on faceted inverted rim bowls, or the manner and spacing of fluted decoration show clear similarities and differences in execution (Figure 6.7). In addition to the mode of technical execution, differences between vessels also exist in the expression of motifs. For example, in the number of concentric circles in the sun motif or spokes in a wheel, and in the size of vessels.

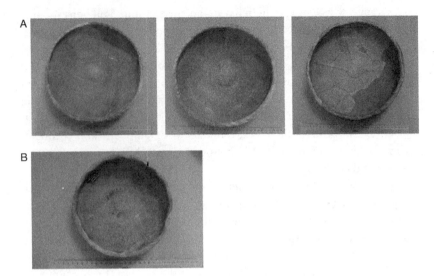

FIGURE 6.7 A) Turban rim vessels showing the same technical signature in the execution of the twist of the rim that were probably made by the same potter, and B) turban rim vessel made by a different potter with a contrasting signature in twist to the rim (photographs: J. Sofaer).

Although no two vessels at the site are exactly the same, the pronounced similarity between some vessels suggests that in these cases minor variation was the outcome of the handmade. In other words, handmade objects lend themselves to variation through slight changes in gestures, materials or firing during the process of manufacture, even if a potter aimed to create an exact copy of a pre-existing vessel. The existence of widely varying technical signatures for the same vessel type within a single chronological horizon also suggests, however, that exact replication of a singular original was not required. These differences exist both within and between grave assemblages, so for larger depositions it is possible to infer that more than one potter made vessels contributing to a single burial, or that a single potter made vessels for more than one interment.

What seems to be going on here is then a matter of scales of difference (Flohr Sørensen 2013). There are objects which are close to being exact copies of each other (whether consciously or unconsciously), and objects which are versions of other objects but do not pretend to copy them faithfully. Indeed, the existence of several different forms of iteration of the same vessel type or decoration suggests a cultural comfort with a level of difference. On one hand, general similarities between vessels of the same type allowed for their identification, but on the other hand, there was a creative space in which it was possible to play with alterity or otherness. It is probably naïve to view the difference between vessels in contemporary Western terms of self-expression since the production of objects was strongly constrained by tradition. Nonetheless, they have their own integrity as 'original copies' (cf Flohr Sørensen 2013).

Mimesis at Vukovar Lijeva Bara

Mimesis was woven into the fabric of the ceramics at Vukovar Lijeva Bara on many different levels. It existed in illusions generated through decoration, the expression of shape and its role in the intertwining of narratives, the subtle revelation of the copy and its assimilation to an original, the expression of cosmology in the ceramics, and in the way that the uniqueness of vessels was cultivated. These were not separate but interrelated aspects where the relationship and tension between original and copy acted as a fundamental impulse for creativity.

CHAPTER 7

Performance

The Production of Knowledge

In 2010 the pioneering performance artist Marina Abramović held a major retrospective at the Museum of Modern Art in New York. The exhibition included approximately fifty works spanning more than four decades of her early interventions and sound pieces, video works, installations, photographs, solo performances and collaborative performances made with Ulay (Uwe Laysiepen) (Biesenbach 2010). In an endeavour to transmit the presence of the artist and make her historical performances accessible to a larger audience, the exhibition also included live re-performances of Abramović's works by other people, as well as a new, original work performed by Abramović herself called *The Artist Is Present* in which she sat motionless every day for three months during the period of the retrospective, a total of 600 hours (Biesenbach 2010).

Abramović deliberately choreographs or sets up possibilities for particular kinds of physical experiences through sets of instructions to herself as the performer and/or to the audience that act like a kind of manual. They frequently refer to or involve objects. For example, in *Rhythm 10* (1973) she set out to explore concepts of ritual, gesture, time and repetition making use of twenty knives and two tape recorders. She rhythmically jabbed a knife aimed between the splayed fingers of her hand. Each time she cut herself, she would pick up a new knife from the row of twenty she had set up, and record and rewind the operation (Biesenbach 2010). She has also created work which relates living to dead bodies (Sofaer 2012). Her performances differ from theatre or acting inasmuch as they are about real rather than acted or superficial experiences (Abramović 2010). For her, Russian roulette is a metaphor for the difference between acting and performance; whereas an actor uses a fake gun and feigns death, a performance artist uses a loaded gun and risks death (Biesenbach 2010: 19). The power of the performance lies in knowing the corporeal reality of the performer's experience even if we as the audience cannot, or would not want to, experience it ourselves. In other words, it is an authentic sensory experience lived by Abramović in which the body is literally altered or made to behave in particular ways rather than its theatrical representation. Abramović has frequently talked about the training and preparation that she undergoes prior to her physically demanding performances in order to carry them out (Abramović 1996; Biesenbach 2010). In her work, performance is itself a form of practice-based research into the human condition in which her body is both subject and medium (Sofaer 2012). Indeed, performance art has been described as a search for body knowledge (Warr 2000: 14).

Themes of preparation, the body, knowledge, process, transformation, temporality, and the role of objects are critical to understanding the intrinsic link between creativity and performance. In the first part of this essay, I want to explore this connection by drawing on these intertwined themes as they may be expressed in a variety of different types of performance. The second part further takes them on through an exploration of the performance of mortuary rituals at the Middle Bronze Age site of Cârna (Cîrna) in Romania, in which ceramics played a critical role.

Creativity and Performance: Preparation, the Body, Knowledge, Process, Transformation, Temporality, and the Role of Objects

Performance takes several forms. As in the contemporary performance art of Abramović, it may be 'real' rather than as acted – in other words, performance is the real-time experience of people using real objects. Metaphors of theatricality and role playing have been used to understand the ways that people act in everyday life (Goffman 1959; Butler 1993, 2004), or in ritual settings where people are possessed by spirits or believed to have transformed into other beings while in trance-like states (Turner 1987; Schechner 1988); performance theorist Richard Schechner has called this 'actualizing' (Schechner 1988). Performance, as it is perhaps more commonly perceived, may also be a matter of acting, in which case it is understood that the action is 'staged', that objects are unusable fakes, and that the person takes on a temporary persona or personae as an actor. In this case, as in cinema or Western theatre traditions, performance requires the temporary suspension of reality by the audience.

In all these different types, performance can be understood as the 'dramatization of creative thought as a means of producing knowledge' (Sofaer 2006: 94). This may be articulated within the performance product – the staging of ideas to an audience – but it also takes place as 'the dramatisation of creative thought *in the creative process itself*, where the staging of a "position" gives life to ideas' (Sofaer 2006: 94). In other words, performances do not just 'happen' spontaneously but may be thought-through, premeditated events that also require practical creative strategies during processes of conceptualisation and planning in order to find solutions as to *how* to perform. As the writer Katherine Mansfield put it, inspiration requires 'terrific hard gardening' (Ghiselin 1985: 19).

Preparation for performance is not just a mental process but can take many forms, including the acquisition of objects (props), the preparation of specific locations or spaces for performance (the stage), the planning and practicing of movement (choreography), and the arrangement and learning of movement, words or music in a particular order (scripts or scores). Critical to preparation for performance is the development of skill. On one level this is about the mastery of specific techniques of the body in the sense described by Marcel Mauss (1935), for example, the precision and strength of the hand techniques of the pianist or the dexterity of the juggler (cf Schechner 1985). On another it is about the interpretation and transmission of a performance text or performance secrets (Schechner 1985): the qualities of the performance that give rise to an emotional or affective response. In other words, preparation for performance includes the acquisition of both non-discursive (practical) knowledge and discursive (cognitive) knowledge (Budden and Sofaer 2009), be that by individuals or as part of the formation of a group (Schechner 1985).

Learning each of these aspects of performance can take place formally or informally. For example, within many theatre traditions formal training takes place in drama schools or during rehearsals. Here the creativity of the performers is understood to be cultivated through the training process (Schechner 1988). Schechner describes three ways in which creativity of the performer can be articulated. The first is through the creation of a role or character; communicating a 'picture' through 'the art of the actions of human beings' (1985: 251) by putting oneself in the shoes of the character to express emotions or motivations. The second is what happens, for example, in Japanese Noh or ballet. Here the performance text or score is fixed. It is there to be learned and presented by the performer. There is no research into emotions or motivations as the text or score is considered complete in itself. Instead the energy of the performers goes into mastering the score which is passed down the generations more or less intact. Only the greatest masters have sufficient 'force' to make changes in scores. The third is where the performer(s) develop their own completely new performance from scratch through improvisation, although paradoxically the ability to successfully improvise is also seen to require training in the abandonment of the script.

There are, nonetheless, cases where a lack of formal preparation is seen as critical to the authenticity of performance. Schechner (1985) describes a cultural insistence that the young Balinese girls who become sanghyang dedari trance dancers do not have any training. In this case a lack of formal teaching is critical to the authenticity of the possession of the girls by the spirits of the dedari, or divine nymphs. Yet while the sanghyang dedari do not actually rehearse, they do undergo training and preparation. Every person in a Balinese village has seen sanghyang dedari dancing, and by the time a girl is eight or nine she has seen many performances. How to dance, therefore, has been absorbed by the sanghyang dedari dancers over the years. Girls are selected by the temple priests and undergo an extended period of warm-up for the dance over several weeks in which they gradually become more and more subject to the ecstasy produced by intoxicating music and incense, and are subject to specific behavioural restrictions (Covarrubias 1937; Schechner 1985). As Schechner recounts,

> In watching sanghyang dedari myself, I, like many others . . . am moved by their grace, simplicity, and naiveté and by their feats of balance and fire walking achieved while in trance. But their skill as dancers, measured against what fully trained Balinese dancers do, is nothing special. What is spectacular is the sanghyang dedari performance taken as a totality: trances, feats, dancing, intensity of participation by the whole village. It is this participation that makes people exaggerate the dancing skills of the little girls.
>
> (1985: 248)

The girls do not perform their dance according to a predetermined choreography and may end their performance at any point. Here creativity lies in the freedom of the girls to move as they wish in a variety of styles since they are not expected to present a particular kind of dance but instead move as the goddesses demand.

The outcomes of these different kinds of learning parallel those described in relation to the making of objects, in particular ceramics and textiles, where different learning schemes allow for different degrees of creativity. Thus highly scaffolded (closely supervised) methods of learning, where large parts of the chaîne opératoire are presented to the student in one go, inhibit innovation and result in close reproduction of existing types. Loosely scaffolded learning (that based around trial and error), where the *chaîne opératoire* is divided up for the learner, results in experimentation and new forms (Greenfield, 2000; Wallaert-Pêtre, 2001; Greenfield, Maynard, and Childs 2003). These ideas have recently been applied to the interpretation of objects in prehistoric contexts (Budden 2008; Føssy 2012).

Creativity in social performance, however, is a different matter. While the roles that people perform in everyday life are, like the sanghyang dedari dancers, also absorbed over the years, albeit on a more profound level, they are the accumulated product of experience and, importantly, repetition (Butler 1993). In this sense people are active in the construction of their own identities through an ongoing embodied process grounded in active engagement with one's material surroundings and with others (Toren 1999; Sofaer 2011). The particular role that one plays at any given point in time, according to Erving Goffman (1959), is configured through a series of frames of reference such that a person is always him- or herself but simultaneously the role; at the moment of writing I am an academic, when my kids call I become a mother, and in the supermarket I am a consumer. Thus social performance creates knowledge about the identity of the person at the moment of performance; individuals are a particular identity at a particular point in time. The difference between 'real life' social performance, ritual performance, theatrical and contemporary per-formance art lies in the degree of choice available to people and in the consequences of their actions. Whereas social performance is highly con-strained and the consequences of transgression may be socially divisive, ritual performance is anti-structural and may sometimes be creative, carni-valesque or playful (Schechner 1987) while simultaneously reinforcing established structures (Turner 1969). Performance in the sense of acting, as well as in modern performance art, offers an arena for radical choices that are denied in the social context (Sofaer 2006).

Performance, and the creativity embedded within it, is thus a social process (Turner 1987) in which both the expression of creativity and its constraints are culturally and contextually defined. There is a continuous dynamic process linking performative behaviour with social and ethical structure: the way people think and organise their lives and identify individual and group values (Schechner 1987; Turner 1987). It is through this play that performance gives rise to knowledge, including under-standings of situations, characters, physical body states, emotions, or identities.

Performance is also a paradigm of process (Schechner 1988) since performance is action over time; it is essentially linked to temporality because it is a creation of limited duration. Time can also be deployed within performance. As Schechner points out, 'performances gather their energies almost as if time and rhythm were concrete, physical pliable things. Time and rhythm can be used in the same way as text, props, costumes and the bodies of the performers and the audience' (1985: 11). Within performance art there are long-standing debates over whether it should be recorded because it then loses its momentariness, which is seen as essential to the performance experience. No two performances are ever the same. Furthermore, performance has transformative qualities, whether that is the transformation of those doing the performing – the 'taking on' of a role or character – or the potential that it has for a transformative effect on the audience, their emotions or attitudes. It may also effect social transformations. With regard to ritual performance, despite assumptions to the contrary, Turner points out that, 'ritual is not necessarily a bastion of social conservatism; its symbols do not merely condense cherished sociocultural values. Rather, through its liminal processes, it holds the generating source of culture and structure' (1987: 158). In addition, while performances may take place between particular points in time, the preparation for performance and the potential reverberations that follow it mean that a performance has time depth on either side, and this has the potential to lend a performance its own chronology.

Performance is about relations between people, whether that is between the performers themselves or between performers and audience. Creativity can therefore be understood as a group phenomenon as well as the preserve of individuals (Littleton and Mercer 2012). Collaboration or 'social creativeness' (Turner 1987: 32) may be directed, but the performers share common aims in working together to bring the performance to fruition. Modern examples of this include film and stage direction, or the conducting of an orchestra. It also occurs in ritual performances of contemporary Western society where, for example, the wedding planner or funeral director organises the component parts of the performance and supports the protagonists in carrying out their roles. Performers touch the audience and some kind of collaboration, or collective theatrical life, is born (Schechner 1985).

Objects can play an important role in connecting people in performances. They are cultural media that provide modes of communication (Singer 1972), offering tangible means of creating relations between people. For instance, in the film *The Wizard of Oz* (1939) the moment that Glinda, the Good Witch of the North (Billie Burke), puts the ruby slippers on Dorothy (Judy Garland), a bond is created between the characters, and Dorothy is protected from the intangible (evil) by the tangible (the magical shoes). Objects can also create physical (not just metaphorical) links between people, such as in sword fighting or eating together from a shared bowl. Although not all performances require objects, dance or poetry being cases in point, some kinds of performance are predicated on an engagement with or through objects, such as juggling or magic shows. In some cases objects become extensions of the body during performance, as in playing a musical instrument. Objects, therefore, can play a critical role in the constitution of creative subjectivity (Hayward 1990).

Paradoxically, however, the very recognition of objects as props within performance can collapse interactions with them back into a mode of appropriation of the object rather than highlighting the subject–object relationship (Clarke, Gough, and Watt 2010: 2). Discussing the role of objects in contemporary performance, analysts have drawn on Martin Heidegger's (1975) essay 'The Thing' to argue that the theatre can be charged with annihilating the social meaning of an object by transforming its 'thingness' into just another means by which the spectacle may be advanced (Clarke, Gough, and Watt 2010). The aim of this reduction is to promote the escape of the object from individual associations or representations and to promote its affective qualities such that it creates responses and, through the mimetic process, provokes the recollection of events (see 'Mimesis' this volume). The audience thus takes a step back from conceptualisation or creating conscious associations and instead engages in a connection with objects on an emotional or visceral level. Provocatively, it has been suggested that '[i]t might even be the case that, like the menacing toys prowling in some depraved Gepetto's workshop, objects truly flourish only in that midnight reality that shields them from our view. Perhaps entities are actually rendered bland or uni-dimensional only through their contact with humans' (Harman 2002: 92, cited in Clarke, Gough, and Watt 2010). In other words, the human creative imagination and emotional response to objects are most powerfully articulated when we are deprived of our 'normal' means of creating meaning through direct interaction with them. Just as the absence of a lover 'makes the heart grow fonder', so too the concealment of an object engages the capacity for creativity, altering its qualities (and the qualities of the event of which it was part) in the memory and imagination.

Creativity and Performance: The Case of Cârna

The cemetery of Cârna is one of the best-published and most studied sites belonging to the Žuto Brdo-Gârla Mare group. The group is traditionally understood to straddle the Romanian Middle and Late Bronze Age, although there is little agreement regarding absolute dates. Dates of 2000–1100 BC (Hänsel 1976), 1600–1150 BC (Crăciunescu 2007), and 1650–1250/1200 (Şandor-Chicideanu 2003) have been proposed, although recent assessments based on radiocarbon dates from a range of sites have placed it at 1900–1400 BC, followed by a Bistreţ-Işalniţa group that makes the transition to the Iron Age (Chicideanu 1986, 1992; Lazăr 2011; Motzoi-Chicideanu 2011).

The Žuto Brdo-Gârla Mare group extended along both banks of the River Danube along the flood plain between the modern city of Belgrade in Serbia and Corabia in south-west Romania, where the river Olt meets the Danube (Crăciunescu 2007; Motzoi-Chicideanu 2011). Cârna is in Romania and, in fact, is a complex of contemporary cemeteries in the vicinity of the Bistreţ-Cârna lake, an area that is periodically flooded by the Danube (Motzoi-Chicideanu 2011) (Figure 7.1). The site of Cârna-Grindul Tomii is the best known of these, being the subject of a detailed monograph (Dumitrescu 1961) and a number of subsequent studies (Hachmann 1968; Hänsel 1968, 1976; Şandor-Chicideanu 2003; Reich 2007; Motzoi-Chicideanu 2011). Excavations in 1942, 1955, and 1956 revealed 116 cremation graves, although it is likely that the cemetery was somewhat larger; estimates exceed more than 200 graves (Dumitrescu 1961). The site was certainly part of a tradition of burial in large cemeteries (Motzoi-Chicideanu 2011). As with other Žuto Brdo-Gârla Mare sites, it is likely that the cemetery was associated with a nearby settlement (Şandor-Chicideanu 2003; Schuster, Kogălniceanu, and Morintz 2008), although the settlements are little investigated (Şandor-Chicideanu 2003; Motzoi-Chicideanu 2011).

Although a lack of comprehensive reporting of grave cuts and fills places some limits on interpretation, Vladimir Dumitrescu's (1961) otherwise impressive monograph on the site and his excellent reconstructions of the positioning of the ceramics offer detailed insights into the burial rite. This is complemented by data from excavations of other nearby Žuto Brdo-Gârla Mare sites (Şandor-Chicideanu 2003). The majority of graves at Cârna were single burials, although there were six double and two triple burials, inasmuch as cremated remains were found in more than one vessel in the grave (Dumitrescu 1961). The cremated bones were placed into urns

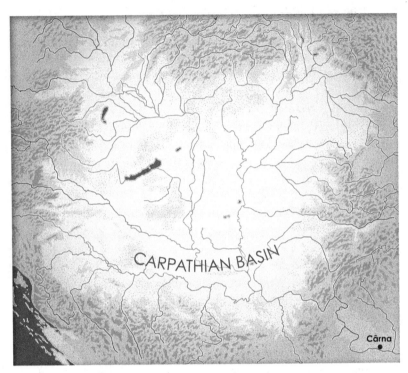

FIGURE 7.1   Map of the Carpathian Basin showing the location of Cârna.

with an effort made to position the bones in more or less anatomical order such that the cranial bones were placed on the top of other cremated remains (Dumitrescu 1961; Motzoi-Chicideanu 2011). The urns were placed within large grave pits (Dumitrescu 1961) although the size of graves may have varied within and between Žuto Brdo-Gârla Mare sites. For example, at Ostrovogania grave pits only 30–45 cm wide were recorded (Şandor-Chicideanu 2003), whereas at Gârla Mare itself the grave pits appear to have been quite substantial in size (G. Crăciunescu, personal communication 24 November 2012). Commonly a small quantity of the cremated bones was scattered at the base of the pit prior to the placing of the urn (Motzoi-Chicideanu 2011). The pits were evenly spaced within the cemetery (Motzoi-Chicideanu 2011), suggesting a desire for discrete burials and the use of grave markers to distinguish these. The grave fill was of the same material as surrounding soil with no evidence for any form of funerary architecture (Dumitrescu 1961). Recent excavations at the type site of Gârla Mare have a rather homogenous fill, suggesting that they were backfilled rapidly as a single event (G. Crăciunescu, personal communication 24 November 2012).

Ceramics were the main category of object deposited with the deceased; a total of 416 vessels were recovered during the excavations (Dumitrescu 1961). Metal and bone artefacts were also found but were rather infrequent, occurring in only eleven graves (Dumitrescu 1961). The number of vessels used in any given burial was variable, being between one and thirteen. The range of vessel types includes large two-handled globular amphorae with long cylindrical or funnel necks and everted rims used as urns, large globular vessels without handles but with similar necks also used as urns, cups of different kinds, jugs, a range of deep and shallow bowls with and without handles, pedestalled vessels, double vessels and vessels with bird-shaped protomes (Dumitrescu 1961; Motzoi-Chicideanu 2011). As in other Žuto Brdo-Gârla Mare cemeteries, anthropomorphic clay figurines were also sometimes included in the deposition (Dumitrescu 1961; Şandor-Chicideanu and Chicideanu 1990); these were found in eight graves.

Despite the relatively wide number and range of ceramic forms in the cemetery, their positioning within the burial was rather standardised (cf Motzoi-Chicideanu 2011: fig. 289). In some of the more elaborate burials two or three cups or other small vessels were placed within the urn on top of the cremated remains. More commonly a combination of small shallow and large deep bowls were used to cap the top of the urn. The smaller bowl was placed right side up, the base sitting in the neck of the urn as if to plug it, while the larger bowl was placed upside down over the small bowl and resting on the rim of the urn as if forming a lid. Frequently a range of different kinds of small vessels such as cups, jugs, or pedestalled vessels were nested within the small bowl. Small vessels, in particular cups and occasionally figurines, were also placed around the neck of the urn. These were held in place by being balanced or wedged against its exterior surface by the bowl used to form a lid. In some cases the whole ensemble was crowned rather precariously with a vessel perched on top of the bowl lid (Figure 7.2). The ceramics, therefore, were regularly assembled in such a way as to make a nested stack of vessels with predictable positions within the stack for vessels of particular type and size, but each stack differs in the precise combination and number of vessels of any given type used. Occasionally, rather than stacking the vessels, a single vessel was placed in the grave or the ceramics were placed in a group or groups in the grave pit, but this was relatively rare. Only seven out of the 116 burials contained a single vessel, and in only four burials were the vessels in groups without any nesting or stacking.

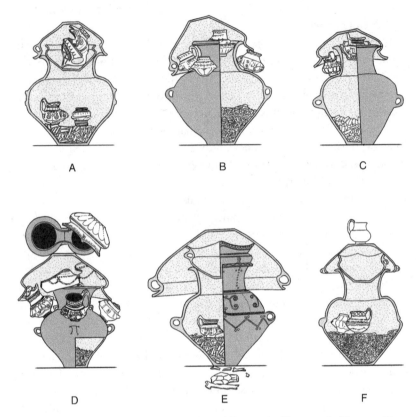

FIGURE 7.2   Pottery stacks in graves at Cârna: A) grave iv, B) grave vii, C) grave viii,
D) grave x, E) grave xi, F) grave xiv (redrawn after Dumitrescu 1961).

The ceramics are richly decorated and designed to be highly visual.
The most frequent motifs are spirals, zigzags, swags, meanders, triangles,
diamonds, circles, and concentric circles (Şandor-Chicideanu 2003).
These were combined in complex iterations with the result that no two
vessels are identical even though they draw on the same repertoire of
motifs. The decoration was symmetrical on either side of the vessel and
was realised through a combination of incised and stamped or impressed
decoration that was inlaid with white paste (Dumitrescu 1961; Şandor-
Chicideanu 2003: 91–97, pl. 199, 201). The effect of inlay is to create a
contrast between the decoration and the background against which it sits.
Many of the ceramics were low fired and often pale, so the inlays offered a
way of increasing the visual resolution of the decoration. The surfaces of

some vessel types, in particular bowls and cups, were almost completely covered with decoration. Despite this apparent freedom in the assembly of motifs, the manufacturing techniques used for individual Žuto Brdo-Gârla Mare vessel forms were relatively rigid with specific forms made in distinct ways. For instance, amphorae were made in sections using a slab technique for the body. Straight-sided bowls were coiled. Shallow bowls with evoluted corners and everted rims (so-called porringers) were thumbed out despite their large size, presumably in order to be able to control the complex shape.

The internal chronology of Cârna has been the subject of considerable study based on ceramic typology and the combination of this with metal objects (Hachmann 1968; Hänsel 1968, 1976; Reich 2002, 2007). Recent work has suggested, however, that the cemetery belongs to a single phase and that the variations within the site are the product of social differences rather than chronological ones. It has been proposed that the cemetery can be divided into eastern and western areas; the eastern area consisting of 36 graves with meander-decorated ceramics and the western area with 80 graves containing predominantly grooved ceramics (Chicideanu 1986, Motzoi-Chicideanu 2011). Each of these areas can be further divided into two, reflecting the organisation of the community into four kin groups (Motzoi-Chicideanu 2011). Other research based on ceramic forms and motifs has also suggested the importance of kin groups at the site (Reich 2002, 2007), although here the existence of three funerary areas, each belonging to a family group, has been suggested with the chronologically oldest graves in the centre of the family plot.

The Žuto Brdo-Gârla Mare group, like other contemporary Bronze Age groups in the region, has been understood as a stratified society (Chicideanu 1986; Vulpe 2010; Vulpe, Petrescu-Dîmboviţa, and László 2010; Palincaş 2012). Analysis of differential burial at the site has classified the graves in terms of wealth. Thus forty-two of the graves have been classed as 'poor', fifty-four of 'medium wealth', fifteen as 'rich', and five as 'very rich', with numerous ceramics, metalwork and figurines being found in them (Coles and Harding 1979). More recent analysis has suggested that gender may have been influential in the burial rite, with the graves of males containing a greater number and wider range of pottery than those of females (Chicideanu 1986; Motzoi-Chicideanu 2011). How this may have been related to the relative status of men and women is, however, subject to debate as it has been pointed out that the figurines depict women with elaborate costumes that contained several metal objects (Palincaş 2012). It has also been suggested that the number of ceramics in the grave was related to the capacity of the deceased to give feasts in life (Motzoi-Chicideanu 2011). Interestingly, some of the more well-furnished graves are those containing the figurines which have been more widely reported as being found in the graves of children (Şandor-Chicideanu and Chicideanu 1990). A link between age and relative position within the cemetery has also been described with children's graves having been placed close to those of men, leading to suggestions of inherited status for children (Chicideanu 1986). The burial rite was likely linked, therefore, to a number of aspects of social identity including kinship, status, gender, and age. Yet the mode of burial is remarkably consistent throughout the interments at the site. It drew upon shared principles in arrangement, and it is to these, and to the performance of the burial, that I now wish to turn.

The Performance of Burial at Cârna

Funerary rites have sometimes been described in terms of choreography and drama, taking on the idea of performance by discussing the deliberate and mindful movement of those arranging the funeral in the placement of the body and objects (Sørensen 2004a, 2004b; Sofaer and Sørensen 2013). The burial rite at Cârna can be understood as a series of pre-planned and ordered choreographed sequences of movement that followed a script. Although no two burials are exactly the same in terms of the replication or positioning of objects deposited with the deceased – indeed they show substantial variation – each burial followed the same basic sequence of events. At each stage within the sequence particular actions of the body were required in order to perform the funeral rite. These are most clearly archaeologically accessible with regard to the actions within the grave itself. Here the choreography of interment drew upon a shared script. Differences between burials represent various levels of the elaboration of the script rather than fundamentally different actions. The script may have gone something like this:

Script for a Modest Cârna Funeral (Grave VIII)

A group of mourners gathers at the graveside carrying ceramic vessels and a basket containing the cremated remains of the deceased. They place the vessels and the basket on the ground at the edge of the pit.

Mourners 1 and 2: Enter the grave pit.
Mourner 3: Hands the basket down to Mourner 1.

Mourner 1: Takes the basket. Standing at the side of the pit, s/he takes a handful of the remains and scatters them in the centre to mark the location for burial.

Mourner 3: Hands down a large urn to Mourners 1 and 2.

Mourners 1 and 2: Take the urn and place it upon the ashes of the deceased. They place their hands in the basket containing the cremated remains and scoop them up, carefully avoiding the cranial bones. They take turns to place the remains in the urn. They continue this action until only the cranial bones are left, finally removing them from the basket and placing them on top of the rest of the body within the urn.

Mourner 3: Turns to a pile of earth beside the grave and begins to throw and shovel it into the grave pit, carefully avoiding the urn.

Mourners 1 and 2: Carefully work the backfill around the urn, gradually fixing it in place, until the earth comes up to a level just below the shoulder of the urn. They stay in the pit but gradually get raised higher up as they stand on top of the backfill.

Mourner 3: Picks up a small bowl and hands it down to Mourner 1.

Mourner 1: Moves to the side of the grave and takes the bowl. S/he turns to the urn and places it square, right side up, in the neck of the urn.

Mourner 3: Picks up a cup and hands it down to Mourner 2.

Mourner 2: Moves to the side of the grave and takes the cup. S/he turns to the urn and places it on its base in the centre of the bowl.

Mourner 3: Picks up a cup and hands it down to Mourner 1.

Mourner 1: Moves to the side of the grave and takes the cup.

Mourner 3: Picks up a large bowl and hands it down to Mourner 2.

Mourner 2: Moves to the side of the grave and takes the bowl.

Mourners 1 and 2: Turn and move to the urn. Mourner 1 places the cup on the steep shoulder of the urn, continuing to hold on to it so that it does not slip off. Mourner 2 turns the bowl upside down and carefully places it at an angle over the top of the vessels sitting in the neck of the urn and over the cup held by Mourner 1 such that it holds the cup on the outside in place. Mourner 1 gingerly withdraws her/his hands. Mourner 2 does the same.

Mourner 3: Turns to a pile of earth beside the grave and again begins to throw and shovel it into the grave pit, carefully avoiding the ceramic stack.

> Mourners 1 and 2: Carefully work the backfill around the vessels, so that they are not dislodged. When the ceramics have been covered and the pit has been filled with earth, they step out of the pit.
>
> All Mourners: Take any remaining soil and pile it over the grave to mark it.
>
> For a less elaborate funeral fewer mourners enter the grave pit and a smaller number of vessels are nested, stacked and balanced. Conversely, for a more elaborate funeral more mourners enter the grave pit and a larger number of vessels are nested, stacked and balanced.

While the archaeology clearly indicates the order of the placement of the vessels and the manner of the construction of the ceramic stack, my script is, of course, conjectural on many other levels. For example, we do not know if the cremated remains were placed in the urn at the cremation pyre or in the pit. Nor do we know if different parts of the sequence were carried out by the same or by different individuals. This script is based upon the minimum number of people that would be required to carry out the performance, but it is, for instance, possible that different people (family members or friends) each placed a vessel in the stack, in an analogous manner to people taking turns to give speeches or readings at a modern funeral. The number of people participating in the funeral described earlier could therefore potentially vary between three and five. Certainly, in some of the more complicated stacks, more than one person would have been required in order to ensure the vessels were held in place during its building. For narrower graves where there was not room for the mourners to move around within the grave, it is possible that the construction of the stack took place from the edge of the pit, the mourners kneeling or bending over it. With regard to the tricky procedure of backfilling the grave without disturbing or knocking down precariously balanced vessels, I have here suggested that the infilling of the grave took place in stages during the rite and formed part of the performance, such that the urn was surrounded with earth and fixed in place before other vessels were placed on top of it. This would help to position the vessels held in place around the rim of the urn. It is also possible, however, that the complete stack of vessels was put in place before backfilling the grave, but this would increase the chances of dislodging vessels during the backfilling process; the positioning of some of the figurines and smaller vessels are difficult to explain should this method have been used. The archaeology suggests that, in the main, the vessels were in situ and some had been assisted in their positioning by the use of the backfill.

Whatever the precise choreography, the drama of such a performance must have had great potency, heightened by the emotions of the mourners. The skilled placement and balancing of the pottery in, on, and around the urn may have had a certain tension – perhaps akin to that we might experience during a circus act – as a result of the potential for it to slip either during the placement itself or during the process of backfilling. The gradual concealment and disappearance of the ceramics through the placement of vessels and the process of backfilling the grave played with notions of visibility and invisibility much like modern theatrical staging, lending the performance time and rhythm. The large grave pit worked like a stage in the round providing a space within which performance could take place and allowing onlookers access to the performance that took place within it.

At Cârna the narrative of burial employed a complex intertwining of different modes of performance in which ceramics played a vital role. On one hand, the performance was real or, in Schechner's (1988) terms, 'actual'; the funeral was a real-life, real-time event that involved the creation of a pottery stack in which people took the parts of mourners. On the other hand, the highly visual although variably fired ceramics that were arranged within the burial may have been largely useless for day-to-day use and therefore were props made specifically for the performance. The shapes and sizes of the vessels were also carefully chosen in order to facilitate a successful 'balancing act' during the funeral. Thus, vessels with angular bodies and rims were placed on the urn as their shape would have been easier to hold in place than a more spherical form. Bowls with decoration on the underside were most frequently placed upside down so as to be displayed. The way in which the ceramics were used, therefore, has more in common with a theatrical event; they were display objects or 'imitations' rather than objects with day-to-day functions, although they may momentarily have attained the status of 'real' during the performance through the mimetic process (see 'Mimesis' this volume). One might speculate that an audience's suspension of disbelief is particularly easy in the funeral context, since what could be more real than death.

Given that the number and choice of the ceramics and the location of the burial within the cemetery may have been related to status, gender, age and kin group (Chicideanu 1986; Reich 2002, 2007; Motzoi-Chicideanu 2011), the deliberate highlighting of the ceramics at the heart of the funeral ritual served to create understandings about who people were. The performance of the funeral thus created knowledge about the identity of the deceased and, potentially, their relationship with the mourners. The vessels were not simply passive carriers of symbolic capital; they were deliberately deployed in an active manner during the performance of the funeral rite and were integral to it. Irrespective of the precise meanings of the ceramics and grave depositions, it is clear that the messages to be conveyed during the funeral were worked out in advance and choices were made through the acquisition of appropriate resources prior to the event, in particular through the selection and acquisition of the ceramic vessels that were to form the centrepiece of the funeral performance. The choice of vessels and their positioning had implications for the number of people required to collaborate in building the stack, each of whom knew his or her role. Thus the choreography of the performance was already determined in the planning stage with little room for improvisation on the day of the funeral. In other words, the creativity embedded within the funeral resided in its planning as well as in the performance of the funeral event itself, during which the ceramic stack was built.

Given that no two burials at Cârna are identical, this suggests that there was a degree of choice available in planning the performance, albeit within limits set by the need to convey knowledge of the deceased and what was appropriate for them. The performers did not move in any way they wished during the funeral, but they could creatively draw upon a repertoire since each of the elements of the funeral relied upon prior acquisition of knowledge as to how to carry out a burial appropriately. The large number of burials within the cemetery of Cârna-Grindul Tomii and the contemporary cemeteries just a few kilometres distance from the site suggest that, even if a cemetery was in use for several hundred years, an understanding of how to perform a Žuto Brdo-Gârla Mare funeral would have been familiar to the mourners. It must have been a script and performance with which they were familiar, having witnessed or participated in funerals on a number of occasions within living memory. Learning how to perform a funeral, therefore, was an accumulated product of experience but may also possibly have involved a more scaffolded practicing of the body gestures required to successful execute some of the delicate balancing of combinations of vessels in the funeral performance. Choices made in terms of which vessels to combine may have involved deliberate decisions to creatively play with material culture in order to provide a visually stunning 'send-off' for the deceased.

A striking aspect of this creativity is the use of material culture to effect transformation. Individual vessels were brought together to build a new entity – the pottery stack – in which the partly reconstituted body of the deceased was placed at its heart. The pottery stack was more than just the sum of its parts. Rather, when finished it was a unified construction where the ceramics that formed its different elements held the other constituent ceramics together much like a three-dimensional jigsaw puzzle or a dry stone wall in which the stones are held together by their neighbours. This reconfiguration of the vessels to form something new has resonance with notions of the rite of passage in which the final stage is the rite of incorporation or the birth of something new (van Gennep 1909; Hertz 1960; Bloch and Parry 1982). The building of the pottery stack was only one part of a longer process, from the moment of death to the erection of a grave marker, that involved a series of transformations and performances, including the act of cremation itself, in which both the deceased and the mourners took part. In this sense the transformation of the body of the deceased through cremation, and the transformation of several individual ceramic vessels into a single stack, were complementary elements of the funeral rite.

The funeral thus created an opportunity for a reconfiguring of the relationship between the mourners and the deceased through performance. Within these performances people worked together with a shared aim. In the context of the burial, this was directed towards the creation of the pottery stack as a new entity and the filling of the grave pit. Even if not formally directed, this was a co-ordinated effort that linked people together in social creativeness (Turner 1969, 1987). The objects also provided a physical, albeit transient, link between those carrying out the funeral as they worked together to balance the vessels. Importantly, the funeral ritual was predicated upon engagement with objects. The ceramics acted not just to contain the ashes of the deceased but also potentially to reinforce community ties between the living through the very act of building the stack and burying it.

It may be argued that the complexity of some of the pottery stacks, and indeed the elaborate decoration on some of the vessels themselves, reveal a level of baroque elaboration that was intended to impress and awe those attending the funeral. In this sense the vessels were deliberately deployed to create a spectacle for the living as much as a 'good send-off' for the deceased. They were appropriated as 'things' in the Heideggerian sense over and above their semantic, symbolic or economic associations with the identity of the deceased. The notion that 'the dead do not bury themselves' and that funerals may be as much, if not more, about the living than the dead is now well established within archaeological analyses (Barrett 1990).

In the context of understanding creativity, what is important here are the tactics that were used to create such impressions. The ways in which ceramics were deployed in the funeral aimed to elicit particular emotional responses in the mourners through putting on a good show, as well as referencing identity; the burial created emotional as well as intellectual knowledge. Once vessels were concealed within a pottery stack, and once the stack was buried under the soil, pottery and the performance, along with the deceased, were consigned to memory. This concealment was the counterpart to the display of ceramics that was a necessary part of the funeral. It formed part of a performance strategy that offered future creative possibilities for memory and imagination to walk hand in hand for the living.

A Return to the Beginning

The burials at Cârna expressed creativity in both conceptualisation and execution. Although they reiterated shared principles with other burials in the cemetery and the wider cultural context, each was also a 'one off' performance in which flexibility and novelty were expressed. Here creativity in the deployment of ceramics was embedded within performance as a social process linked to the community's desire to articulate the identity of the deceased but also, and perhaps more powerfully, to express its emotional needs.

Although modern and Bronze Age performances differ in many ways, given that all performances are expressions of creative thought as a means of producing knowledge, it is appropriate to end this essay by returning to its starting point in the work of Marina Abramović. Responding to a question about the relevance and continuing power of live performance in the digital age, Abramović replied,

> Documentation, photographs, video – all this is secondhand. The performance's time is art. You have to be in the place where things happen. Then it really makes sense. If the performance has some kind of element of transformation . . . If it's bad, it's bad and you leave. But if it's not bad, it's really good and you never forget it in your life.
>
> (Pikul 2010)

The creativity in the burials at Cârna lay in exactly such an attempt to make an impact, so that the mourners would never forget what they had experienced. Perhaps it was intended that in remembering the performance, the deceased might also be remembered.

CHAPTER 8

Failure

Creativity and Risk

Failure is intrinsic to the human experience. It is painful and haunting and comes laced with shame, anger, despair, guilt, inadequacy and frustration – emotions we usually wish away or hide (O'Gorman and Werry 2012). In modern Britain we are told that failure is bad. It is to be avoided in order to preserve one's dignity. Yet at the same time, failure is to be confronted and overcome. A slew of self-help books enjoin us to rediscover our self-esteem by getting over the fear of failure that holds us back in achieving our goals. Here mistakes become opportunities or revelations; in the somewhat ironic words of the playwright and novelist Samuel Beckett, 'Fail again. Fail better' (Beckett 1983). Failure is thus reclaimed as a self-improving experience from which we learn and become more resilient.

Failure is also a persistent threat within the creative process. The creation story of the Maya told within the *Popol Vuh*, or Book of the People, illustrates the universality of the close link between creativity and failure. It recounts the four attempts of the gods to create living beings. At first they made animals, but these could not speak and therefore could not worship the gods. So the gods then made men of mud, but these were too crumbly, lopsided and lacked knowledge. The gods realised that they were a mistake and let them dissolve away in water. Then they made men from wood. These looked like men and could procreate but lacked hearts and minds and could not understand. Again, they were unsatisfactory, so eventually the gods destroyed them. Finally they made men from maize dough. These men talked, had minds, were good and handsome, and finally the gods were satisfied (Goetz and Morley 1950). In this parable of persistence, the new comes about through a process of learning and experimentation with materials and form. It suggests that, even when something appears at first glance to be successful, it may not be fully satisfactory or appealing and may need to be rethought.

Failure has been increasingly theorised as the twin of creativity. This identification arises from often contrasting and incompatible philosophical and political positions. On one hand, scholars in art criticism, queer studies, literary theory and performance studies have rehabilitated failure by championing it as a means of unravelling the certainties of knowledge, competence, representation, normativity, and authority. They argue that failure is the counterpoint to modernity's empty promises of progress and betterment (O'Gorman and Werry 2012). Here insecurity and uncertainty offer an impetus for creative endeavour (Pallasmaa 2009), but the impossibility of solving problems or the inevitability of responding in a way that is never quite good enough (be that a response to global issues such as climate change, or on a smaller scale such as an artist working on a new idea) implies the inevitability of failure. In the words of philosopher Gilles Deleuze, 'A creator who isn't grabbed around the throat by a set of impossibilities is no creator. A creator is someone who creates their own impossibilities, and thereby creates possibilities . . . without a set of impossibilities, you won't have the line of flight, the exit that is creation' (1995: 133). Yet precisely because the task ahead is never really achievable, because the creative act cannot be 'finished', the protagonist will be dogged by a greater or lesser sense of their own failure (Jeanes 2006). This is productive failure: a failure from which new understandings, insights, or objects arise (Sofaer and Sofaer 2008).

On the other hand, the importance of failure is fast becoming a cannon within the history of science and modern management theory in which failure is identified as part of the process of innovation. In this case failure is part of the march of progress. It is a means to an end. As Thomas Edison is reported to have said, 'I have not failed 10,000 times. I have successfully found 10,000 ways that will not work'. Furthermore, when an object has been invented, not all ideas will be culturally successful and may have variable uptake. In a Western capitalist system, the drive for success in an ever-changing environment demands that new ideas are constantly developed in the anticipation that only a fraction of these will ultimately be fruitful.

Failure can thus be understood as productive and necessary. In this final essay, I want to explore the relationship between creativity and failure, and to consider different kinds of risks or possibilities for failure that exist within both the process of making objects and in their social reception. My case study focuses upon two very different individual artefacts. The first is an

Early Bronze Age Nagyrév jug from the site of Százhalombatta in Hungary. The second is a Late Bronze Age vessel from the site of Lăpuş in Romania.

Creativity, Risk and Failure

The possibility for failure arises from the risk that is embedded in the physical nature of the process of making things (Adamson 2010). The nature of this risk was explored by the furniture maker David Pye in his discussion of the contrast between the 'free' workmanship of risk and the 'regulated' workmanship of certainty. Workmanship of risk is 'workmanship using any kind of technique or apparatus in which the quality of the result is not predetermined but depends on the judgment, dexterity and care which the maker exercises as he works. The essential idea is that the quality of the result is continually at risk during the process of making' (Pye 1968: 20). Workmanship of certainty is found in mass production and in its pure state in automation. In workmanship of this sort, the result is predetermined and unalterable once production begins. In writing with a pen, for example, the outcome is completely dependent upon the actions of the writer and is the workmanship of risk, whereas the way that the same words appear upon the page are predetermined and replicable when produced by printing and are therefore the workmanship of certainty.

Within the production of objects it is possible to move backwards and forwards between these two different kinds of workmanship. The use of tools to lend the process pre-defined parameters – such as a mould, a plane set to a desired depth, or regulated kilns – decreases the level of risk within the processes of making an object. Yet even in using tools, the involvement of the human hand means that it is not possible to eliminate risk. Risks exist, for example, in the choice or mixing of materials, in making a mistake through the slip of the hand, or in the control of technologies including pyrotechnology. The specific kinds of risks run by craftspeople are particular to the material being worked with and specific points in the *chaîne opératoire* (Kuipers 2013). Likewise, the extent to which errors may be catastrophic to the outcome or can be modulated through the correction of mistakes, as well as the ability to start again and recycle resources, varies with material and point in the making process. In clay, for example, it is possible to reshape or correct errors as long as the clay is damp. The most risky part of the process lies in the firing. This sets in chain an irreversible series of events that reflects not only firing conditions themselves, but also decisions made by the potter earlier in the making process. For example, this is the point at which large inclusions in the clay matrix, such as pebbles, can result in spalling or cracking of the vessel during firing. Yet it is precisely because of the risk involved in making things by hand that Pye (1968) argues that objects possess a particular richness. This arises from the range of creative possibilities and variability in outcome that can only be produced through the workmanship of risk, including aesthetic qualities, shape, and the ingenuity of the maker. This does not in itself mean that handmade objects are necessarily any good or better than mass-produced objects – both have the potential to be good and bad quality – but it does lend them particular resonance and diversity.

The chance of something going wrong in the making process is related to the skill of the maker. There are potentially different levels of risk for different people with different levels of aptitude and skill in making the same object. The risk of failure is increased when doing something for the first time (even if it has been done by others) and decreases as experience is accumulated. What constitutes skill in respect of any given material or object, however, is culturally defined since skill is learnt and learning is a social process (Adamson 2007; Budden 2008). Furthermore, the extent to which something can go wrong before it is considered a failure and the degree of tolerance of error – in other words what is deemed to constitute failure – is both a cultural and personal matter.

On a cultural level, the degree of risk taken in making an object depends on the social desirability of such risk-taking – in other words, what makes taking a risk worthwhile (van der Leeuw 1989; Adamson 2007). Within the learning process, culturally acceptable levels of risk and tolerance of error may be expressed in the degree of guidance provided to a novice and the opportunities available for him or her to learn independently through making errors. Learning inevitably involves failing, but the extent to which mistakes are prevented and corrected depends on culturally specific learning systems (Greenfield 2000). In highly scaffolded learning systems the transmission of knowledge is closely controlled, and mistakes are caught early and corrected, leading to close reproduction of existing material forms. By contrast, in loosely scaffolded or unscaffolded learning novices acquire skills more independently, including by trial and error, resulting in greater experimentation and diversity of outcome (Greenfield 2000; Wallaert-Pêtre 2001; Greenfield, Maynard, and Childs 2003) (see 'Performance' this volume). Different learning systems thus reflect contrasting cultural attitudes to risk in learning and to objects as the outcome of the learning process; in more conservative societies failure may not be tolerated, whereas in others risk of failure is more acceptable. Following this line of thinking, one might suggest that the more diverse and variable the material culture within a given context, the more relaxed were social attitudes to failure and serendipity; something not going quite as anticipated leads to incorporation or rejection of actions and ideas next time round. Such social attitudes to learning may also be linked to the availability of resources. Where resources or raw materials are scarce or precious in terms of investment in their preparation, risks are potentially more costly and learning may therefore be more closely supervised (Herzfeld 2004).

On a personal level, craftspeople can modulate the risk that they take either by playing safe and staying with what they know, or by pushing the boundaries of materials or new expressions. Ethnoarchaeological work indicates that it is not in the best interest of craftspeople to produce poorly made objects since it results in damage to their reputation (Longacre, Xia, and Tao 2000). In a discussion of reasons for poorly executed pottery it has been noted that once potters can no longer satisfy the necessary criteria for production, they simply stop potting (Crown 2001). Yet in some objects it is also possible to recognise the deliberate taking of risk, the flaunting of skill, and the pushing of the boundaries of materials by confident, creative craftspeople. Craft theorist Glenn Adamson describes such an attitude in his discussion of Michael Baxandall's (1980) work on German Renaissance wood sculptures (Adamson 2007). Baxandall was curator of sculpture at the Victoria and Albert Museum in London, and his research highlighted the role of material properties and their manipulation in the creative process. Following a distinctly archaeological turn, he suggested that the thought process of the carver was preserved within the wood and could therefore be traced from sculpture (Adamson 2007). In particular, the northern Renaissance sculptors used local lime wood, which suffered from radial cracking known as 'starshake' as a result of uneven shrinkage in drying. The carvers had to read these lines, which became determining factors in the sculptural compositions. Some opted for a relaxed, more stable and less risky approach to carved form; others flaunted the properties of material by creating 'knowingly hazardous' shapes that curved along the lines of potential fracture (Baxandall 1980: 32). As Adamson (2007) points out, skill as management of risk is not just a technical matter, but was fixed within the decision-making process and the stylistic sensibility of the sculptor. Similarly, architect Frank Gehry's distinctive design of the Guggenheim Museum in Bilbao is a case of deliberately creating 'resistances', in other words, making things difficult for himself and his team (Sennett 2008). Gehry sought to create an impression of light and water bouncing off the exterior of the building. As a response to local environmental regulations, he eventually turned to quilted titanium, a novel material for the building's skin, which in turn impacted upon his understanding of the stability of the structure, allowing him to work in new ways through developing new skills (Sennett 2008). For both Renaissance wood carvers and twentieth century architect, creativity was not simply a sudden moment of inspiration but was embedded within knowledge of materials and skill in working with them, as well as the expression of insights and ideas. Skill is not just knowing how to do something but knowing how to make something seem 'just right' (Adamson 2007). It therefore both includes and excludes; it permits and restricts actions and outcomes (Adamson 2007).

Tradition forms part of the knowledge base that simultaneously opens up and closes down opportunities for creativity. To make something is to have learned how to make it within a particular tradition. Cooking is a case in point. Many people know how to bake chocolate cake, but whether we make American brownies, plain or iced English chocolate sponge, or elaborately decorated Austrian Sacher torte depends on the tradition in which we were taught. It has been suggested that great artists rarely speak of the dimension of freedom in their work, choosing instead to emphasise the role of restrictions and constraints in their materials and artistic medium, the cultural and social situation, the shaping of their personality and style, and the identification of their own territory and personal limits (Pallasmaa 2009). For example, modernist composer Igor Stravinsky argued that artistic strength and meaning can only come from tradition and embraced 'the resistance of material and technique' as important counterforces in his composition (Stravinsky, cited in Pallasmaa 2009: 113). In his view, an artist who deliberately seeks novelty is trapped in his very aspiration (Pallasmaaa 2009: 113): 'His art becomes unique, indeed, in the sense that its world is totally closed and it does not hold any possibility for communication' (Stravinsky in Pallasmaa 2009: 113). Likewise, in the case of objects, because they are modes of communication through which social relations are articulated, and changes in the material world impact on social life (Sofaer and Sørensen 2002), objects need to be recognisable in form or application to the people who use them. Thus, for example, the keyboard of a computer follows the same familiar configuration as its predecessor the typewriter. Similarly, early metal in Europe was used to make ornaments that were used in a manner that reiterated existing social dynamics (Sofaer Derevenski 2000). Moving too far outside tradition poses a double risk of failure: first a risk of producing an object of dubious quality and second a risk of cultural rejection since the meaning of the object may not be widely understood.

Novelty, however, is a relative concept. Novelty can only be identified in relation to what came before and with respect to the constraints and opportunities offered by the tradition within which people work. Furthermore, although today there is a constant search for the new in Anglo-American society that takes the value of novelty for granted (Bauman 2007), elsewhere the degree to which it is valued is culturally specific, and the subtlety of its identification may be unpredictable. Innovators, therefore, are frequently confronted with uncertainty. They are obliged to adopt hypotheses or beliefs about actors they hope to mobilise with their projects but can never be completely sure that these actors will behave as they should (Akrich 1993). When they do not, and objects do not find a place within existing social understandings (cf Sofaer and Sørensen 2002), such objects become creative failures.

In the making of objects, possibilities for failure are therefore related to the knowledge and skill of the maker in working with materials, cultural and personal attitudes to risk, and the reception of the new by others; even if an object is technically well executed it may not be socially acceptable. In the following section I want to further explore these possibilities through two contrasting individual objects.

Creativity and Failure I: The Case of a Nagyrév Jug from Százhalombatta

The site of Százhalombatta is situated on the right bank of the Danube, 30 km south of Budapest in Hungary (Figure 8.1) (see 'Recycling' this volume). It is one of the largest and best-preserved Bronze Age temperate tell settlements in central Europe. The site today is 200 m by 100 m in size, although it is estimated that up to one-third of its original area may have been destroyed during clay extraction by a local brick factory and erosion by the River Danube (Poroszlai 2000). The site was first occupied at the end of the Early Bronze Age (the classic Nagyrév [Szigetszentmiklós] to late Nagyrév [Kulcs] transition). It was continuously inhabited through the Middle Bronze Age Vatya period and Vatya-Koszider horizon at the end of the Middle Bronze Age, to the start of the Late Bronze Age. There followed an hiatus in occupation until the Urnfield phase of the Late Bronze Age, during which the site was again in use into the Iron Age.

Among the rich ceramic assemblage from the site is a small Early Bronze Age Nagyrév jug dating to 2500–2000 BC (Figure 8.2A). The vessel is approximately 12 cm in height and is a common vessel form typical of the

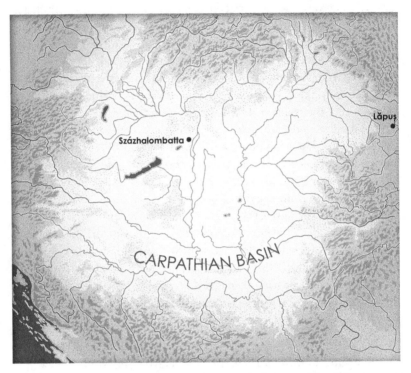

FIGURE 8.1 Map of the Carpathian Basin showing the location of Százhalombatta and Lăpuş.

period in Nagyrév sites in the Budapest region (Kalicz-Schreiber 1984). Like others of its kind, the vessel was made in distinct sections. A cone-shaped body made by coiling was attached within a thumbed out inverted conical, slightly pedestalled base. The two sections were pressed together; finger impressions made as a result of this process can be felt on the inside of the vessel while those on the exterior were smoothed out. Nevertheless, there was no attempt at hiding the join between the two sections on the outside of the vessel. Instead the overlap between them was deliberately highlighted. The flat everted rim was formed by bending over the clay towards the outside of the jug. Below the rim, a handle was attached by piercing a hole in the vessel wall and inserting the end of the handle through it, thereby creating a kind of a peg joint (Sofaer 2006). The lower end of the handle was similarly attached, and the joins at both ends were smoothed inside and out. Compared to others of its kind (Figure 8.2B), however, this particular jug differs in several respects. This vessel appears to

FIGURE 8.2   A) Poorly made Nagyrév jug from Százhalombatta, and B) well-made
Nagyrév jug from Százhalombatta (photographs: S. Budden).

be somewhat more 'scruffy' and 'ugly' than many of its contemporaries. It is
made from less well-prepared clay with quartz inclusions clearly visible in
the fabric. The thickness of the vessel wall is greater than in others of its
type. The join between the sections is reasonably well executed albeit
slightly uneven in places, but the rim and handle are irregular and
lumpy. Finally, the vessel surface is unburnished, whereas other Nagyrév
jugs are typically highly burnished. Although well-made jugs are not
necessarily 'perfect', often displaying slight unevenness in manufacture,
and no two are entirely identical, compared to other vessels of the same type
this particular jug falls far short of the ideal.

This 'scruffy' pot expresses the workmanship of risk that is embedded
within the creative process of making by hand. It is an entirely handmade
object in which the dexterity of its maker – or rather in this case the relative
lack of dexterity – is expressed within the finished product. This vessel
represents a much lower level of skill in its manufacture than other similar
vessels (Budden 2008; Budden and Sofaer 2009). In recent studies of
ceramic production at Százhalombatta, Hungary, it was observed that
simple vessel forms such as cups with less well-prepared clays showed
relatively greater numbers of errors than more technically demanding
fine wares with highly levigated clays, thin walls, complex shapes and
embellishments (Budden 2008; Budden and Sofaer 2009). This pattern
runs contrary to what one might expect inasmuch as it could be anticipated

that where potters of similar ability make a range of different vessels, then those that are more technically challenging ought to display more errors than vessels that are technically easier. Given that the prevalence of error decreases from easier to more complex vessel forms, it has been suggested that this reflects a gradient of potting experience and that a structured system of moderately scaffolded apprenticeship operated at the site (Budden 2008; Budden and Sofaer 2009; Sofaer and Budden 2013). Less skilled potters for whom there was a greater risk of making mistakes therefore learnt their craft on easier vessel forms made from less valuable resources, for which there was a higher social tolerance of error. More experienced or master potters made complex fine wares using better-prepared clays for which the social tolerance of error was much lower (Budden 2008; Budden and Sofaer 2009; Sofaer and Budden 2013). Within the hierarchical social structure of apprenticeship, failure, therefore, may have formed part of the constitution of identity since unskilled potting defined apprentices but would have imperiled masters' claims to authority (Budden and Sofaer 2009).

At Százhalombatta, although the vessels were still useable, the failure of apprentice potters to produce error-free vessels was part of a learning process in which the accumulation of skill promised future perfection. Such a process must have required potters to reflect upon their work to understand why and how they had failed in order to improve next time. In this sense failure made visible the places where creative aspirations and material realities collided (Werry and O'Gorman 2012). It forced people to think critically and to respond when making something new. It also marked how value was made and measured (Werry and O'Gorman 2012), this residing not only in perfection but in the learning process of making itself. Furthermore, such attitudes were not unique to Százhalombatta. It can also be seen in Nagyrév vessels from other sites including, for example, at Dunaújváros, where vessels of the same type with a range of different kinds of errors in all stages of the chaîne opératoire from clay preparation to firing can be identified (Horváth and Keszi 2004; Budden 2008). Risk and the associated possibility of failure, therefore, seems to have been culturally acceptable in Nagyrév contexts and to have been widely understood as part of the potting process.

Creativity and Failure II: The Case of a Vessel from Lăpuş

The site of Lăpuş in northwest Romania is one of the most intensively investigated cemeteries in the eastern Carpathian Basin (Kacsó,

Metzner-Nebelsick and Nebelsick 2011) (Figure 8.1). It lies in an isolated valley in the eastern part of the Lăpuş River depression in northern Transylvania and consists of at least seventy barrows with complex construction sequences containing a range of different kinds of cremation burials (Teržan 2005; Pop 2009; Kacsó, Metzner-Nebelsick, and Nebelsick 2011). The barrows were distributed in a series of seven clusters which may have been part of a much larger monumental funerary complex extending over more than a kilometre within the valley (Kacsó, Metzner-Nebelsick, and Nebelsick 2011). The site has traditionally been dated to the thirteenth–twelfth centuries BC, falling within the Romanian Late Bronze Age and has been divided into three phases (Lăpuş 1–3) primarily on the basis of ceramic typology (Kacsó 1971, 1975, 2004). A recent series of radiocarbon dates on material associated with typologically later pottery types has yielded dates of between 1610–1490 BC and 1310–1190 BC, indicating that building activity took place in the late fourteenth and early thirteenth centuries BC, with activities in a single barrow (barrow 26) taking place over a duration of at least 100 years (Kacsó, Metzner-Nebelsick, and Nebelsick 2011). This suggests that earlier phases of use of the site must also be pushed back in date.

Finds from the cemetery include ceramic vessels; metal objects including daggers, pins, fibulae, miniature axes, tools and gold beads; as well as bone and stone items (Kacsó, Metzner-Nebelsick, and Nebelsick 2011). Of these, ceramics are by far the most numerous. Among these are fragments of a tall high-necked vessel (approximately 67.5 cm high), now heavily reconstructed, found in tumulus 5. This was richly decorated with incised so-called *Kerbschnitt* decoration cut out of the clay in a manner akin to woodcarving, and modelled animal head protomes in the form of bovids (Kacsó 2001, 2011) (Figure 8.3A). The technical execution of the vessel is outstanding, expressed not only in the precision of the complex exterior decoration, the fine detail of the modelling and quality of the burnishing, but also in the evident control of the firing; given the large size of the vessel and the narrowness of the protomes extending from the vessel, it would have been extremely challenging to control the thermal dynamic. Here it is possible to identify a deliberate taking of technical risk, flaunting of skill in a range of different vessel forming, decorating and modelling techniques, and a pushing of the boundaries of materials. This is a virtuoso ceramic object that reached new heights in a sophisticated and showy use of materials and skill.

FIGURE 8.3   A) Vessel from Lăpuș tumulus 5, and B) vessel from Lăpuș tumulus 4
(photographs: J. Sofaer).

This vessel is one of a very small number of objects with similar form
and modelled animal head or phallic protomes. Three are currently
known from Lăpuș from tumuli 2, 4 and 5. Each of these vessels, however, is individual. They differ from each other in form as well as in the
articulation of decoration with different choices in terms of its realism or
abstraction, and in the choice of subject for the protomes. The vessel
from tumulus 5, however, follows a distinctly different decorative logic to
those from tumuli 2 and 4 (Figure 8.3B). The latter two vessels, with
symmetrically placed incised anthropomorphic motifs at the quarter
points of the vessel shoulder set above incised swags and triangles, have
incised cone-shaped motifs placed above an incised band running
around the neck and zoomorphic and/or solar motifs set above this.
The lower part of each vessel was probably undecorated and lacked the
chunky *Kerbschnitt* notable on the vessel from tumulus 5. The vessel
from tumulus 5 may also have been decorated only on its upper half
(although the fragmentation of the vessel makes this uncertain), but in
contrast to the iconographic representations on the other two vessels and
the extraordinary realism of its modelled bovid protomes, the excised

Kerbschnitt decoration is highly abstract. The surface decoration is a series of bands of interlocking triangles (or zigzags in relief depending on which aspect one chooses to emphasise) set within incised borders. The decoration flows across the neck of the pot like threads in a fabric cut across the bias. The awareness of the geometry of the vessel is rather different to the other two vessels from Lăpuş. This is a clear attempt at all-over decorative coverage rather than the division of the vessel into segments. The triangles at the end of the bands are often slightly smaller than those in the middle, suggesting a playing with perspective in order to draw the eye to the midpoint and give an impression of 'flow' down the vessel.

The excised decoration on the vessel from tumulus 5 refers back to Middle Bronze Age Suciu de Sus pottery such as that from the type site in the neighbouring valley approximately 5 kilometres east of Lăpuş, or from the site of Oarţa de Jos (see Kacsó 2011). Suciu de Sus vessels, in particular bowls, are decorated with curvilinear and spiral motifs augmented with zigzags made by cutting out triangles, using the distinctive *Kerbschnitt* technique in which the clay is carved. On some vessels chisel marks can be seen in the clay as a result of this technique. These marks were not smoothed out by potters, thereby deliberately lending a flavour of woodcarving to the decorated surface of the ceramic vessel. Similar highly elaborate vessels have been found at Lăpuş and define its early phases (Kacsó 1971, 1975, 2004). The vessel from tumulus 5, therefore, sits within this clay-carving tradition to an extent that its contemporaries from tumuli 2 and 4 do not. Yet it also differs from Suciu de Sus pottery in vessel shape and in the application of realistically modelled three-dimensional protomes that are otherwise alien to the highly abstract Suciu de Sus tradition. It further differs from the bulk of contemporary pottery found at the site, which, on the whole, is much less fine in quality, although there are some exceptionally large and technically complex vessels. It also contrasts with subsequent channelled pottery forms which include large high-necked vessels, similar to the Gáva pottery of the eastern Hungarian Plain, with black exterior and red interior surfaces, as well as a number of other smaller forms (Kacsó 1975; Kacsó, Metzner-Nebelsick, and Nebelsick 2011).

The vessel from tumulus 5 thus both sits within, and emerges from, an established tradition of how to decorate ceramics. Its maker(s) used the knowledge and skills developed within it, playing with an established idiom in new ways to create something distinctly new. Yet in pushing the boundaries of tradition this vessel also simultaneously moves away from it and from the small number of other similar contemporary vessels on a number of levels. Not only did its maker(s) take deliberate technical risks (risks that they successfully pulled off), but they were also running a risk with regard to the object's social reception. At present, no other similar vessel is known, leaving that from tumulus 5 as a 'one off' unique object. Vessels that are thought to follow it in the chronological sequence at Lăpuş are substantially different in form and decoration. Of course, it is dangerous to base arguments upon negative evidence (more such vessels may be out there somewhere), but given the current state of knowledge it appears that this kind of vessel did not have a wide uptake. Even if one argues that it was a 'special' vessel made for a particular setting, and that it may have been used and enjoyed by its owners, it does not appear to have been copied or desired outside that single context. In short, the creative ideas expressed in the vessel did not take off. Despite its imaginative and technical brilliance, with regard to its social reception the vessel from tumulus 5 may be considered a creative failure.

Creativity, Failure and Archaeology

Thinking through failure in archaeology is methodologically challenging. Things and materials may be recycled, thereby mitigating the entry of failures to the archaeological record. Furthermore, with the exception of wasters in kilns, contextual data for failure in ceramic production is rare. There may have been many vessels which were 'one offs' or creative experiments, but even if it is possible to identify 'unique' or different vessels, given the potential gaps in the archaeological record it is difficult to know just how unique they really were. In addition, the temporal resolution of the archaeological record frequently lacks sufficient detail to be able to place these within a sequence of creative developments. On the whole, archaeologists are not geared towards looking for failure; we always tend to look at what succeeds, not what falls by the wayside.

In its inevitable incompleteness, the very attempt to understand creativity as an aspect of human life might too constitute a kind of productive failure. While it may be a postmodern trap to fetishise failure – to wallow in its inevitability – it also offers a caesura, a breathing space, rather than a full stop or exclamation mark (Bharucha 2012). If creativity and failure go hand in hand and we want to investigate creativity, then we are left with a dilemma. Either we believe that the data cannot stand up to the investigation of failure and we accept our own creative failure as archaeologists, or we start to think through our data in new ways in order to access failure as an authentic aspect of human experience. Human life is fragile and fraught with struggle as well as success.

Afterword

I started this book by arguing for the study of the 'unstudiable' notion of creativity in archaeology. Yet, as the poet Joseph Brodsky put it, 'In the business of writing, what one accumulates is not expertise but uncertainties' (1986: 17). It is in the recognition of what is not well understood, as well as what is known, that archaeology moves forward. While I hope that I have shown that the complex and nuanced concept of creativity can be explored in the Bronze Age, creativity is not a finite notion. Hence no discussion of creativity can ever be complete. There are other themes that I could have chosen to explore within this book and other case studies that I might have used as examples. In writing this volume I have necessarily been selective in my choices and have aimed to discuss a range of different creative practices in order to convey the breadth of creativity in clay in the Bronze Age in the Carpathian Basin. It would therefore be wrong to end with some kind of ostentatious statement about what creativity 'is' or 'is not'. Rather than attempt a global understanding or model of creativity, my ambitions have been more modest. Through explorations of the particular ways that people acted in making and using clay objects, I have aimed to expose understandings of creativity as both process and outcome. I have tried to open up new questions and to offer a fresh series of understandings of the potentials of prehistoric clay objects to the reader. Throughout I have stressed that creativity is a cultural and material phenomenon. Consequently I have taken an unashamedly contextual direction in its investigation. I have focussed on independent individual case studies with different data sets and on a single material.

I did not go to the Carpathian Basin to hunt down particular predetermined 'types' of creativity. Instead the themes explored within this book took shape around the material that I have had the great privilege to study over several years. Nonetheless, the selection of the themes and case studies raises questions regarding the typicality of those that I have chosen. I do not believe that the people who made and used the objects that I have discussed here were uniquely creative in relation to their contemporaries, although the specific articulation of creativity was culturally embedded. Nor do I suggest that the creativity that they expressed was qualitatively the same. The case studies reveal a spectrum of creativity (Liep 2001) from the practice-based solutions and on-going problem-solving of the everyday, seen for example in the recycling and creative destruction of ceramics at Százhalombatta, to the specific local conditions that provided the environment for concentrated bursts of novelty or originality as seen in the Beaker mélange in the Budapest region or the burials at Cârna. Creativity is not just a matter of what we perceive today as 'beauty', as shown in my discussion of the vessels from Velika Gorica and Dobova, but it exists in a range of material responses to everyday living as well as in singular events. It may be expressed in contrasting ways under different social, economic, and political conditions in a wide range of settings outside those designated as 'art'.

To argue for the contextuality of creativity in terms of contrasting practices in the making and use of clay objects is not, however, to advocate for the mutual exclusivity of the themes discussed in this volume. In each essay I have chosen to highlight a particular way of thinking through creativity that surfaces particularly clearly in individual objects, sites, or cultural units at a given point in time. Drilling down into any one of these might well reveal the coexistence of a range of creative responses. Thus, for example, while I have chosen to discuss mimesis through the specific example of Vukovar Lijeva Bara because of its many dimensions expressed at the site, it may be possible to see mimesis at play in many of the case studies discussed here. Indeed, as the relationship between original and copy is a fundamental aspect of creativity (Benjamin 1933) and can be said to sit beneath the development of ceramic types and their uptake, mimesis might exist in almost all Bronze Age settings, albeit in particular perhaps more reduced ways than at Vukovar Lijeva Bara. Similarly, all Bronze Age ceramic objects were handmade. 'Thinking hands' (Pallasmaa 2009) must therefore have been at work in the creation of the new throughout the region. All creative acts run the risk of technical or social failure. Although this can be modulated by the skill of the potter and his or her understanding of social boundaries, failure is an inevitable and therefore ubiquitous aspect of human existence. It must therefore have coexisted alongside creative acts. The potentially widespread nature of the different themes discussed in this volume begs the question as to how each of these aspects of creativity might be articulated differently in other cultural contexts in the region. For example, although I have here chosen to discuss the design of Swedish helmet bowls, the question of how other ceramic forms were designed and with what rationale provokes consideration of other contemporary vessel types and decoration, as well as temporal shifts in these. Such questions are beyond the scope of this volume but offer directions for future research.

Although creativity is an extraordinary human capacity, creativity in the Bronze Age was embedded in the ordinary and familiar preoccupations of people: the making and reuse of things, responses to pre-existing objects and to making sense of the world through cosmology, the negotiation of human relationships and encounters with other communities, and the performance of identity. Despite the contemporary relevance of the ways that Bronze Age people creatively used clay, the manner of this creativity may seem somewhat alien to modern eyes. The use of clay as a critical medium for the expression of creativity, while familiar to Bronze Age people, is far from our own experience today. Although we may use china cups and plates or have ceramic tiles in the bathroom, on the whole we tend to take clay for granted. We are largely unfamiliar with its potentials, and we use clay for a relatively restricted range of purposes. Furthermore, while the rich, complex and dynamic clay cultures of the Bronze Age in the Carpathian Basin often seem to be infused with resourcefulness, innovation and imagination, there is a prevailing sense that this was quite carefully regulated and controlled. Such a notion of regulated creativity may seem antithetical to a modern creative ideal where to be creative is to be radical, 'out of the box' or an individual free thinker. Yet, as I have indicated in this volume, Bronze Age creativity was not a free-for-all. It existed in the space between the existing and the new, emerging from the recombination of existing body and social practices, ideas and materials. It was about the ways actions, imagination and emotions were played out in specific settings to construct new realities through material expression.

The use of clay in the Carpathian Basin provides the 'red thread' that has run throughout this volume. In coming to grips with creativity in clay, my investigation has also raised new questions: What are the creative potentials of other materials? Are these qualitatively different to clay? What aspects of creativity might other materials express in particular contexts in comparison, and in conjunction, with clay? A study of different materials might also offer ways into understanding creativity at different scales. The beauty of clay is that it offers the possibility of highly local detailed insights. This local variability in ceramics contrasts with the widespread similarity of metalwork throughout large parts of the Carpathian Basin. This may suggest contrasts in Bronze Age attitudes to different materials with distinct material-specific expressions of creativity and a different range of analytical themes appropriate to the investigation of creativity in other media (see Bender Jørgensen, Sofaer, and Sørensen forthcoming).

The approach that I have taken to the investigation of creativity in the present volume is doubtless the product of my own creative context. I gladly acknowledge my own desire to use the distinctive strengths and methodological directions of archaeology in order to position the discipline in relation to fundamental questions of contemporary relevance. Yet, as I hope this volume has shown, the potential contribution of archaeology goes beyond such an agenda. The 'moral significance' of material things is that they lie outside the self (Crawford 2011: 16), but because objects are made by people they are also of the self. Thus archaeology's twin focus on the social and the material not only offers methodological possibilities but is also an appropriate and fruitful avenue through which to critically investigate creativity. I end this book in the hope that an understanding of creativity – in the making and use of objects, in the places that it is expressed, in its many forms and associations – may open up the investigation of a full range of rich and varied human experiences in the past.

Introduction

Adamson, G. 2010. Introduction to 'Forms in the Realms of Matter', from *The Life of Forms in Art* by Henri Focillon. In G. Adamson (ed), *The Craft Reader*. Oxford: Berg, pp. 360–365.

Arendt, H. 1958. *The Human Condition*. 2nd ed. 1998. Chicago: University of Chicago Press.

Barnett, H. 1953. *Innovation: The Basis of Cultural Change*. New York: McGraw-Hill.

Benjamin, W. 1933 [1978]. *On the Mimetic Faculty*. In P. Demetz (ed), *Reflections: Essays, Aphorisms, Autobiographical Writings*. Trans. E. Jephcott. New York: Schocken, pp. 720–722.

Blandino, B. 2003. *Coiled Pottery*. London: Bloomsbury Publishing PLC.

Boas, F. 1955. *Primitive Art*. London: Dover.

Boden, M. 1994. What Is Creativity? In M. Boden (ed), *Dimensions of Creativity*. Cambridge, MA: MIT Press, pp. 75–118.

Boden, M. A. 2003. *The Creative Mind: Myths and Mechanisms*. London: Routledge.

Boden, M. A. 2009. Life and Mind. *Minds and Machines* 19(4): 453–463.

Bohm, D. 1996. *On Creativity*. London: Routledge.

Bóna, I. 1975. *Die Mittlere Bronzezeit Ungarns und ihre sudostlichen Bezielumgen*. Budapest: Akadémia Kiadó.

de Certeau, M. 1984 [1988]. *The Practice of Everyday Life*. Berkeley: University of California Press.

Deleuze, G. 1995. *Negotiations*. Trans. M. Joughin. New York: Columbia University Press.

Focillon, H. 1989. *Life of Forms in Art*. Trans. C. Hogan and G. Kubler. New York: Zone Books.

Fogarty, E. 1937. *Rhythm*. London: George Allen and Unwin.

Gibson, C. 2010. Creative Geographies: Tales from the 'Margins'. *Australian Geographer* 41(1): 1–10.

Hallam, E. and Ingold, T. 2007. *Creativity and Cultural Improvisation*. Volume 44 of Association of Social Anthropologists Monographs. Oxford: Berg.

Hänsel, B. 1968. *Beiträge zur Chronologie der mittleren Bronzezeit im Karpatenbecken*. Bonn: Habelt.

Harding, A. 2013. Trade and Exchange. In H. Fokkens and A. Harding (eds), *The Oxford Handbook of the European Bronze Age*. Oxford: Oxford University Press, pp. 370–381.

Ingold, T. 2011. *Being Alive: Essays on Movement, Knowledge and Description*. London: Routledge.

Ingold, T. 2013. *Making: Anthropology, Archaeology, Art and Architecture*. London: Routledge.

Jeanes, E. 2006. 'Resisting Creativity, Creating the New'. A Deleuzian Perspective on Creativity. *Creativity and Innovation Management* 15(2): 127–134.

Kacsó, C. 2011. *Repertoriul Arheologic Al Judetului Maramureş*. Bibliotheca Marmatia 3. Baia Mare: Muzeul Judetean De Istorie Şi Arheologie Maramureş.

Keller, C. 2001. Thought and Production: Insights of the Practitioner. In M. Schiffer (ed), *Anthropological Perspectives on Technology*. Albuquerque: University of New Mexico Press, pp. 33–45.

Koestler, A. 1964. *The Act of Creation*. London: Hutchinson.

Kristiansen, K. 2000. *Europe before History*. Cambridge: Cambridge University Press.

Kristiansen, K. and Larsson, T. 2005. *The Rise of Bronze Age Society: Travels, Transmissions and Transformations*. Cambridge: Cambridge University Press.

Leach, J. 2004. *Creative Land. Place and Procreation on the Rai Coast of Papua New Guinea*. New York: Berghahn.

Liep, J. 2001. Introduction. In J. Liep (ed), *Locating Cultural Creativity*. London: Pluto Press, pp. 1–13.

Merleau-Ponty, M. 1962. *Phenomenology of Perception*. Trans. C. Smith. London: Routledge & Kegan Paul.

Michelaki, K. 2008. Making Pots and Potters in the Bronze Age Villages of Kiszombor-Új-Élet and Klárafalva-Hajdova in Hungary. *Cambridge Archaeological Journal* 18(3): 327–352.

Mithen, S. 1998. *Creativity in Human Evolution and Prehistory*. London: Routledge.

Morris, R. 1970. Some Notes on the Phenomenology of Making: The Search for the Motivated. *Artforum* 8(8): 62–66.

Mozsolics, A. 1967. *Bronzefunde des Karpatenbeckens*. Budapest: Akadémiai Kiadó.

Pallasmaa, J. 2009. *The Thinking Hand. Existential and Embodied Wisdom in Architecture*. Chichester: Wiley.

Piazza, G. 1997. Materials, Relationships and Languages: Interview with Giovanni Piazza. Reported in L. Gandini 2005. From the Beginning of the *Atelier* to Materials as Languages: Conversations with Reggio Emilia. In L. Gandini, L. Hill,

L. Cadwell, and C. Schwall (eds), *In the Spirit of the Studio: Learning from the Atelier of Reggio Emilia.* New York: Teachers College Press, pp. 6–15.

Pringle, H. 2013. The Origins of Creativity. *Scientific American* 308: 36–43.

Pye, D. 1968. *The Nature and the Art of Workmanship.* Cambridge: Cambridge University Press.

Sennett, R. 2009. *The Craftsman.* London: Penguin.

Sofaer, J. 2006. Pots, Houses and Metal: Technological Relations at the Bronze Age Tell at Százhalombatta, Hungary. *Oxford Journal of Archaeology* 25(2): 127–147.

Sofaer, J. 2011. Human Ontogeny and Material Change at the Bronze Age Tell of Százhalombatta, Hungary. *Cambridge Archaeological Journal* 21(2): 217–227.

Sternberg, R. 1998. *Handbook of Creativity.* Cambridge: Cambridge University Press.

Taylor, C. 1989. *Sources of the Self: The Making of the Modern Identity.* Cambridge, MA: Harvard University Press.

Thrift N, 2000, Afterwords. *Environment and Planning D: Society and Space* 18(2): 213–255.

Toren, C. 1999. *Mind, Materiality and History. Explorations in Fijian Ethnography.* London: Routledge.

Vicze, M. 2011. *Bronze Age Cemetery* at Dunaújváros-Duna-dűlő. Dissertationes Pannonicae Series IV, Volume 1. Eötvös Loránd University, Institute of Archaeological Sciences, Budapest.

Visy, Z. (ed). 2003. *Hungarian Archaeology at the Turn of the Millennium.* Budapest: Ministry of National Cultural Heritage, Teleki László Foundation.

Wagner, R. 1981. *The Invention of Culture.* Chicago: University of Chicago Press.

Wilf, E. 2011. Sincerity versus Self-Expression: Modern Creative Agency and the Materiality of Semiotic Forms. *Cultural Anthropology* 26(3): 462–484.

1 Hands

Adamson, G. 2007. *Thinking through Craft.* Oxford: Berg.

Adorno, T. 1979. Functionalism Today. *Oppositions* 17: 31–41.

Bâ, A. H. 1976. African Art: Where the Hand Has Ears. Reprinted in G. Adamson (ed), 2010. *The Craft Reader.* Oxford: Berg, pp. 379–385.

Bachelard, B. 1982. *Water and Dreams: An Essay on the Imagination of Matter.* Dallas, TX: The Pegasus Foundation.

Bailey, D. W. 2005. *Prehistoric Figurines: Representation and Corporeality in the Neolithic.* Abingdon: Routledge.

Balen, D. and Rendić Miočević, A. 2012. *The Magic of Play.* Zagreb: Archaeological Museum in Zagreb.

Barley, N. 1994. *Smashing Pots: Works of Clay from Africa.* Washington DC: Smithsonian Institution Press.

Becker, S. Forthcoming. Creativity as Sensual Cosmology: The Case of Bird Iconography in Late Bronze and Early Iron Age Europe. In L. Bender Jørgensen, J. Sofaer, and M. L. S. Sørensen with G. Appleby, S. Becker, S. Bergerbrant, S. Coxon, K. Grömer, F. Kaul, D. Maričević, S. Mihelić, A. Rast-Eicher, and H. Rösel-Mautendorfer, *Creativity in the Bronze Age*. Manuscript in preparation.

Bender Jørgensen, L. 2013. Spinning Faith. In M. L. S. Sørensen and K. Rebay-Salisbury (eds), *Embodied Knowledge*. Oxford: Oxbow, pp. 128–136.

Benjamin, W. 1968 [1992]. *Illuminations*. Edited and introduced by H. Arendt. New York: Schocken Books.

Biehl, P. F. 2006. Materialität, Variabilität und Individualität kommunikativen Handelns in der Vorgeschichte. In S. Conrad, R. Einicke, A. Furtwängler, H. Löhr, and A. Slawisch (eds), *Pontos Euxeinos. Beiträge zur Archäologie und Geschichte des Antiken Schwarzmeer- und Balkanraumes*. Schr. Zentrum Arch. u. Kulturgesch. Schwarzmeerraum 10. Weissbach: Beier & Beran, pp. 23–34.

Biehl, P. F. 2008. 'Import', 'Imitation' or 'Communication'? Figurines from the Lower Danube and Mycenae. In P. F. Biehl and Y. Ya. Rassamakin (eds), *Import and Imitation in Archaeology*. Langenweißbach: Beier & Beran, pp. 105–124.

Blier, S. P. 1987. *The Anatomy of Architecture. Ontology and Metaphor in Batammaliba Architectural Expression*. Chicago: University of Chicago Press.

Blischke, J. 2002. *Gräberfelder als Spiegel der historischen Entwicklung während der mittleren Bronzezeit in mittleren Donaugebiet*. Universitätsforschungen zur Prähistorischen Archäologie 80. Bonn: Rudolf Habelt.

Bondár, M. 2012. A New Late Copper Age Wagon Model from the Carpathian Basin. In P. Anreiter, E. Bánffy, L. Bartosiewicz, W. Meid, and C. Metzner-Nebelsick (eds), *Archaeological, Cultural and Linguistic Heritage. Festschrift for Erzsébet Jerem in Honour of Her 70th Birthday*. Budapest: Archaeolingua, pp. 71–83.

Bondár, M. and Székely, G. 2011. A New Early Bronze Age Wagon Model from the Carpathian Basin. *World Archaeology* 43(4): 538–553.

Budd, P. and Taylor, T. 1995. The Faerie Smith Meets the Bronze Industry: Magic Versus Science in the Interpretation of Prehistoric Metal-Making. *World Archaeology* 27(1): 133–143.

Budden, S. 2008. Skill amongst the Sherds: Understanding the Role of Skill in the Early to Late Middle Bronze Age in Hungary. In I. Berg (ed), *Breaking the Mould: Challenging the Past through Pottery, Manchester 2006*. British Archaeological Reports International Series 1861. Oxford: BAR, pp. 1–17.

Budden, S. and Sofaer, J. 2009. Nondiscursive Knowledge and the Construction of Identity: Potters, Potting and Performance at the Bronze Age Tell of Százhalombatta, Hungary. *Cambridge Archaeological Journal* 19(2): 203–220.

Bulatović, A. 2013. Birds Images on Serbian Bronze Age Ceramics. In B. Rezi, R. Németh, and A. Berecki (eds), *Bronze Age Crafts and Craftsmen*. Proceedings of the International Colloquium from Târgu Mureș. Târgu Mureș: Editura MEGA, pp. 23–31.

Cardoso, R. 2008 [2010]. Craft versus Design: Moving beyond a Tired Dichotomy. In G. Adamson (ed), *The Craft Reader*. Oxford: Berg, pp. 321–332.

Carroll, C. and Carroll, R. 2012. *Mudras of India: A Comprehensive Guide to the Hand Gestures of Yoga and Indian Dance*. London: Singing Dragon.

Chicideanu, I. 1995. Cultura Gârla Mare. In C. Stoica, M. Rotea, and N. Boroffka (eds), *Comori Ale Epocii Bronzului Din România [Treasures of the Bronze Age]*. Bucharest: Ministerul Culturii and Muzeul Naţional De Istorie A României, pp. 171–181.

Childe, V. G. 1929. *The Danube in Prehistory*. Oxford: Clarendon Press.

David, N. 1990. *Vessels of the Spirit: Pots and People in North Cameroon* [Video]. Calgary: University of Calgary.

Dumitrescu, V. 1961. *Necropola Incineraţie Din Epoca Bronzului De La Cîrna*. Biblioteca De Arheologie IV. Bucharest: Editura Academiei Republicii Populare Romîne.

Gamble, C. 2007. *Origins and Revolutions: Human Identity in Earliest Prehistory*. Cambridge: Cambridge University Press.

Garašanin, D. 1972. *The Bronze Age of Serbia*. Beograd: National Museum Beograd, catalogue of the exhibition.

Garašanin, M. 1983. Dubovačko-Žutobrdska Grupa. In A. Benac (ed), *Praistorija Jugoslavenskih Zemalja IV. Bronzano Doba*. Sarajevo: Akademija nauka i umjetnosti Bosne i Hercegovine, Centar za balkanolosoška ispitivanja, pp. 520–535.

Grömer, K., Rösel-Mautendorfer, H., and Bender Jørgensen, L. 2013. Visions of Dress – Recreating Bronze Age Clothing from the Danubian Region. *Textile: The Journal of Cloth and Culture* 11(3): 218–241.

Guba, S. and Szeverényi, V. 2007. Bronze Age Bird Representations from the Carpathian Basin. *Communicationes Archaeologicae Hungariae* 2007, pp. 75–110.

Hagen, S. 2002. 'The Bone Collector'. Review of Charles LeDray, Sculpture 1989–2002, Institute of Contemporary Art, Philadelphia, May 10–July 14, 2002. *Philadelphia City Paper*, May 30, 2002 edition.

Hahn, H. P. 2012. Words and Things: Reflections on People's Interaction with the Material World. In J. Maran and P. W. Stockhammer (eds), *Materiality and Social Practice: Transformative Capacities of Intercultural Encounters*. Oxford: Oxbow, pp. 4–12.

Harding, A. 2000. *European Societies in the Bronze Age*. Cambridge: Cambridge University Press.

Heidegger, M. 1971. *Poetry, Language, Thought*. Trans. A. Hofstadter. New York: Harper and Row.

Heidegger, M. 1977. *What Calls for Thinking*. New York: Harper and Row.

Hoffiller, V. 1928. Idol od Ilovače iz Dalja. *VHAD* XV: 249–256.

Høgseth, H. B. 2013. The Language of Craftsmanship. In M. L. S. Sørensen and K. Rebay-Salisbury (eds), *Embodied Knowledge*. Oxford: Oxbow, pp. 95–105.

Horváth, L. A., Korom, A., Terei, Gy., Szilas, G., and Reményi, L. 2005. Előzetes jelentés az épülő Kőérberek, Tóváros-Lakópark területén folyó régészeti feltárásról [Preliminary report on the archaeological excavation conducted parallel to the construction on the territory of the Kőérberek, Tóváros Residental District]. *Aquincumi Füzetek* 11: 137–167.

Ingold, T. 1998. From Complimentary to Obviation: On Dissolving the Boundaries between Social and Biological Anthropology, Archaeology and Psychology. *Zeitschrift für Ethnologie* 123: 21–52.

Ingold, T. 2013. *Making: Anthropology, Archaeology, Art and Architecture*. London: Routledge.

Jockenhövel, A. 1997. Die Vogel-Sonnen-Barke: Symbol der mitteleuropäischen Urnenfelderkultur. In *Von der Höhlenkunst zur Pyramide: Vorzeit und Altertum*. Leipzig: Mannheim, pp. 258–262.

Jovanović, M. 2011. *Masters of Clay and Wheat*. Novi Sad: Museum of Vojvodina.

Kalicz, N. 1968. *Die Frühbronzezeit in Nordostungarn*. Archaeologia Hungarica 45. Budapest: Akadémiai Kiadó.

Kalicz-Schreiber, R. 2010. *Ein Gräberfeld der Spätbronzezeit von Budapest-Békásmegyer*. Institut für Archäologische Wissenschaften der Eötvös Loránd Universität. Edited by G. V. Szabó and G. Váczi. Budapest: L'Harmattan, Ungarn.

Kiss, V. 2003. Potters in Transdanubia. In Z. Visy (ed), *Hungarian Archaeology at the Turn of the Millenium*. Budapest: Ministry of National Cultural Heritage, Teleki László Foundation, pp. 150–151.

Kiss, V. 2007. Contacts along the Danube: A Boat Model from the Early Bronze Age. In I. Galanaki, H. Tomas, Y. Galanakis, and R. Laffineur (eds), *Prehistory across Borders*. Proceedings of the International Conference Bronze and Early Iron Age Interconnections and Contemporary Developments between the Aegean and the Regions of the Balkan Peninsula, Central and Northern Europe. University of Zagreb, 11–14 April 2005. *Aegaeum* 27. Université de Liège and University of Texas at Austin.

Kiss, V. 2011. The Role of the Danube in the Early and Middle Bronze Age of the Carpathian Basin. In G. Kovács and G. Kulcsár (eds), *Ten Thousand Years along the Middle Danube. Life and Early Communities from Prehistory to History*. Budapest: Archaeolingua, pp. 211–239.

Knappett, C. 2005. *Thinking through Material Culture: An Inter-Disciplinary Perspective*. Philadelphia: University of Pennsylvania Press.

Knappett, C. 2012. Meaning in Miniature: Semiotic Networks in Material Culture. In M. Jessen, N. Johannsen, and H. J. Jensen (eds), *Excavating the Mind: Cross-Sections through Culture, Cognition and Materiality*. Arhus: Arhus University Press, pp. 87–109.

Kohring, S. 2013. Conceptual Knowledge as Technologically Materialized: A Case Study of Pottery Production, Consumption and Community Practice. In M. L. S. Sørensen and K. Rebay-Salisbury (eds), *Embodied Knowledge*. Oxford: Oxbow, pp. 106–116.

Kovács, T. 1972a. Askoi, Bird-Shaped Vessels, Bird-Shaped Rattles in Bronze Age Hungary. *Folia Archaeologica* 23: 7–28.

Kovács, T. 1972b. Bronzkori harangszoknyás szobrok a Magyar Nemzeti Múzeum gyüjteményében [Bronze Age Bell-Skirted Statuettes in the Collection of the Hungarian National Museum]. *Archaeologiai Értesítő* 99: 47–52.

Kovács, T. 1973. Representations of Weapons on Bronze Age Pottery. *Folia Archaeologica* XXIV: 7–31.

Kovács, T. 1977. *The Bronze Age in Hungary.* Budapest: Corvina Press.

Kovács, T. 1981. Bronzezeitliche Tradition in der hallstattzeitlichen Kunst Transdanubiens. In C. Eibner and A. Eibner (eds), *Die Halstattkultur. Symposium Steyr 1980.* Linz: Amt der Oö. Landesregierung, Abt Kultur, pp. 65–78.

Kreiter, A., Budden, S., and Sofaer, J. 2004 [2006]. Early and Middle Bronze Age Storage Vessel Building Techniques in Hungary. *Ősrégészeti Levelek (Prehistoric Newsletter)*: 85–91.

Krstić, D. 1985. Karakteristike sahranjivanja na nekropoli bronzanog doba u Korbovu [Burying Characteristics of the Bronze Age Cemetery in Korbovo]. *Zbornik Narodnog muzeja* XI-1, Beograd.

Krstić, D. 2003. *Glamija: nekropola bronzanog doba u Korbovu [Glamija: Bronze Age Necropolis in Korbovo].* Arheoloske monografije, Band 15. Belgrade: Nationalmuseum Beograd.

Lakoff, G. and Johnson, M. 1999. *Philosophy in the Flesh: The Embodied Mind and Its Challenge to Western Thought.* New York: Basic Books.

Lave, J. and Chaiklin, S. (eds). 1993. *Understanding Practice: Perspectives on Activity and Context.* Cambridge: Cambridge University Press.

Lave, J. and Wenger, E. 1991. *Situated Learning: Legitimate Peripheral Participation.* Cambridge: Cambridge University Press.

Leslie, E. 1998. Walter Benjamin: Traces of Craft. *Journal of Design History* 11(1): 5–13.

Letica, Z. 1973. *Antropomorfne figurine bronzanog doba u Jugoslaviji.* Dissertationes et Monographiae. Beograd: Filozofski Fakultet. Savez Arheoloških Društava Jugoslavije.

Majnarić-Pandžić, N. 1982. O porijeklu srednjobrončanodobne antropomorfne plastike u jugoslavenskom Podunavlju. *Opuscula Archaeologica* 7: 47–61.

Maričević, D. and Sofaer, J. 2012. Creativity in Clay: Bird-Shaped and Bird-Ornamented Ceramic Objects in the Middle and Late Bronze Age in the Middle and Lower Danube Regions. Paper presented at the EAA Conference, Helsinki.

Marzke, M. 1992. Evolutionary Development of the Human Thumb. *Hand Clinics* 8(1): 1–8.

Marzke, M. 1997. Precision Grips, Hand Morphology, and Tools. *American Journal of Physical Anthropology* 102: 91–110.

Mauss, M. 1935 [2006]. Les techniques du corps. In N. Schlanger (ed), *Marcel Mauss: Techniques, Technology and Civilisation.* Trans. B. Brewster. Oxford: Durkheim Press, pp. 77–95. [Previously published in *Economy and Society* 1973.]

Medović, P. 2006. *Vojvodina u Praistoriji od Neandertalaca do Kelta.* Novi Sad: Platoneum.

Merleau-Ponty, M. 1992. *Phenomenology of Perception*. London: Routledge.

Milleker, B. 1905. A *Vattinai Ōstelep*. Temesvár: n.p.

Morris, R. 1970. Some Notes on the Phenomenology of Making: The Search for the Motivated. *Artforum* 8(8): 62–66.

Neagoe, M. I. 2011. Reprezentări din lut ale piciorului uman în cadrul culturii Žuto-Brdo – Gârla Mare. *Sebus* 3: 109–134

Okada, Y. and Kamiya, K. 2010. みかんのむかた (Mikan no mukata) [Of Peeled Tangerine]. Tokyo: Shogakukan.

Palincaş, N. 2010. Reconfiguring Anatomy: Ceramics, Cremation and Cosmology in the Late Bronze Age in the Lower Danube. In K. Rebay-Salisbury, M. L. S. Sørensen, and J. Hughes (eds), *Body Parts and Bodies Whole*. Oxford: Oxbow, pp. 72–89.

Palincaş, N. 2012. Investigating Bronze Age Social Organisation in the Lower Danube Region. The Case of the Žuto Brdo-Gârla Mare Area. *Istros* XVIII: 13–38.

Pallasmaa, J. 2000. *Tapio Wirkkala: Eye, Hand and Thought*. Helsinki: Werner Söderström Oy.

Pallasmaa, J. 2005. *The Eyes of the Skin: Architecture and the Senses*. Chichester: Wiley.

Pallasmaa, J. 2009. *The Thinking Hand: Existential and Embodied Wisdom in Architecture*. Chichester: Wiley.

Parker Pearson, M. and Richards, C. 1994. Ordering the World: Perceptions of Architecture, Space and Time. In M. Parker Pearson and C. Richards (eds), *Architecture and Order. Approaches to Social Space*. London: Routledge, pp. 1–33.

Poroszlai, I. 2000. Excavation Campaigns at the Bronze Age Tell Site at Százhalombatta-Földvár. In I. Poroszlai and M. Vicze (eds), *Százhalombatta Archaeological Expedition Annual Report 1*. Százhalombatta: Archaeolingua, pp. 13–73.

Premk, A., Popovic, P., and Bjelajac, Lj. 1984. Izvestaj o sondaznim iskopavanjima u 1980 godini, *Djerdapske sveske* II: 111–134.

Reich, C. 2005. Vogelmensch und Menschvogel. Bronzezeitliche Vogel-Mensch-Darstellungen im mittleren und unteren Donauraum. In B. Horejs, R. Jung, E. Kaiser, and B. Teržan (eds), *Interpretationsraum Bronzezeit. Festschrift Bernhard Hänsel*. Bonn: Rudolf Habelt, pp. 231–239.

Şandor-Chicideanu, M. 2003. *Cultura Žuto Brdo-Gârla Mare. Contribuţii la cunoaşterea epocii bronzului la Dunărea Mijlocie şi Inferioară*. Cluj-Napoca: Editura Nereamia Napocae.

Şandor-Chicideanu, M. and Chicideanu, I. 1990. Contribution to the Study of the Gârla Mare Anthropomorphic Statuettes. *Dacia* 34: 53–76.

Schumacher-Matthäus, G. 1985. *Studien zu bronzezeitlichen Schmucktrachten im Karpatenbecken*. Marburger Studien zur Vor- und Frühgeschichre 6. Mainz: Philipp von Zabern.

Sennett, R. 2009. *The Craftsman*. London: Penguin Books.

Sherratt, A. 1983. The Secondary Exploitation of Animals in the Old World. *World Archaeology*, 15(1): 90–104.

Shusterman, R. 2012. *Thinking through the Body: Essays in Somaesthetics.* Cambridge: Cambridge University Press.

Šimić, J. 2000. *Kulturne skupine s inkrustiranom keramikom u brončanom dobu sjeveroistočne Hrvatske [Cultural Groups with Encrusted Ceramics in the Bronze Age in North-east Croatia].* Osijek: Muzej Slavonije Osijek.

Slepian, M. L. and Ambady, N. 2012. Fluid Movement and Creativity. *Journal of Experimental Psychology: General* 141: 625–629.

Sofaer, J. 2006. Pots, Houses and Metal: Technological Relations at the Bronze Age Tell at Százhalombatta, Hungary. *Oxford Journal of Archaeology* 25(2): 127–147.

Sofaer, J. and Budden, S. 2013. Many Hands Make Light Work: Potting and Embodied Knowledge at the Bronze Age Tell at Százhalombatta, Hungary. In M. L. S. Sørensen and K. Rebay-Salisbury (eds), *Embodied Knowledge.* Oxford: Oxbow, pp. 117–127.

Sørensen, M. L. S. and Rebay-Salisbury, K. (eds). 2013. *Embodied Knowledge.* Oxford: Oxbow.

Sturt, G. 1923 [Reprinted 1993]. *The Wheelwright's Shop.* Cambridge: Cambridge University Press.

Szathmári, I. 2003a. Beiträge zu den Vogeldarstellungen der bronzezeitlichen Tell-Kulturen. In E. Jerem and P. Raczky (eds), *Morgenrot der Kulturen. Frühe Etappen der Menschheitsgeshichte in Mittel- und Südosteuropa. Festschrift für Nándor Kalicz zum 75. Geburtstag.* Budapest: Archaeolingua, pp. 513–523.

Szathmári, I. 2003b. The Florescence of the Middle Bronze Age in the Tisza Region: The Füzesabony Culture. In Z. Visy (ed), *Hungarian Archaeology at the Turn of the Millenium.* Budapest: Ministry of National Cultural Heritage, Teleki László Foundation, pp. 156–157.

Szentmiklosi, A. 2006. Relations of the Cruceni-Belegiš Culture with the Žuto Brdo-Gârla Mare Culture. *Analele Banatului S.N.* XIV(1): 229–270.

Tárnoki, J. 2003. The Expansion of the Hatvan Culture. In Z. Visy (ed), *Hungarian Archaeology at the Turn of the Millenium.* Budapest: Ministry of National Cultural Heritage, Teleki László Foundation, pp. 145–148.

Thomas, B. and Szentléleky, T. 1959. *Vezető a veszprémi Bakonyi Múzeum régészeti kiállitásához [Guide to the Archaeological Exhibition of the Bakony Museum of Veszprém].* Budapest: Múzeumok Közp. Prop. Irodája.

Todorović, J. 1977. *Praistorijska Karaburma II. Nekropola bronzanog doba. Prehistoric Karaburma II [The Necropolis of the Bronze Age].* Dissertationes et monographiae XIX. Monografije 4. Belgrade: City of Belgrade Museum.

Tompa, F. 1935. *25 Jahre Urgeschichtsforschung in Ungarn.* Berlin: Bericht der Römisch-Germanischen Kommission.

Trbuhović, V. 1956–57. Plastika vrsacko-zutobredske grupe. *Starinar n.s.* 7–8: 132.

Vasić, V and Vasić, R. 2000. Función depuradora de los humedales I: una revisión bibliográfica sobre el papel de los macrófitos. *Boletín SEHUMED* IV(16): 131–139.

Vukmanović, M. and Popović, P. 1996. Predmeti kultne namene na nalazi tima bronzanog doba na Djerdapu [Cult Objects on Bronze Age Sites in the Iron Gate]. *Zbornik Radova Narodnog Muzeja* 16(1): 89.

Wade, J. A. 1989. The Context of Adoption of Brass Technology in Northeastern Nigeria and Its Effects on the Elaboration of Culture. In S. E. van der Leeuw and R. Torrence (eds), *What's New? A Closer Look at the Process of Innovation*. One World Archaeology 14. London: Unwin Hyman, pp. 225–244.

Wendrich, W. 2012. Archaeology and Apprenticeship: Body Knowledge, Identity, and Communities of Practice. In W. Wendrich (ed), *Archaeology and Apprenticeship: Body Knowledge, Identity, and Communities of Practice*. Tucson: University of Arizona Press, pp. 1–19.

Wirth, S. 2006. Vogel-Sonnen-Barke. In H. Beck, D. Geuenich, and H. Steuer (eds), *Reallexikon der Germanischen Altertumskunde*. Berlin/New York: Walter de Gruyter, pp. 552–563.

2 Recycling

Bauman, Z. 2005. *Liquid Life*. Cambridge: Polity Press.

Bergerbrant, S. Forthcoming. Creativity and Textile Tools in Middle Bronze Age Százhalombatta-Földvár. In L. Bender Jørgensen, J. Sofaer, and M. L. S. Sørensen with G. Appleby, S. Becker, S. Bergerbrant, S. Coxon, K. Grömer, F. Kaul, D. Maričević, S. Mihelić, A. Rast-Eicher, and H. Rösel-Mautendorfer, *Creativity in the Bronze Age*. Manuscript in preparation.

Bóna, I. 1975. *Die Mittlere Bronzezeit Ungarns und Ihre Südöstlichen Beziehungen*. Archaeologia Hungarica IL. Budapest: Akadémiai Kiadó.

Brysbaert, A. and Vetters, M. 2012. Buried, Wasted, Half-Done and Left-Over: In Search of the Artisans among Their 'Rubbish'. Paper presented at the conference Craft and People: Agents of Skilled Labour in the Archaeological Record. 1–2 November 2012. London: British Museum.

Budden, S. and Sofaer, J, 2009. Nondiscursive Knowledge and the Construction of Identity. Potters, Potting and Performance at the Bronze Age Tell of Százhalombatta, Hungary. *Cambridge Archaeological Journal* 19(2): 203–220.

Budden, S., 2007. Renewal and Reinvention: The Role of Learning Strategies in the Early to Late Bronze Age of the Carpathian Basin. Unpublished PhD, University of Southampton.

Budden, S., 2008. Skill amongst the Sherds: Understanding the Role of Skill in the Early to Late Middle Bronze Age in Hungary. In I. Berg (ed), *Breaking the Mould: Challenging the Past through Pottery, Manchester 2006*. British Archaeological Reports International Series 1861. Oxford: BAR, pp. 1–17.

Douglass, J. and Heckman, R. 2012. Pots and Agriculture: Anasazi Rural Household Production, Long House Valley, Northern Arizona. In J. Douglass and N. Gonlin (eds), *Ancient Households of the Americas: Conceptualizing What Households Do*. Boulder: University of Colorado, pp. 189–218.

Earle, T. and Kristiansen, K. (eds). 2010. *Organizing Bronze Age Societies. The Mediterranean, Central Europe and Scandinavia Compared.* Cambridge: Cambridge University Press.

Gandini, L. 2005. From the Beginning of the Atelier to Materials as Languages: Conversations with Reggio Emilia. In L. Gandini, L. Hill, L. Cadwell, and C. Schwall (eds), *In the Spirit of the Atudio: Learning from the Atelier of Reggio Emilia.* New York: Teachers College Press, pp. 6–15.

Gandini, L. and Kaminsky, I. 2005. Remida, the Creative Recycling Center in Reggio Emilia: An Interview with Elena Giacopini, Graziella Brighenti, Arturo Bertoldi, and Alba Ferrari. *Innovations in Early Education* 12(3): 1–13.

Guerra, M. and Zuccoli, F. 2012. Finished and Unfinished Objects: Supporting Children's Creativity through Materials. *Procedia – Social and Behavioral Sciences* 51: 721–727.

Harding, A. 2000. *European Societies in the Bronze Age.* Cambridge: Cambridge University Press.

Ingold, T. 1986. *Evolution and Social Life.* Cambridge: Cambridge University Press.

Ingold, T. and Hallam, E. 2007. Creativity and Cultural Improvisation: An Introduction. In E. Hallam and T. Ingold (eds), *Creativity and Cultural Improvisation.* Oxford: Berg, pp. 1–24.

Jeanes, E. 2006. 'Resisting Creativity, Creating the New'. A Deleuzian Perspective on Creativity. *Creativity and Innovation Management* 15(2): 127–134.

Jury, L. 2004. 'Fountain' Most Influential Piece of Modern Art. *The Independent* 2 December 2004.

Knappett, C. 2005. *Thinking through Material Culture. An Interdisciplinary Perspective.* Philadelphia: University of Pennsylvania Press.

Kovács, G. 2008. Geoarchaeological Investigation of Százhalombatta-Földvár Bronze Age Tell Settlement in Hungary. Unpublished PhD thesis, University of Cambridge.

Kovács, T. 1969. A százhalombattai bronzkori telep [The Bronze Age Settlement at Százhalombatta]. *Archaeologiai Értesítő* 96: 161–169.

Kreiter, A. 2005. Middle Bronze Age Ceramic Finds from Százhalombatta-Földvár, Hungary. In I. Poroszlai and M. Vicze (eds), *Százhalombatta Archaeological Expedition. Report 2.* Százhalombatta: Matrica Museum, pp. 9–19.

Kreiter, A. 2007. *Technological Choices and Material Meanings in Early and Middle Bronze Age Hungary: Understanding the Active Role of Material Culture through Ceramic Analysis.* British Archaeological Reports International Series 1604. Oxford: Archaeopress.

Kreiter, A., Bajnóczi, B., Sipos, P., Szakmány G., and Tóth, M. 2007. Archaeometric Examination of Early and Middle Bronze Age Ceramics from Százhalombatta-Földvár, Hungary. *Archeometriai Műhely* 2: 33–46.

Larson, A. 2000. Sustainable Innovation through an Entrepreneurship Lens. *Business Strategy and the Environment* 9: 304–317.

Leach, J. 2004. Modes of Creativity. In E. Hirsch and M. Strathern (eds), *Transactions and Creations. Property Debates and the Stimulus of Melanesia*. New York: Berghahn Books, pp. 151–175.

Liep, J. 2001. Introduction. In J. Liep (ed), *Locating Cultural Creativity*. London: Pluto Press, pp. 1–13.

Marton, H. 2012. The Resonance of Gabbroic Clay in Contemporary Ceramic Works. Paper presented at the conference Insight from Innovation: New Light of Archaeological Ceramics. 19–21 October 2012. University of Southampton.

Neuwirth, R. 2006. *Shadow Cities: A Billion Squatters, A New Urban World*. London: Routledge.

Piazza, G. 1997. Materials, Relationships and Languages: Interview with Giovanni Piazza. Reported in L. Gandini 2005. From the Beginning of the *Atelier* to Materials as Languages: Conversations with Reggio Emilia. In L. Gandini, L. Hill, L. Cadwell, and C. Schwall (eds), *In the Spirit of the Studio: Learning from the Atelier of Reggio Emilia*. New York: Teachers College Press, pp. 6–15.

Pope, R. 2005. *Creativity. Theory, History, Practice*. London: Routledge.

Poroszlai, I., 1996. *Excavations at Százhalombatta 1989–1995*. Százhalombatta: Matrica Museum.

Poroszlai, I., 2000. Excavation Campaigns at the Bronze Age Site at Százhalambatta-Földvár. In I. Poroszlai and M. Vicze (eds), *Százhalombatta Archaeological Expedition SAX Annual Report 1*. Százhalombatta: Archaeolingua, pp. 13–73.

Poroszlai, I. 2003. Fortified Centres along the Danube. In Z. Visy (ed), *Hungarian Archaeology at the Turn of the Millenium*. Budapest: Department of Monuments of the Ministry of Cultural Heritage, pp. 151–155.

Rice, P. 1984. *Pots and Potters: Current Approaches in Ceramic Archaeology*. Los Angeles: University of California, Institute of Archaeology.

Roy, R. 2000. Sustainable Product-Service Systems. *Futures* 32(3–4): 289–299.

Savage, P. 2010. The Germ of the Future? Ghetto Biennale: Port-au-Prince. *Third Text* 24(4): 491–495.

Schumpeter, J. 1942. *Capitalism, Socialism, and Democracy*. New York: Harper & Row.

Skibo, J. 2013. *Understanding Pottery Function*. New York: Springer.

Sofaer, J. 2006. Pots, Houses and Metal. Technological Relations at the Bronze Age Tell at Százhalombatta, Hungary. *Oxford Journal of Archaeology* 25(2): 127–147.

Sofaer, J. with contributions by Bech, J.-H., Budden, S., Choyke, A., Eriksen, B. V., Horváth, T., Kovács, G., Kreiter, A., Mühlenbock, C., and Stika, H.-P. 2010. Technology and Craft. In T. Earle and K. Kristiansen (eds), *Organizing Bronze Age Societies*. Cambridge: Cambridge University Press, pp. 185–217.

Sofaer, J. 2011. Human Ontogeny and Material Change at the Bronze Age Tell of Százhalombatta, Hungary. *Cambridge Archaeological Journal* 21(2): 217–227.

Sofaer, J., Sørensen, M. L. S., and Vicze, M. 2012. Notes from a Bronze Age Tell: Százhalombatta-Földvár, Hungary. *The European Archaeologist* 38: 15–16.

Sofaer, J., Vicze, M., and Sørensen, M. L. S. Forthcoming. *Life on a Bronze Age Tell: The Pottery from Levels 1–7, Százhalombatta, Hungary. SAX Report IV.* Százhalombatta: Matrica Museum.

Sørensen, M. L. S. with contributions by Bech, J.-H., Kulcsarne-Berzsenyi, B., Kristiansen, K., Mühlenbock, C., Prescott, C., and Vicze, M. 2010. Households. In T. Earle and K. Kristiansen (eds), *Organizing Bronze Age Societies.* Cambridge: Cambridge University Press, pp. 122–154.

Springer, T. and Grebe, A. (eds). 2003. *Gold und Kult der Bronzezeit* (exhibition catalogue). Nürnberg: Verlag des Germanischen Nationalmuseums.

Van Gijn, A. and Hofman, C. 2008. Were They Used as Tools? An Exploratory Functional Study of Abraded Potsherds from Two Pre-colonial Sites on the Island of Guadeloupe, Northern Lesser Antilles. *Caribbean Journal of Science* 44(1): 21–35.

Vicze, M. 1992. Die Bestattungen der Vatya-kultur. In W. Meier-Arendt (ed), *Bronzezeit in Ungarn. Forschungen in Tell-Siedlungen an Donau und Thiess.* Frankfurt am Main: Museum für Vor- un Frühgeschichte, Archaeologisches Museum, pp. 92–95.

Vicze, M. 2005. Excavation Methods and Some Preliminary Results of the SAX Project. In I. Poroszlai and M. Vicze (eds), *Százhalombatta Archaeological Expedition. Report 2.* Százhalombatta: Archaeolingua, pp. 65–77.

Vicze, M. 2011. Bronze Age Cemetery at *Dunaújváros-Duna-dűlő.* Dissertationes Pannonicae Series IV, Volume 1. Budapest: Eötvös Loránd University, Institute of Archaeological Sciences.

Vicze, M. and Poroszlai, I. 2004. Százhalombatta – Földvár. In J. Kisfaludi (ed), *Archaeological Investigations in Hungary 2003.* Budapest: Kulturális Örökségvédelmi Hivatal, pp. 290–293.

3 Design

Adamson, G. 2007. *Thinking through Craft.* Oxford: Berg.

Behrens, R. 1998. Art, Design and Gestalt Theory. *Leonardo* 31(4): 299–303.

Benjamin, W. 1968 [1992]. *Illuminations.* Edited and introduced by H. Arendt. London: Fontana Books.

Bohm, D. 1996 *On Creativity.* London: Routledge

Bóna, I. 1975. *Die Mittlere Bronzezeit Ungarns und Ihre Südöstlichen Beziehungen.* Archaeologia Hungarica IL. Budapest: Akadémiai Kiadó.

Bourdieu, P. 1968. Outline of a sociological Theory of Art Perception. *International Social Science Journal* 20(Winter): 589–612.

Budden, S., 2008. Skill amongst the Sherds: Understanding the Role of Skill in the Early to Late Middle Bronze Age in Hungary. In I. Berg (ed), *Breaking the Mould: Challenging the Past through Pottery, Manchester 2006.* British Archaeological Reports International Series 1861. Oxford: BAR, pp. 1–17.

Cardoso, R. 2008 [2010]. Craft versus Design: Moving beyond a Tired Dichotomy. In G. Adamson (ed), *The Craft Reader.* Oxford: Berg, pp. 321–332.

Cox, G. 2005. *Cox Review of Creativity in Business: Building on the UK's Strengths.* London: HM Treasury.

Crown, P. 2007. Life Histories of Pots and Potters: Situating the Individual in Archaeology. *American Antiquity* 72: 677–690.

Csányi, M. 1982–1983. A nagyrévi kultúra leletei a Közép-Tiszavidékről. *SzMMÉ* 1982–83: 33–65.

Csányi, M. 2003. Tiszaug-Kéménytetõ: A Bronze Age Settlement in the Tiszazug. In Z. Visy (ed), *Hungarian Archaeology at the Turn of the Millennium.* Budapest: Ministry of National Cultural Heritage, pp. 143–144.

Gibson, J. 1979. *The Ecological Approach to Visual Perception.* Boston, MA: Houghton Mifflin.

Girić, M. 1971. *Mokrin. The Early Bronze Age Necropolis.* Beograd: Smithsonian Institution / The Archaeological Society of Yugoslavia.

Görsdorf, J., Marková, K., and Furmánek, V. 2004. Some New 14 C Data to the Bronze Age in Slovakia. *Geochronometria* 23: 79–91.

Hegmon, M. 1992. Archaeological Research on Style. *Annual Review of Anthropology* 21: 517–536.

Heidegger, M. 1950. The Thing. Reprinted in G. Adamson (ed). 2010. *The Craft Reader.* Oxford and New York: Berg, pp. 404–408.

Kaul, F. 1998. *Ships on Bronzes. A Study in Bronze Age Religion and Iconography.* Copenhagen: National Museum of Denmark.

Kaul, F. 2004. Bronzealderens ikonografiske motiver og deres fremkomst i en fromativ fase. In G. Milstreu and H. Prøhl (eds), *Prehistoric Pictures as Archaeological Source.* Gotarc Serie C. Arkeologiska Skrifter 50. Göteborg: Göteborgs Universitet, pp. 85–119.

Kaul, F. 2005. Bronze Age Tripartite Cosmologies. *Prähistorische Zeitschrift* 80(2): 135–148.

Knappett, C. 2005. *Thinking through Material Culture. An Interdisciplinary Perspective.* Philadelphia: University of Pennsylvania Press.

Kristiansen, K. and Larsson, T. 2005. *The Rise of Bronze Age Society. Travels, Transmissions and Transformations.* Cambridge: Cambridge University Press.

Kuijpers, M. 2012. The Sound of Fire, Smell of Copper, Feel of Bronze, and Colours of the Cast: Sensory Aspects of Metalworking Technology. In M. L. S. Sørensen and K. Rebay-Salisbury (eds), *Embodied Knowledge.* Oxford: Oxbow, pp. 137–150.

Leslie, E. 1998. Walter Benjamin: Traces of Craft. *Journal of Design History* 11(1): 5–13.

Nichol, L. 1997 [2004]. Foreword. In D. Bohm (ed), *On Creativity.* Routledge Classics Edition. Oxford: Routledge, pp. xv–xxxiii.

Norman, D. 1988. *The Design of Everyday Things.* New York: Doubleday.

Norman, D. 2004. *Emotional Design. Why We Love (or Hate) Everyday Things.* New York: Basic Books.

Petroski, R. 1997. *Invention by Design. How Engineers Get from Thought to Thing.* Cambridge, MA: Harvard University Press.

Pope, R. 2005. *Creativity. Theory, History, Practice.* London: Routledge.

Poroszlai, I. 2003. Fortified Cenres along the Danube. In Z. Visy (ed), *Hungarian Archaeology at the Turn of the Millennium.* Budapest: Ministry of National Cultural Heritage, pp. 151–155.

Poroszlai, I. and Vicze, M. 2004. *Százhalombatta Története A Bronzkortól Napjainkig. A Százhalombattai 'Matrica' Múzeum Állandó Kiállításának Katalógusa.* Százhalombatta: Matrica Múzeum.

Pye, D. 1968. *The Nature and the Art of Workmanship.* Cambridge: Cambridge University Press.

Rast-Eicher, A. and Bender Jøgensen, L. 2013. Sheep Wool in Bronze Age and Iron Age Europe. *Journal of Archaeological Science* 40: 1224–1241.

Reschreiter, H. and Kowarik, K. 2009. The Staircase: A Technical Masterpiece. In A. Kern, K. Kowarik, A. Rausch, and H. Reschreiter (eds), *Kingdom of Salt. 7000 Years of Hallstatt.* Veröffentlichungen der Prähistorischen Abteilung (VPA) 3. Vienna: The Natural History Museum of Vienna, pp. 61–63.

Risatti, H. 2007. *A Theory of Craft. Function and Aesthetic Expression.* Durham: University of North Carolina Press.

Schreiber, R. 1984. Szimbolikus ábrázolások korobronzkori edényeken (Symbolische darstellungen an frübronzezeitlichen Gefässen). *Archaeológiai Értesítő* 111: 3–28.

Sofaer, J. 2011. Human Ontogeny and Material Change at the Bronze Age Tell of Százhalombatta, Hungary. *Cambridge Archaeological Journal* 21: 217–227.

Sofaer, J. 2013. Cosmologies in Clay: Swedish Helmet Bowls in the Middle Bronze Age of the Carpathian Basin. In S. Bergerbrant and S. Sabatini (eds), *Counterpoint: Essays in Archaeology and Heritage Studies in Honour of Professor Kristian Kristiansen.* Oxford: Archaeopress. pp. 361–365.

Sofaer, J. Forthcoming. Pots as Stories. In L. Bender Jørgensen, J. Sofaer, and M. L. S. Sørensen with G. Appleby, S. Becker, S. Bergerbrant, S. Coxon, K. Grömer, F. Kaul, D. Maričević, S. Mihelić, A. Rast-Eicher, and H. Rösel-Mautendorfer, *Creativity in the Bronze Age.* Manuscript in preparation.

Sofaer, J. and Budden, S. 2012. Many Hands Make Light Work: Embodied Knowledge at the Bronze Age Tell at Százhalombatta, Hungary. In M. L. S. Sørensen and K. Rebay-Salisbury (eds), *Embodied Knowledge.* Oxford: Oxbow, pp. 117–127.

Sofaer Derevenski, J. and Sørensen, M. L. S. 2002. Becoming Cultural: Society and the Incorporation of Bronze. In B. Ottaway and E. C. Wager (eds), *Metals and Society: Papers from a Session Held at the European Association of Archaeologists Sixth Annual Meeting in Lisbon 2000.* British Archaeological Reports International Series 1061. Oxford: Archaeopress, pp. 117–121.

Sørensen, M. L. S. and Appleby, G. Forthcoming. The Making of a New Material – From Copper to Bronze. In L. Bender Jørgensen, J. Sofaer, and M. L. S. Sørensen with

G. Appleby, S. Becker, S. Bergerbrant, S. Coxon, K. Grömer, F. Kaul, D. Maričević, S. Mihelić, A. Rast-Eicher, and H. Rösel-Mautendorfer, *Creativity in the Bronze Age*. Manuscript in preparation.

Stafford, B. M. 2007. *Echo Objects. The Cognitive Work of Images*. Chicago: University of Chicago Press.

Tasić, N. 1972. The Mokrin Necropolis and Its Position in the Development of the Early Bronze Age in Voivodina. In S. Foltiny (ed), *Mokrin II. The Early Bronze Age Necropolis*. Kikinda: Narodni Museum, pp. 9–28.

van Toorn, J. 1994. Design and Reflexivity. *Visible Language* 28(4): 316–325.

Vicze, M. 2009. Nagyrév Symbolism Revisited: Three Decorated Vessels from Százhalombatta and Dunaújváros. *Tisicum: A Jász-Nagykun-Szolnok Megyei Múzeumok Évkönyve XIX* (2009): 309–318.

Vicze, M. 2011. Bronze Age Cemetery at *Dunaújváros-Duna-dűlő*. Dissertationes Pannonicae Series IV, Volume 1. Budapest: Eötvös Loránd University, Institute of Archaeological Sciences.

Wallance, D. 1956. *Shaping America's Products*. New York: Reinhold.

Wells, P. 2012. *How Ancient Europeans Saw the World: Vision, Patterns, and the Shaping of the Mind in Prehistoric Times*. Princeton, NJ: Princeton University Press.

Wildenhain, M. 1957. Asilomar Conference Proceedings. A Ceramist Speaks on Design. Reprinted in G. Adamson (ed). 2010. *The Craft Reader*. Oxford and New York: Berg, pp. 569–574.

4 Margins

Archetti, E. P. 2001. Football and Polo: Tradition and Creolization in the Making of Modern Argentina. In J. Liep (ed), *Locating Cultural Creativity*. London: Pluto Press, pp. 93–105.

Banks, M. 1996. *Ethnicity: Anthropological Constructions*. London: Routledge

Bauman, Z. 2004. *Identity. Conversations with Benedetto Vecchi*. Cambridge: Polity Press.

Blok, A. and Jensen, T. E. 2012. *Bruno Latour: Hybrid Thoughts in a Hybrid World*. London: Routledge.

Bourdieu, P. 1993. *The Field of Cultural Production*. Cambridge: Polity Press.

Brodie, N. 1997. New Perspectives on the Bell Beaker Culture. *Oxford Journal of Archaeology* 16(3): 297–314.

Bush, R. and Habib, A. (eds). 2012. *Marginality and Exclusion in Egypt*. London: Zed Books Ltd.

Chomsky, N. 1964. *Current Issues in Linguistic Theory*. The Hague: Mouton.

Choyke, A. and Bartosiewicz, L. 2005. Skating with Horses: Continuity and Parallelism in Prehistoric Hungary. *Revue de Paléobiologie* 10: 317–326.

Gibson, C. 2010. Guest Editorial – Creative Geographies: Tales from the 'Margins'. *Australian Geographer* 41(1): 1–10.

Csikszentmihalyi, M. 1988. Society, Culture, and Person: A Systems View of Creativity. In R. J. Sternberg (ed), *The Nature of Creativity*. Cambridge: Cambridge University Press, pp. 325–339.

Czene, A. 2008. Bell Beakers at Budakalász. In M. Gyöngyössy (ed), *Perspectives of the Past. Excavations of the Last Decade in Pest County*. Szentendre: Pest Megyei Múzeumok Igazgatósága.

Dawdy, S. L. (ed). 2000. 'Creolization'. *Historical Archaeology* 34(4): 1–133.

Desideri, J. 2011. *When Beakers Met Bell Beakers. An Analysis of Dental Remains.* British Archaeological Reports International Series 2292. Oxford: Archaeopress.

Dogan, M. and Pahre, R. 1990. *Creative Marginality: Innovation at the Intersections of Social Sciences.* Boulder, CO: Westview Press.

Dogan, M. 1999. Marginality. In M. A. Runco and S. R. Pritzer (eds), *Encyclopedia of Creativity*. Vol. 2, I–Z. San Diego, CA: Academic Press, pp. 179–184.

Dvořák, P. 1992. *Die Gräberfelder der Glockenbecherkultur in Mähren I. Katalog der Funde.* Brno: Petr Dvořák.

Endrődi, A. 1992. A korabronzkori Harangedény kultúra telepe és temetője Szigetszentmiklós határában [The Settlement and Cemetery of the Bell Beaker Culture in the District of Szigetszentmiklós]. In P. Havassy and L. Selmeczi (eds), *Régészeti kutatások az Mo autópálya nyomvonalán I. Archäologische Forschungen auf der Strasse der Autobahn Mo. I. BTM Műhely* 5: 83–201.

Endrődi, A. 2002. New Data on the Late Copper Age and Early Bronze Age Settlement History of Budapest – Csepel Island. *Budapest Régiségei* XXXVI: 115–129.

Endrődi, A. 2003. Characteristic Elements of the Settlement Structure in the Early Bronze Age Settlement at Budapest-Albertfalva. In C. Kacsó (ed), *Bronzezeitliche Kulturerscheinungen im Karpatischen Raum. Die Beziehungen zu den benachbarten Gebieten. Bibliotheca Marmatia* 2(2003): 151–157.

Endrődi, A. 2005. Kora Bronzkori Ház- És Településrekonstrukció A Harangedény-Csepel-Csoport Budapest (XI. Kerület)-Albertfalva LelőHelyén [Reconstruction of an Early Bronze Age House and Settlement at the Budapest Albertfalva Site of the Bell Beaker–Csepel Group]. *Ősrégészeti Levelek* 7: 128–134.

Endrődi, A. 2012. Early Bronze Age Headdress. Markers of the Social Status in the Bell Beaker–Csepel Group. *Archaeologiai Értesítő* 137: 7–26.

Endrődi, A. 2013. Recent Data on the Settlement History and Contact System of the Bell Beaker–Csepel Group. In A. Anders and G. Kulcsár (eds), with G. Kalla, V. Kiss, and G. V. Szabó, *Moments in Time*. Papers Presented to Pál Raczky on His 60th Birthday. Ősrégészeti Társaság / Prehistoric Society Eötvös Loránd University. Budapest: L'Harmattan, pp. 693–705.

Endrődi, A. and Pásztor, E. 2006. Symbolism and Traditions in the Society of Bell Beaker–Csepel Group [A szimbolizmus és a tradíciók szerepe a Harangedény–Csepel-csoport társadalmában]. *Archaeologiai Értesítő* 131: 7–25.

Endrődi, A., Gyulai, F., and Reményi, L. 2008. The Roles of the Environmental and Cultural Factors in the Everyday Life of Bell Beaker–Csepel Group. *Millenni. Studi di Archeologia Preistorica* 6: 235–256.

Eriksen, T. H. 2003. Creolization and Creativity. *Global Networks* 3(3): 223–237.

Ferguson, L. 1992. *Uncommon Ground: Archaeology and Early African America, 1650–1800*. Washington, DC: Smithsonian Institution Press.

Florida, R. 2002. *The Rise of the Creative Class*. New York: Basic Books.

Fokkens, H., Achterkamp, Y. and Kuipers, M. 2008. Bracers or Bracelets? About the Functionality and Meaning of Bell Beaker Wrist-Guards. *Proceedings of the Prehistoric Society* 74: 109–140.

Gibson, C. 2010. Guest Editorial – Creative Geographies: Tales from the 'Margins'. *Australian Geographer* 41(1): 1–10.

Gibson, C. and Connell, J. 2004. Cultural Industry Production in Remote Places: Indigenous Popular Music in Australia. In D. Power and A. Scott (eds), *The Cultural Industries and the Production of Culture*. London and New York: Routledge, pp. 243–258.

Hájek, L. 1968. *Kultura zvoncovitých pohárů v Čechách*, Archeologické Studijní Materiály 5, Praha: n.p.

Hannerz, U. 1987. The World in Creolisation. *Africa* 57: 546–559.

Hannerz, U. 1992. *Cultural Complexity: Studies in the Social Organization of Meaning*. New York: Columbia University Press.

Harrison, R. 1980. *The Beaker Folk: Copper Age Archaeology in Western Europe*. London: Thames and Hudson.

Heyd, V. 1998, *Die Glockenbecherkultur in Süddeutschland*, Zum Stand der Forschung einer Regionalprovinz entlang der Donau. In M. Benz and S. Van Willigen (eds), Some New Approaches to the Bell Beaker 'Phenomenon'. Lost Paradise . . . ? Proceedings of the 2nd Meeting of the 'Association Archéologie et Gobelets', Feldberg (Germany), 18–20 April 1997. British Archaeological Reports International Series 690, Oxford, pp. 87–106.

Heyd, V. 2005. The Eastern Periphery of the Bell Beaker Phenomenon and Its Relation with the Aegean Early Bronze Age. In I. Galanaki, Y. Galanakis, R. Laffineur, (eds), *Between the Aegean and Baltic Seas. Prehistory across Borders*. Proceedings of the International Conference 'Bronze and Iron Age Interconnections and Contemporary Developments between the Aegean and the Regions of the Balkan Peninsula, Central and Northern Europe'. 11–14 April 2005. University of Zagreb, *Aegaeum* 27, 91–104.

Heyd, V., Husty, L. and Kreiner, L. 2004. *Siedlungen der Glockenbecherkultur in Süddeutschland und Mitteleuropa*. Arbeiten zur Archäologie Süddeutschlands. Büchenbach: Dr Faustus Verlag.

Hirsch, E. 2004. Boundaries of Creation: The Work of Credibility in Science and Ceremony. In E. Hirsch and M. Strathern (eds), *Transactions and Creations. Property Debates and the Stimulus of Melanesia*. New York: Berghahn Books, pp. 176–192.

Ilon, G. 2005. Bucsu, Hosszú Aszú-dűlő. In *Régészeti Kutatások Magyarországon 2004 – Archaelogical Investigations in Hungary 2004*, Budapest: Kulturális Örökségvédelmi Hivatal, p. 179.

Ingold, T. 2007. Introduction. Part I. Modes of Creativity in Life and Art. In E. Hallam and T. Ingold (eds), *Creativity and Cultural Improvisation*. Oxford: Berg, pp. 45–54.

Inskip, S. 2013. *Islam in Iberia or Iberian Islam. Bioarchaeology and the Analysis of Emerging of Islamic Identity in Early Medieval Spain*. Unpublished PhD thesis, University of Southampton.

Kalicz-Schreiber, R. 1981. Möglichkeiten zur feineren Gliederung der Nagyrév-kultur in Budapest. In N. Kalicz and R. Kalicz-Schreiber (eds), *Die Frühbronzezeit im Karpatenbecken und in den Nachbargebieten. Internationales Symposium 1977 Budapest–Velem*. Budapest: Mitteilungen des Archäologischen Instituts der Ungarischen Akademie der Wissenschaften Beiheft 2, pp. 81–87.

Kalicz-Schreiber, R. 1984. Komplex der Nagyrév-Kultur. In N. Tasić (ed), *Kulturen der Frühbronzezeit des Karpatenbeckens und Nordbalkans*. Beograd: Balkanološki Institut SANU, pp. 133–190.

Kalicz-Schreiber, R. 1997. Kora Bronzkori Temetkezesek A Csepel-Sziget keleti partján (Frühbronzezeitliche Bestattungen Am Östlichen Ufer Der Csepel-Insel Bei Budapest) *Budapest Régiségei* 31: 177–197.

Kalicz-Schreiber, R. 1998/1997. A Somogyvár-Vinkovci kultúra és a Harangedény-Csepel-csoport Budapest kora bronzkorában [Die Somogyvár-Vinkovci-Kultur und die Glockenbecher in der Frühbronzezeit von Budapest]. *Savaria* 24(1998/1999): 83–114.

Kalicz-Schreiber, R. and Kalicz N. 1998/2000. A harangedények szerepe a Budapest környéki kora bronzkor társadalmi viszonyainak megjelenítésében [The Role of Bell Beakers in Reflecting Social Relations in the Early Bronze Age of Budapest]. *Archaeologiai Értesítő* 125: 45–78.

Kalicz-Schreiber, R. and Kalicz, N. 1999. A Somogyvár-Vinkovci- Kultur und die Glockenbecher in der Frühbronzezeit von Budapest. *Savaria* 24(3): 83–115.

Koepp, R. 2002. *Clusters of Creativity: Enduring Lessons on Innovation and Entrepreneurship from Silicon Valley and Europe's Silicon Fen*. Chichester: John Wiley.

Koestler, A. 1964. *The Act of Creation*. London: Hutchinson.

Koledin, J. 2008. Prilog Poznavanju rasprostranjenosti zvonastih pehara [A Contribution to the Familiar Distribution of Bell Beakers]. *Rad muzeja Vojvodine* 50: 33–59.

Kristiansen, K. 1998. *Europe before History*. Cambridge: Cambridge University Press.

Kulcsár, G. 2003. The Early Bronze Age. In Z. Visy (ed), *Hungarian Archaeology at the Turn of the Millenium*. Budapest: Ministry of National Cultural Heritage, Teleki László Foundation, pp. 141–142.

Kulcsár, G. 2009. *The Beginnings of the Bronze Age in the Carpathian Basin: The Makó-Kosihy-Čaka and the Somogyvár-Vinkovci Cultures in Hungary*. Budapest: Archeolingua.

Latour, B. 1993. *We Have Never Been Modern*. Trans. C. Porter. New York: Harvester/Wheatsheaf.

Leach, J. 2004. Modes of Creativity. In E. Hirsch and M. Strathern (eds), *Transactions and Creations. Property Debates and the Stimulus of Melanesia*. New York: Berghahn Books, pp. 151–175.

Lévi-Strauss, C. 1966. *The Savage Mind*. London: Weidenfeld and Nicolson.

Liep, J. 2001. Introduction. In J. Liep (ed), *Locating Cultural Creativity*. London: Pluto Press, pp. 1–13.

Lindholm-Romantschuk, Y. 1998. *Scholarly Book Reviewing in the Social Sciences and Humanities: The Flow of Ideas within and among Disciplines*. Westport, CT: Greenwood Press.

Machnik, J. 1991. *The Earliest Bronze Age in the Carpathian Basin*. Bradford: Department of Archaeological Sciences.

Mikołajczak, K. and Szczodrowski, R. 2012. The Bell Beaker Phenomenon. Meanings of Regional Transmission. In H. Fokkens and F. Nicolis (eds), *Background to Beakers. Inquiries into Regional Cultural Backgrounds of the Bell Beaker Complex*. Leiden: Sidestone Press, pp. 177–190.

Pásztor, E. 2009. Prehistoric Cosmologies – A Methodological Framework for an Attempt to Reconstruct Bronze Age Cosmologic Ideas in the Carpathian Basin. In J. A. Rubiño Martín, J. A. Belmonte, F. Prada, and A. Alberdi (eds), *Cosmology Across Cultures*. ASP Conference Series vol. 409, pp. 457–463.

Patay, R. 2008. An Early Bronze Age Cemetery at Szigetszentmiklós. In M. Gyöngyössy (ed), *Perspectives of the Past. Excavations of the Last Decade in Pest County*. Szentendre: Pest Megyei Múzeumok Igazgatósága, pp. 34–35.

Patay, R. 2013. Preliminary Report on the Excavation of the Bell Beaker Cemetery and Settlement at Szigetszentmiklós. Hungary: n.p.

Perry-Smith, J. and Shalley, C. 2003. The Social Side of Creativity: A Static and Dynamic Social Network Perspective. *The Academy of Management Review* 28(1): 89–106.

Piguet, M. and Besse, M. 2009 Chronology and Bell Beaker Common Ware. *Radiocarbon* 51(2): 817–830.

Place, B. 2000. Constructing the Bodies of Ill Children in the Intensive Care Unit. In A. Prout (ed), *The Body, Childhood and Society*. London: Macmillan Press, pp. 172–194.

Pope, R. 2005. *Creativity. Theory, History, Practice*. London: Routledge.

Potrebica, H. 2008. Contacts between Greece and Pannonia in the Early Iron Age with Special Concern to the Area of Thessalonica. In P. Biehl and Y. Rassamakin (eds), *Import and Imitation in Archaeology*. Langenweißbach: Beier & Beran, pp. 187–212.

Price, S. 1999. The Centrality of Margins: Art, Gender, and African American Creativity. In I. Okpewho, C. B. Davies, and A. A. Mazrui (eds), *The African Diaspora: African Origins and New World Identities*. Bloomington: Indiana University Press, pp. 204–226.

Price, T. D., Knipper, C., Grupe, G., and Smrcka, V. 2004. Strontium Isotopes and Prehistoric Human Migration: The Bell Beaker Period in Central Europe. *European Journal of Archaeology* 7(April): 9–40.

Rehman, F., Robinson, V. J., and Shennan, S. J. 1992. A Neutron Activation Study of Bell Beakers and Associated Pottery from Czechoslovakia and Hungary. *Památky archeologické* 83: 197–211.

Renfrew, C., 2001. Symbol before Concept: Material Engagement and the Early Development of Society. In I. Hodder (ed), *Archaeological Theory Today* Cambridge: Polity Press, pp. 122–140.

Robertson, R. 1992. *Globalization: Social Theory and Global Culture*. London: Sage.

Rushdie, S. 1991. *Imaginary Homelands: Essays and Criticism 1981–1991*. London: Granta Books.

Schreiber R. 1973. *A harangedények népe Budapesten. Emlékek Budapest múltjából [Die Glockenbecher-Kultur in Budapest]*. Emlékek Budapest múltjából 19. Budapest: Budapesti Történeti Múzeum.

Schreiber, R. 1975. *A tököli korabronzkori temetők [Frühbronzezeitliche Gräberfelder von Tököl]. Archaeologiai Értesítő* 102: 187–203.

Schreiber, R. 1976. *Die Probleme der Glockenbecherkultur in Ungarn*. In J. N. Lanting and J. D. van der Waals (eds), *Glockenbecher-Symposion. Oberried-Freiburg 1974*. Bossum/Haarlem: Fibula – Van Dishoeck, pp. 183–215.

Scott, A. J. 1999. The Cultural Economy: Geography and the Creative Field. *Media, Culture and Society* 21: 807–817.

Scott, A. J. 2000. *The Cultural Economy of Cities*. Sage: London.

Sofaer, J. 2002. Engendering Context. Context as Gendered Practice in the Early Bronze Age of the Upper Thames Valley, UK. *Journal of European Archaeology* 5: 191 – 211.

Sofaer, J. 2006. *The Body as Material Culture. A Theoretical Osteoarchaeology*. Cambridge: Cambridge University Press.

Sofaer, J. L. 2012. *Art Ambassador: I Do Not Speak French*. Performance Lecture. 3 November 2012. Geneva: Piano Nobile, Festival of new performance.

Sørensen, M. L. S. 2010. Bronze Age Bodiness – Maps and Coordinates. K. Rebay-Salisbury, M. L. S. Sorensen, and J. Hughes (eds), *Body Parts and Bodies Whole: Changing Relations and Meanings*. Oxford: Oxbow Books, pp. 54–63.

Sørensen, M. L. S. and Rebay-Salisbury, K. 2008. Landscapes of the Body: Burials of the Middle Bronze Age in Hungary. *European Journal of Archaeology* 11(1): 49–74.

Strathern, M. 1996. Cutting the Network. *Journal of the Royal Anthropolpgical Institute n.s.* 2: 517–535.

Thomas, J. 1991. Reading the Body: Beaker Funerary Practice in Britain, in Sacred and Profane. P. Garwood, D. Jennings, R. Skeates, J. Toms (eds), *Proceedings of a Conference on Archaeology, Ritual and Religion*, Monograph 32, Oxford: Oxford University Committee for Archaeology, pp. 33–42.

Törnqvist, G. 2011. *The Geography of Creativity*. Cheltenham: Edward Elgar.

Turek, J. 1998. The Bell Beaker Period in North-West Bohemia. In M. Benz and S. Van Willigen (eds), *Some New Approaches to the Bell Beaker 'Phenomenon'. Lost Paradise ... ?* Proceedings of the 2nd Meeting of the 'Association Archéologie et Gobelets', Feldberg (Germany), 18th–20th April 1997. British Archaeological Reports, International Series 690. Oxford: J. and E. Hedges, pp. 107–119.

Turek, J. 2002. Žárové pohřby obdobi zvoncovitých pohárů z Lovosic [The Bell Beaker Cremation Burials from Lovosice]. In P. Čech and Z. Smrž (eds), *Sborník Drahomíru Kouteckému* - Festschrift für Drahomir Koutecký. Most: Ústav archeologické památkové péče severozápadních Čech, pp. 265–270.

Turek, J. 2012. Periferie fenoménu zvoncovitých Pohárů [Periphery of the Bell Beaker Phenomenon]. *Archeologie ve středních Čechách* 16: 183–193, fototAb. 1.

Vander Linden, M. 2006. *Le phénomène campaniforme dans l'Europe du 3ème millénaire avant notre ère. Synthèse et nouvelles perspectives*. British Archaeological Reports International Series 1470. Oxford: Archaeopress.

Vander Linden, M. 2007. What Linked the Bell Beakers in Third Millennium BC Europe? *Antiquity* 81: 343–351.

Vandkilde, H. 2007. *Culture and Change in Central European Prehistory 6th–1st Millennium BC*. Aarhus: Aarhus University Press.

Van der Ploeg, I. 2004. 'Only Angels Can Do without Skin': On Reproductive Technology's Hybrids and the Politics of Body Boundaries. *Body and Society* 10(2): 153–181.

Wake, E. 2003. Contact: Indo-Christian Art. Catalogue. In *Aztecs*. Royal Academy of Arts. London: Thames and Hudson, pp. 343–344, 481–484.

Wilf, E. 2011. Sincerity versus Self-Expression: Modern Creative Agency and the Materiality of Semiotic Forms. *Cultural Anthropology* 26(3): 462–484.

Zoffmann, Z. 2006. A harang alakú edények népének embertani leletei csepel szigetről [Anthropological finds of the Bell Beaker Culture from the Csepel Island]. *Anthropologiai Közlemények* 47: 11–15.

5 Resistance

Alexander, J. 1965. The Spectacle Fibulae of Southern Europe. *American Journal of Archaeology* 69(1): 7–23.

Balen Letunić, D. 1981. Grobovi kasnog brončanog I staijeg željeznog doba iz okolice Karlovaca. *Vjesnik Arheoloskog muzeja u Zagrebu* XIV: 11–23.

Barthes, R. 1967. The Death of the Author. *Aspen* 5+6 (Fall/Winter). Available at ww.ubu.com/aspen/aspen5and6/index.html

Bergmann, J. 1982. *Ein Gräberfeld der jüngeren Bronze- und Eisenzeit bei Vollmarshausen, Kr. Kassel. Kasseler Beiträge zur Vor- und Frühgeschichte 5*. Marburg: Elwert.

Blečić Kavur, M. 2011. The Fastest Way to the *Big Sea*. A Contribution to the Knowledge about the Influence of the UFC on the Territory of the Northern Adriatic. In C. Gutjahr and G. Tiefengraber (eds), *Beiträge zur Mittel- und Spätbronzezeit sowie zur Urnenfelderzeit am Rande der Südostalpen*. Rahden/ Westf.: Verlag Marie Leidorf GmbH, pp. 51–62.

Brunšmid, J. 1898. Groblje sa urnama u Krupačama kod Krašića u Hrvatskoj, *Vjesnik Hrvatskoga Arheoloskoga Drustva*, n.s. III: 137–143.

Buchanan, I. 2000. *Michel de Certeau: Cultural Theorist*. London: Sage.

Črešnar, M. 2010. New Research on the Urnfield Period of Eastern Slovenia. A Case Study of Rogoza Near Maribor. *Arheološki vestnik* 61: 7–119.

de Certeau, M. 1984. *The Practice of Everyday Life*. Berkeley: University of California Press.

de Cléir, S. 2011. Creativity in the Margins: Identity and Locality in Ireland's Fashion Journey. *Fashion Theory: The Journal of Dress, Body & Culture* 15(2): 201–224.

Dizdar, M., Tonc, A., and Ložnjak Dizdar, D. 2011. Rescue Excavations of AS 6 Gornji Vukojevac on the Zagreb – Sisak Motorway Route, Section Velika Gorica South – Lekenik (Ostalo). *Annales Instituti Archaeologici* VII(1): 61–64.

Fiske, J. 1992. Cultural Studies and the Culture of Everyday life. In L. Grossberg, C. Nelson, and P. Treichler (eds), *Cultural Studies*. New York: Routledge, pp. 154–173.

Foucault, M. 1977. *Discipline and Punish*. Trans. A. Sheridan. New York: Pantheon.

Frazer, B. 1999. Reconceptualizing Resistance in the Historical Archaeology of the British Isles: An Editorial. *International Journal of Historical Archaeology* 3(1): 1–10.

Glogović, D. 2002. Noževi culture polja sa žarama iz Hrvatske [Urnfield Culture Knives in Croatia]. *Prilozi Instituta za arheologiju u Zagrebu* 19: 213–220.

Hoffiller, V. 1909. Staro groblje u Velikoj Gorici. *Vjesnik Hrvatskoga Arheoloskoga Drustva*, n.s. X: 120–134.

Hoffiller, V. 1924. Prethistorijske žare iz Velike Gorice kraj Zagreba. In M. Abramić and V. Hoffiller (eds), *Bulićev zbornik. Naučni prilozi posvećeni Franu Buliću prigodom LXXV. Godišnjice njegova života od učenika i prijatelja*. Zagreb/Split: Strena Buliciana, pp. 1–8.

Janik, A. and Toulmin, S. 1973. *Wittgenstein's Vienna*. New York: Simon and Schuster.

Kalicz-Schreiber, R. 2010. *Ein Graberfeld der Spätbronzezeit von Budapest-Békásmegyer*. Budapest: Institut für Archäologische Wissenschaften der Eötvös Loránd Universität and L'Harmattan, Ungarn.

Karavanić, S. 2000. *Prijelaz iz starije u mlađu kulturu polja sa žarama u sjevernoj Hrvatskoj*. PhD thesis, Department of Archaeology, Faculty of Arts and Humanities, University of Zagreb.

Karavanić, S. 2009. *The Urnfield Culture in Continental Croatia*. British Archaeological Reports International Series 2036. Oxford: Archaeopress.

Karavanić, S. 2010. Sljepoočničarke i struktura grobnih priloga na groblju u Velikoj Gorici [Temple Rings and the Structure of Grave Goods Found in the Velika Gorica Graveyard]. *Prilozi Instituta za arheologiju u Zagrebu* 27: 83–94.

Karavanić, S. 2011. The End of the Middle Bronze Age and the Beginning of the Urnfield Culture in Central Croatia. In C. Gutjahr and G. Tiefengraber (eds), *Beiträge zur Mittel- und Spätbronzezeit sowie zur Urnenfelderzeit am Rande der Südostalpen*. Rahden/Westf.: Verlag Marie Leidorf GmbH, pp. 11–36.

Karavanić, S. 2013. The Velika Gorica Cemetery and Related Sites in Continental Croatia. In M. Lochner and F. Ruppenstein (eds), *Brandbestattungen von der mittleren Donau bis zur Ägäis zwischen 1300 und 750 v. Chr. Akten des internationalen Symposiums an der Österreichischen Akademie der Wissenschaften in Wien, 11.-12. Februar 2010. [Cremation Burials in the Region between the Middle Danube and the Aegean, 1300–750 BC. Proceedings of the International Symposium Held at the Austrian Academy of Sciences at Vienna, 11–12 February 2010]*. Wien: Verlag der Österreichischen Akademie der Wissenschaften, pp. 119–133.

Leal, O. 1990. Popular Taste and Erudite Repertoire: The Place and Space of Television in Brasil. *Cultural Studies* 4(1): 19–29.

Leal, O. and Oliver, R. 1988. Class Interpretations of a Soap Opera Narrative: The Case of the Brazilian Novella 'Summer Sun'. *Theory, Culture and Society* 5: 81–99.

Leone, M. 2005. *The Archaeology of Liberty in an American Capital. Excavations in Annapolis*. Berkeley: University of California Press.

Ljubić, Š. 1885. Prvo otkriće predhistoričkih grobja od žara u Hrvatskoj. *Vjesnik Hrvatskoga Arheoloskoga Drustva* VII(1): 65–72.

Ložnjak Dizdar, D. 2009. Grobovi uglednica mlađe faze culture polja sa žaramau sjevernoj Hrvatskoj. Prilog poznavanju ženske nošnje kasnog brončanog doba na prostoru južne Panonije. *Vjesnik Arheoloskog muzeja u Zagrebu*, 3.s., XLII: 157–182.

Miller, D., Rowlands, M., and Tilley, C. (eds). 1989. *Domination and Resistance*. London: Routledge.

Ó Crualaoich, G. 2003. *The Book of the Cailleach: Stories of the Wise-Woman Healer*. Cork: Cork University Press.

Pabst, S. 2012. *The Spectacle Fibulae. An Investigation into Late Bronze and Early Iron Age Female Costume between the Baltic and the Mediterranean*. Rahden/Westf: Marburger Studien zur Vor- und Frühgeschichte.

Pavišić, I. 2003. Novi nalazi fibula u obliku violinskoga gudala u Hrvatskom zagorju Prilog poznavanju razdoblja kulture polja sa žarama u sjeverozapadnoj Hrvatskoj [Neue Funde von Violinbogenfibeln in Hrvatsko Zagorje Beitrag zu Erkenntnissen zur älteren Urnenfelderkultur in Nordkroatien]. *Prilozi Instituta za arheologiju u Zagrebu* 20: 47–56.

Rebay-Salisbury, K. 2012. Inhumation and Cremation: How Burial Practices Are Linked to Beliefs. In M. L. S. Sørensen and K. Rebay-Salisbury (eds), *Embodied Knowledge*. Oxford: Oxbow, pp. 15–26.

Sørensen, M. L. S. and Rebay-Salisbury, K. 2008. From Substantial Bodies to the Substance of Bodies: Analysis of the Transition from Inhumation to Cremation during the Middle Bronze Age in Europe. In J. Robb and D. Boric (eds), *Past Bodies*. Oxford: Oxbow, pp. 59–68.

Sørensen, M. L. S. and Rebay-Salisbury, K. 2009. Landscapes of the Body: Burials of the Middle Bronze Age in Hungary. *European Journal of Archaeology* 11(1): 49–74.

Staré, F. 1957a. Polmesečne britve iz Jugoslavije. *Arheološki vestnik* 3–4: 204–222.

Staré, F. 1957b. *Tombes plates à urne à Dobova en Slovénie et à Velika Gorica en Croatie. Inventaria Archaeologica Corpus des Ensembles Archéologiques, Jugoslavija, fascicule*. I: Y1–Y10. Bonn: Rudolf Habelt Verlag.

Staré, F. 1975. *Dobova*. Brežice: Posavski Muzej Brežice.

Svoljšak, D. and Pogačnik, A. 2001. *Tolmin, prazgodovinsko grobišče I*. Katalog in monografije 34. Ljubljana: Narodni Muzej.

Svoljšak, D. and Pogačnik, A. 2002. *Tolmin, prazgodovinsko grobišče II*. Razprave, Katalog in monografije 35. Ljubljana: Narodni Muzej.

Teržan, B. 1999. An Outline of the Urnfield Culture Period in Slovenia. *Arheološki vestnik* 50: 97–143.

Vicze, M. 2011. *Bronze Age Cemetery at Dunaújváros – Duna-dűlő*. Dissertationes Pannonicae ex Instituto Archaeologico Universitatis de Rolando Eötvös nominatae Budapestinensis provenientes Series IV Volumen 1. Budapest: Eötvös Loránd University, Institute of Archaeological Sciences.

Vinski-Gasparini, K. 1973. Kultura poljia sa žarama u sjevernoj Hrvatskoj. Zadar: Radovi Filozofskog Fakulteta.

Vinski-Gasparini, K. 1983. Kultura polja sa žarama sa svojim grupama. In Đ. Basler, A. Benac, S. Gabrovec, M. Garašanin, N. Tasić, B. Čović, K. Vinski-Gasparini (eds), *Praistorija Jugoslavenskih Zemalja IV Bronzano Doba*. Sarajevo: Akademija nauka i umjetnosti Bosne i Hercegovine. Centar za balkanološka ispitivanja, pp. 547–646.

Vrdoljak, S. 1996. Prapovijesno naselje na Kosovcu kod Bregane (Samobor). *Opuscula Archaeologica Radovi Arheološkog zavoda* 20:179–184.

Weber, C. 1996. *Die Rasiermesser in Südosteuropa*. PBF VIII. Stuttgart: Franz Steiner Verlag.

Wilkie, L. 2000. *Creating Freedom: Material Culture and African-American Identity at Oakley Plantation, Louisiana, 1845–1950*. Baton Rouge: Louisiana State University Press.

Williams, B. 1988. *Upscaling Downtown: Stalled Gentrification in Washington, DC*. Ithaca, NY: Cornell University Press.

6 Mimesis

Balen-Letunić, D. 1996. Pretpovijesna naselja I nekropola vukovarske Lijeve bare. In Ž. Demo (ed), *Vukovar – Lijeva Bara. Povijest jednog arheološkog nalazišta (tragovi, istraživanja, znamenja) [The History of an Archaeological Site (relics, research, renown)]* (exhibition catalogue). Zagreb: The Archaeological Museum in Zagreb, pp. 32–33.

Baudrillard, J. 1988. Simulacra and Simulations. In M. Poster (ed), *Selected Writings*. Stanford, CA: Stanford University Press, pp. 166–184.

Benjamin, W. 1933 [1978]. 'On the Mimetic Faculty'. Trans. E. Jephcott. In P. Demetz (ed), *Reflections: Essays Aphorisms, Autobiographical Writings*. New York: Schocken, pp. 720–722.

Benjamin, W. 1968 [1992]. *Illuminations*. Edited and introduced by H. Arendt. London: Fontana Books.

Benjamin, W. 1999. *The Arcades Project*. Cambridge, MA: Harvard University Press.

Bóna, I. 1975. *Die Mittlere Bronzezeit Ungarns und ihre sudostlichen Bezielumgen*. Budapest: Akadémia Kiadó.

Bradley, R. 2006. Danish Razors and Swedish Rocks: Cosmology and the Bronze Age Landscape. *Antiquity* 80(308): 372–389.

Budden, S. 2007. *Renewal and Reinvention: The Role of Learning Strategies in the Early to Late Middle Bronze Age of the Carpathian Basin*. Unpublished PhD dissertation, Southampton University.

Calderoni, C. 2010. Mimesis and Simulation: Illusory Effects in Music and Film. *This Century's Review* Issue 01/06. Available at http://history.thiscenturysreview.com/issue0106.html.

Crown, P. 2007. Life Histories of Pots and Potters: Situating the Individual in Archaeology. *American Antiquity* 72: 677–690.

Deleuze, G. 1968. *Difference and Repetition*. Columbia: Columbia University Press.

Demo, Ž, 2003. Naseobinski nalazi kasnog bakrenodobnog i mlađeg željeznodobnog sloja u terenskom dnevniku s iskopavanja nalazišta Vukovar-Lijeva bara (1951–1953) [Settlement Finds from the Late Eneolithic and Late Iron Age Strata in the Field Diary of the Excavations at Vukovar-Lijeva Bara (1951–1953)]. *Opuscula Archaeologica* 27: 351–365.

Demo, Ž. 2009. *Ranosrednjovjekono groblje bjelobrdske kulture: Vukovar – Lijeva Bara (X-XI. Stoljeće) [An Early Medieval Cemetery of the Bijelo Brdo Culture: Vukovar Lijeva Bara (10th–11th Centuries)]*. Zagreb: Arheološki muzej u Zagrebu.

Desideri, F. 2005. The Mimetic Bond. Benjamin and the Question of Technology. In A. Benjamin (ed), *Walter Benjamin and Art*. London and New York: Continuum, pp. 108–120.

Dornisch, L. 1989. Ricoeur's Theory of Mimesis: Implications for Literature and Theology. *Literature and Theology* 3(3): 308–318.

Durman, A. (ed). 2007. *One Hundred Croatian Archaeological Sites*. Zagreb: Leksikografski Zavod Miroslav Krleža.

Edwards, P. (ed). 1967. Mimesis. In *The Encyclopedia of Philosophy, Vol. 5 & 6*. New York: Macmillian, p. 335.

Emden, C. J. 2006. *Walter Benjamins Archäologie der Moderne: Kulturwissenschaft um 1930*. Munich: Wilhelm Fink Verlag.

Flohr Sørensen, T. 2013. Original Copies. Seriality, Similarity and the Simulacrum in the Early Bronze Age. *Danish Journal of Archaeology* 1(1): 45–61.

Frazer, J. 1890. *The Golden Bough*. New York and London: Macmillan and Co.

Freud, S. 1899. *Die Traumdeutung [The Interpretation of Dreams]*. Leipzig and Vienna: Franz Deuticke.

Gell, A. 1998. *Art and Agency. An Anthropological Theory*. Oxford: Clarendon Press.

Harrison, R. 2003. 'The Magical Virtue of These Sharp Things': Colonialism, Mimesis and Knapped Bottle Glass Artefacts in Australia. *Journal of Material Culture* 8(3): 311–336.

Hodder, I. 1993. The Narrative and Rhetoric of Material Culture Sequences. *World Archaeology* 25(2): 268–282.

Jeannerod, M. 2002. *La nature de l'esprit. Sciences cognitives et cerveau*. Paris: Odile Jacob.

Jones, A. M. 2005. Between a Rock and a Hard Place: Rock Art and Mimesis in Neolithic and Bronze Age Scotland. In V. Cummings and A. Pannett (eds), *Set in Stone: New Approaches to Neolithic Monuments in Scotland*. Oxford: Oxbow, pp. 107–117.

Karavanić, S. 2009. *The Urnfield Culture in Continental Croatia*. British Archaeological Reports International Series 2036. Oxford: Archaeopress.

Kaul, F. 1998. *Ships on Bronzes. A Study in Bronze Age Religion and Iconography*. Copenhagen: National Museum of Denmark.

Kaul, F. 2004. Bronzealderens ikonografiske motiver og deres fremkomst i en fromativ fase. In G. Milstreu and H. Prøhl (eds), *Prehistoric Pictures as Archaeological Source*. Gotarc Serie C. Arkeologiska Skrifter 50. Göteborg: Göteborgs Universitet, pp. 85–119.

Kaul, F. 2005. Bronze Age Tripartite Cosmologies. *Prähistorische Zeitschrift* 80(2): 135–148.

Kelly, M. (ed). 1998. Mimesis. In *The Encyclopedia of Aesthetics, Vol. 3*. Oxford: Oxford University Press, p. 233.

Kinahan, J. 1999. Towards an Archaeology of Mimesis and Rain-Making in Namibian Rock Art. In P. Ucko (ed), *The Archaeology and Anthropology of Landscape. Shaping Your Landscape*. London: Routledge, pp. 337–358.

Knappett, C. 2002. Photographs, Skeuomorphs and Marionettes: Some Thoughts on Mind, Agency and Object. *Journal of Material Culture* 7(1): 97–117.

Kristiansen, K. and Larsson, T. 2005. *The Rise of Bronze Age Society. Travels, Transmissions and Transformations*. Cambridge: Cambridge University Press.

Leslie, E. 2000. *Walter Benjamin: Overpowering Conformism*. London: Pluto Press.

Mauss, M. and Hubert, H. 1904. A General Theory of Magic. *Année sociologique* 7: 1–146.

Metzner-Nebelsick, C. 2002. *Der 'Thrako-Kimmerische' Formenkreis aus der Sicht der Urnenfelder- und Hallstattzeit im südöstlichen Pannonien*. Rahden/Westf: Verlag Marie Leidorf.

Nakamura, C. 2005. Mastering Matters: Magical Sense and Apotropaic Figurine Worlds of Neo-Assyria. In L. Meskell (ed), *Archaeologies of Materiality*. Oxford: Blackwell, pp. 46–70.

Newbold, R. 2010. Mimesis and Illusion in Nonnus: Deceit, Distrust, and the Search for Meaning. *Helios* 37(1): 81–106.

Pope, R. 2005. *Creativity. Theory, History, Practice*. London: Routledge.

Potolsky, M. 2006. *Mimesis*. New York: Routledge.

Potrebica, H. 2008. Contacts between Greece and Pannonia in the Early Iron Age with Special Concern to the Area of Thessalonica. In P. Biehl and Y. Rassamakin (eds), *Import and Imitation in Archaeology*. Langenweissbach: Beier & Beran, pp. 187–212.

Potrebica, H. and Dizdar, M. 2002. Prilog poznavanju naseljenosti Vinkovaca i okolice u starijem željeznom dobu. [A Contribution to Understanding Continuous Habitation of Vinkovci and Its Surroundings in the Early Iron Age]. *Prilozi Instituta za arheologiju u Zagrebu* 19: 79–100.

Proust, M. 1992. *In Search of Lost Time*. London: Chatto and Windus.

Réjouis, R-M. 2009. Object Lessons: Metaphors of Agency in Walter Benjamin's 'The Task of the Translator' and Patrick Chamoiseau's *Solibo Magnifique*. *French Literature Series* 36(1): 147–159.

Ricoeur, P. 1975. (Trans. 1977) *The Rule of Metaphor: Multi-disciplinary Studies of the Creation of Meaning in Language*. Trans. R. Czerny with K. McLaughlin and J. Costello. Toronto: University of Toronto Press.

Ricoeur, P. 1984. *Time and Narrative*. Chicago: The University of Chicago Press.

Rousseau, J.-J. 1979. *Emile, or On Education*. Trans. A. Bloom. New York: Basic Books.

Seckel, A. 2004. *Masters of Deception. Escher, Dalí and the Artists of Optical Illusion*. New York: Sterling Publishing.

Sofaer, J. 2013. Cosmologies in Clay: Swedish Helmet Bowls in the Middle Bronze Age of the Carpathian Basin. In S. Bergerbrant and S. Sabatini (eds), *Counterpoint: Essays in Archaeology and Heritage Studies in Honour of Professor Kristian Kristiansen*. Oxford: Archaeopress, pp. 361–365.

Sofaer, J. Forthcoming. Pots as Stories. In L. Bender Jørgensen, J. Sofaer, and M. L. S. Sørensen with G. Appleby, S. Becker, S. Bergerbrant, S. Coxon, K. Grömer, F. Kaul, D. Maričević, S. Mihelić, A. Rast-Eicher, and H. Rösel-Mautendorfer, *Creativity in the Bronze Age*. Manuscript in preparation.

Sofaer, J. and Budden, S. 2012. Many Hands Make Light Work: Embodied Knowledge at the Bronze Age Tell at Százhalombatta, Hungary. In M. L. S. Sørensen and K. Rebay-Salisbury (eds), *Embodied Knowledge*. Oxford: Oxbow, pp. 117–127.

Sofaer, J. and Sofaer, J. 2008. The Authenticity of Ambiguity: Writing the Dis/interest Project. In J. Sofaer and D. Arnold (eds), *Biographies and Space*. London: Routledge, pp. 168–193.

Stafford, B. 2007. *Echo Objects. The Cognitive Work of Images*. Chicago: University of Chicago Press.

Taussig, M. 1992. *The Nervous System*. London/New York: Routledge.

Taussig, M. 1993. *Mimesis and Alterity. A Particular History of the Senses*. New York: Routledge.

Taussig, M. 2006. *Walter Benjamin's Grave*. Chicago: University of Chicago Press.

Tkalčec, T., Karavanić, S., and Kudelić, A. 2011. Zaštitna arheološka istraživanja na Starom gradu Dubovcu 2009–2010 [Archaeological Rescue Excavations at Stari Grad Dubovac 2009–2010]. *Annales Instituti Archaeologici / Godišnjak Instituta za archeologiju* VII(1): 74–80.

Vinski, Z. 1955. Prethodni izvještaj o iskopavanju nekropole na Lijevoj bari u Vukovaru 1951., 1952. i 1953. Godine. *Ljetopis Jugoslavenske akademije znanosti i umjetnosti za godinu* 60: 231–255.

Vinski, Z. 1959. Ausgrabungen in Vukovar. *Archaeologia Iugoslavica* III: 99–109.

Vinski-Gasparini, K. 1973. *Kultura polja sa žarama u sjevernoj Hrvatskoj*. Zadar: Radovi Filozofskog Fakulteta.

Vinski-Gasparini, K. 1983. Kultura polja sa žarama sa svojim grupama. In Đ. Basler, A. Benac, S. Gabrovec, M. Garašanin, N. Tasić, B. Čović, and V. Vinski-Gasparini (eds), *Praistorija Jugoslavenskih Zemalja IV Bronzano Doba*. Sarajevo: Akademija nauka i umjetnosti Bosne i Hercegovine. Centar za balkanološka ispitivanja, pp. 547–646.

7 Performance

Abramović, M., 1996. Clean the House. Edited Transcription of an Interview between Scott deLahunta and Marina Abramović Recorded in September 1995. In R. Allsopp and S. deLahunta (eds), *The Connected Body? An Interdisciplinary Approach to the Body and Performance*. Amsterdam: Amsterdam School of Arts, pp. 15–22.

Abramović, M. 2010. Marina Abramović on Performance Art. In K. Biesenbach (ed), *Marina Abramović. The Artist Is Present*. New York: MOMA, p. 211.

Barrett, J. 1990. The Monumentality of Death: The Character of Early Bronze Age Mortuary Mounds in Southern Britain. *World Archaeology* 22(2): 179–189.

Biesenbach, K. (ed). 2010. *Marina Abramović. The Artist Is Present*. New York: MOMA.

Bloch, M. and Parry, J. 1982. *Death and the Regeneration of Life*. Cambridge: Cambridge University Press.

Budden, S. 2008. Skill amongst the Sherds: Understanding the Role of Skill in the Early to Late Middle Bronze Age in Hungary. In I. Berg (ed), *Breaking the Mould: Challenging the Past through Pottery, Manchester 2006*. British Archaeological Reports International Series 1861. Oxford: BAR, pp. 1–17.

Budden, S. and Sofaer, J. 2009. Non-discursive Knowledge and the Construction of Identity. Potters, Potting and Performance at the Bronze Age Tell of Százhalombatta, Hungary. *Cambridge Archaeological Journal* 19(2): 203–220.

Butler, J. 1993. *Bodies That Matter: On the Discursive Limits of Sex*. London: Routledge.

Butler, J. 2004. *Undoing Gender*. New York: Routledge.

Chicideanu, I. 1986. Die Frühthrakische Kultur. Zur Bronzezeit in Sudwest Rumänien. *Dacia*, n.s. 30(1–2): 7–47.

Chicideanu, I. 1992. O descoperire de la începutul primei epoci a fierului de la Cârna. *Studii şi cercetări de istorie veche şi arheologie a Institutului de Arheologie 'Vasile Pârvan' (SCIVA) Review* 43(1): 39–45.

Clarke, L. B., Gough, R., and Watt, D. 2010. Opening Remarks on a Private Collection. *Performance Research: A Journal of the Performing Arts* 12(4): 1–3.

Coles, J. and Harding, A. 1979. *The Bronze Age in Europe. An Introduction to the Prehistory of Europe c.2000–700 BC*. London: Methuen & Co.

Covarrubias, M. 1937. *Island of Bali*. Kuala Lumpur: Oxford University Press.

Crăciunescu, G. 2007. *Sfârşitul Epocii Bronzului În Sud-Vestul României. Cultura Gârla Mare. Expoziţie organizată în capital culturală europeană. Sibiu 7–30 iunie 2007*. Craiova: Editura Universitaria.

Dumitrescu, V. 1961. *Necropola Incineraţie Din Epoca Bronzului De La Cîrna*. Biblioteca De Arheologie IV. Bucharest: Editura Academiei Republicii Populare Romîne.

Føssy, S. 2012. *Rom for variasjon. En studie I bronsealderens tekstilhåndverk*. Trondheim: Norwegian University of Science and Technology.

Ghiselin, B. 1985. Introduction. In B. Ghiselin (ed), *The Creative Process. Reflections on Invention in the Arts and Sciences*. Berkeley: University of California Press.

Goffman, E. 1959. *The Presentation of Self in Everyday Life*. New York: Anchor Books.

Greenfield, P. M. 2000. Children, Material Culture and Weaving. In J. Sofaer (ed), *Children and Material Culture*. London and New York: Routledge, pp. 72–86.

Greenfield, P. M., Maynard, A. E., and Childs, C. P. 2003. Historical Change, Cultural Learning and Cognitive Representation Zinacantec Maya Children. *Cognitive Development* 18: 455–487.

Hachmann, R. 1968. Rezension zu V. Dumitrescu, Necropola de incinerade din epoca bronzului da la Cima. *Germania* 46: 368–370.

Hänsel, B. 1968. *Beiträge zur Chronologie der mittleren Bronzezeit in Karpatenbecken*. Bonn: Habelt.

Hänsel, B. 1976. *Beiträge zur regionalen und chronologischen Gliederung der älteren Hallstattzeit an den unteren Donau*. Bonn: Habelt.

Harman, G. 2002. *Tool-Being: Heidegger and the Metaphysics of Objects*. Chicago: Open Court.

Hayward, P. 1990. Introduction. Technology and the (Trans)formation of Culture. In P. Hayward (ed), *Culture, Technology and Creativity in the Late Twentieth Century*. London: John Libbey, pp. 1–12.

Heidegger, M. 1975. 'The Thing' in *Poetry, Language, Thought*. Trans. A. Hofstadter. New York: Harper & Row, pp. 163–187.

Hertz, R. 1960. *Death and the Right Hand*. Trans. R. Needham and C. Needham. New York: Free Press.

Lazăr, S. 2011. *Sfârşitul Epocii Bronzului Şi Începutul Epocii Fierului În Sud-Vestul României*. Craiova: Editura Universitaria.

Littleton, K. and Mercer, N. 2012. Communication, Collaboration and Creativity: How Musicians Negotiate a Collective 'Sound'. In D. Hargreaves, D. Miell, and R. Macdonald (eds), *Musical Imaginations: Multidisciplinary Perspectives on Creativity, Performance and Perception*. Oxford: Oxford University Press, pp. 233–241.

Mauss, M. 1935 [2006]. Trans. B. Brewster. Les techniques du corps. In N. Schlanger (ed), *Marcel Mauss: Techniques, Technology and Civilisation*. Oxford: Durkheim Press, pp. 77–95. [Previously published in *Economy and Society* 1973.]

Motzoi-Chicideanu, I. 2011. *Obiceiuri funerare în Epoca Bronzului la Dunărea Mijlocie şi Inferioară*. Bucharest: Editura Academiei Române.

Palincaş, N. 2010a. Living for the Others: Gender Relations in Prehistoric and Contemporary Archaeology of Romania. In L. H. Dommasnes, T. Hjørungdal, S. MontónSubías, M. Sánchez Romero, and N. Wicker (eds), *Situating Gender in European Archaeology*. Budapest: Archaeolingua, pp. 93–116.

Palincaş, N. 2010b. Reconfiguring Anatomy: Ceramics, Cremation and Cosmology in the Late Bronze Age in the Lower Danube. In K. Rebay-Salisbury, M. L. S. Sørensen, and J. Hughes (eds), *Body Parts and Bodies Whole: Changing Relations and Meanings*. Oxford: Oxbow, pp. 72–89.

Palincaş, N. 2012. Investigating Bronze Age Social Organisation in the Lower Danube Region. The Case of the Žuto Brdo-Gârla Mare Area. *Istros* XVIII: 13–38.

Pikul, C. 2010. Interview with Marina Abramović. Body Issues: Marina Abramović's New MOMA Reterospective. *Elle* 11 March 2010. Available at www.elle.com/cul ture/art-design/a10958/body-issues-marina-abramovics-new-moma-retrospective-435627.

Reich, C. 2002. Das Gräberfeld von Cîrna. *Praehistorische Zeitschrift* 77(2): 159–179.

Reich, C. 2007. *Das Gräberfeld von Szeremle und die Gruppen mit inkrustierter Keramikentlang der mittleren und unteren Donau*. Berlin: Staatliche Museen zu Berlin.

Şandor-Chicideanu, M. 2003. *Cultura Žuto Brdo-Gârla Mare. Contribuţii la cunoaşterea epocii bronzului la Dunărea Mijlocie şi Inferioară*. Cluj-Napoca: Editura Nereamia Napocae.

Şandor-Chicideanu, M. and Chicideanu, I. 1990. Contribution to the Study of the Gârla Mare Anthropomorphic Statuettes. *Dacia* 34: 53–76.

Schechner, R. 1985. *Between Anthropology and Theatre*. Philadelphia: University of Pennsylvania Press.

Schechner, R. 1987. Victor Turner's Last Adventure. In V. Turner, *The Anthropology of Performance*. New York: PAJ Publications, pp. 7–20.

Schechner, R. 1988. *Performance Theory*. London: Routledge.

Schuster, C., Kogălniceanu, R., and Morintz, A. 2008. *The Living and the Dead. An Analysis of the Relationship between the Two Worlds during Prehistory at the Lower Danube*. Târgoviște: Editura Cetatea De Scaun.

Singer, M. 1972. *When a Great Tradition Modernizes*. New York: Praeger.

Sofaer, J. 2011. Human Ontogeny and Material Change at the Bronze Age Tell of Százhalombatta, Hungary. *Cambridge Archaeological Journal* 21(2): 217–227.

Sofaer, J. 2012. Touching the Body. The Living and the Dead in Osteoarchaeology and the Performance Art of Marina Abramović. *Norwegian Archaeological Review* 45(2): 135–150.

Sofaer, J. and Sørensen, M. L. S. 2013. Death and Gender. In S. Tarlow and L. Nilsson-Stutz (eds), *Oxford Handbook of the Archaeology of Death and Burial*. Oxford: Oxford University Press, pp. 527–542.

Sofaer, J. L. 2006. Beam Me Up, Scotty: Navigating Processes. In C. Bannerman, J. Sofaer, and J. Watt (eds), *Navigating the Unknown: The Creative Process in Contemporary Performing Arts*. London: Middlesex University Press/ResCen, pp. 92–101.

Sørensen, M. L. S. 2004a. The Grammar of Drama: An Analysis of the Rich Early Bronze Age Grave at Leubingen, Germany. In T. Kienlin (ed), *Die Dinge als Zeichen: Kulturelles Wissen und materielle Kultur*. Universitätsforschungen zur prähistorischen Archäologie 127. Bonn: Habelt, pp. 283–291.

Sørensen, M. L. S. 2004b. Stating Identities: The Use of Objects in Rich Bronze Age Graves. In J. Cherry, C. Scarre, and S. Shennan (eds), *Explaining Social Change: Studies in Honour of Colin Renfrew*. Cambridge: McDonald Institute for Archaeological Research, pp. 167–176.

Turner, V. 1969. *The Ritual Process*. London: Routledge and Kegan Paul.

Turner, V. 1987. *The Anthropology of Performance*. New York: PAJ Publications.

Toren, C., 1999. *Mind, Materiality and History: Essays in Fijian Ethnography*. London: Routledge.

van Gennep, A. 1909 [1960]. *The Rites of Passage*. London: Routledge and Kegan Paul.

Vulpe, A. 2010. Reprezentarea statutului social in obiectul arheologic. In M. Petrescu-Dîmbovița and A. Vulpe (eds), *Istoria Românilor. Vol. 1*. Bucharest: Editura Enciclopedică, pp. 352–365.

Vulpe, A., Petrescu-Dîmbovița, M., and László, A. 2010. Epoca metalelor. In M. Petrescu-Dîmbovița and A. Vulpe (eds), *Istoria Românilor. Vol. 1*. Bucharest: Editura Enciclopedică, pp. 207–395.

Wallaert- Pêtre, H. 2001. Learning How to Make the Right Pots: Apprenticeship Strategies and Material Culture, a Case Study in Handmade Pottery from Cameroon. *Journal of Anthropological Research* 57(4): 471–493.

Warr, T. 2000. Preface. In T. Warr and A. Jones. *The Artist's Body*. London: Phaidon Press, pp. 11–15.

8 Failure

Adamson, G. 2007. *Thinking through Craft*. Oxford: Berg.

Adamson, G. 2010. Introduction to *The Nature and the Art of Workmanship* by David Pye. In G. Adamson (ed), *The Craft Reader*. Oxford: Berg, p. 341.

Akrich, M. 1993. A Gazogene in Costa Rica. In P. Lemonnier (ed), *Technological Choices. Transformation in Material Cultures since the Neolithic*. London: Routledge, pp. 289–337.

Bauman, Z. 2007. *Liquid Times*. Cambridge: Polity Press.

Baxandall, M. 1980. *The Limewood Sculptors of Renaissance Germany*. New Haven, CT: Yale University Press.

Beckett, S. 1983. *Worstward Ho*. London: John Calder.

Bharucha, R. 2012. On Failing Failure: A Letter to Margaret Werry. *Performance Research: A Journal of the Performing Arts* 17(1): 101–104.

Budden, S. 2008. Skill amongst the Sherds: Understanding the Role of Skill in the Early to Late Middle Bronze Age in Hungary. In I. Berg (ed), *Breaking the Mould: Challenging the Past through Pottery, Manchester 2006*. British Archaeological Reports International Series 1861. Oxford: BAR, pp. 1–17.

Budden, S. and Sofaer, J, 2009. Nondiscursive Knowledge and the Construction of Identity. Potters, Potting and Performance at the Bronze Age Tell of Százhalombatta, Hungary. *Cambridge Archaeological Journal* 19(2): 203–220.

Crown, P. L. 2001. Learning to Make Pottery in the Prehispanic American Southwest. *Journal of Anthropological Research* 57: 451–469.

Deleuze, G. 1995. *Negotiations*. Trans. M. Joughin. Now York: Columbia University Press.

Goetz, D. and Morley, S. G. (eds). 1950. *Popol Vuh: The Sacred Book of the Ancient Quiché Maya By Adrián Recinos*. 1st ed. Norman: University of Oklahoma Press.

Greenfield, P. 2000. Children, Material Culture and Weaving. Historical Change and Developmental Change. In J. Sofaer (ed), *Children and Material Culture*. London: Routledge, pp. 72–86.

Greenfield, P. M., Maynard, A. E., and Childs, C. P. 2003. Historical Change, Cultural Learning and Cognitive Representation in Zinacantec Maya Children. *Cognitive Development* 18: 455–487.

Herzfeld, M. 2004. *The Body Impolitic: Artisans and Artifice in the Global Hierarchy of Value*. Chicago: University of Chicago Press.

Horváth, J. and Keszi, T. 2004. *The Treasures of Intercisa Museum II. The Catalogue of the Permanent Prehistoric Exhibition of Intercisa Museum*. Dunaújváros: Intercisa Múzeum.

Jeanes, E. 2006. 'Resisting Creativity, Creating the New'. A Deleuzian Perspective on Creativity. *Creativity and Innovation Management* 15(2): 127–134.

Kacsó, C. 1971, Unele considerații cu privire la geneza ceramicii din necropola tumulară de la Lăpuș. *Marmatia* 2: 36–54.

Kacsó, C. 1975. Contributions à la connaissance de la culture de Suciu de Sus à la lumière de recherches faites à Lăpuș. *Dacia*, n.s. 19: 45–68.

Kacsó, C. 2001. Zur chronologischen und kulturellen Stellung des Hügelgräberfeldes von Lăpuș. In C. Kacsó (ed), *Der nordkarpatische Raum in der Bronzezeit. Symposium Baia Mare 7.-10. Oktober 1998*. Bibliotheca Marmatia 1. Baia Mare: Muzeul Judetean De Istorie Și Arheologie Maramureș, pp. 231–278.

Kacsó, C. 2004. *Mărturii arheologice*. Baia Mare: Muzeul Judetean De Istorie Și Arheologie Maramureș.

Kacsó, C. 2011. *Repertoriul Arheologic Al Judetului Maramureș*. Bibliotheca Marmatia 3. Baia Mare: Muzeul Judetean De Istorie Și Arheologie Maramureș.

Kacsó, C., Metzner-Nebelsick, C., and Nebelsick, L. 2011. New Work at the Late Bronze Age Tumulus Cemetery of Lăpuș in Romania. In E. Borgna and S. Müller Celka (eds), *Ancestral Landscapes: Burial Mounds in the Copper and Bronze Ages (Central and Eastern Europe – Balkans – Adriatique – Aegean, 4th–2nd Millennium B.C.)*. Proceedings of the International Conference Held in Udine, May 15th–18th 2008. Travaux de la Maison de l'Orient et de la Méditerranée 61. Lyon: Maison de l'Orient et de la Méditerranée, pp. 341–354.

Kalicz-Schreiber, R. 1984. Komplex der Nagyrév-Kultur. In N. Tasić (ed), *Kulturen der Frühbronzezeit des Karpatenbeckens und Nordbalkans*. Beograd: Balkanološki Institut SANU, pp. 133–190.

Kuipers, M. 2013. Creative Copies: The Importance of Repetition for Creativity. Paper presented at the conference Creativity: An Exploration through the Bronze Age and Contemporary Responses to the Bronze Age. 10–11 April 2013. Cambridge.

Longacre, W. A., Xia, J., and Tao, Y. 2000. I Want to Buy a Black Pot. *Journal of Archaeological Method and Theory* 7(4): 273–293.

O'Gorman, R. and Werry, M. 2012. On Failure (On Pedagogy): Editorial Introduction. *Performance Research: A Journal of the Performing Arts* 17(1): 1–8.

Pallasmaa, J. 2009. *The Thinking Hand. Existential and Embodied Wisdom in Architecture*. Chichester: John Wiley.

Pop, D. 2009. Comments on the State of Research of Suciu de Sus Culture and Lăpuș Group. *Marmatia* 9(1): 101–145.

Poroszlai, I. 2000. Excavation Campaigns at the Bronze Age Site at Százhalombatta-Földvár. In I. Poroszlai and M. Vicze (eds), *Százhalombatta Archaeological Expedition SAX Annual Report 1*. Százhalombatta: Archaeolingua, pp. 13–73.

Pye, D. 1968. *The Nature and the Art of Workmanship*. Cambridge: Cambridge University Press.

Sennett, R. 2008. *The Craftsman*. London: Allen Lane.

Sofaer, J. 2006. Pots, Houses and Metal. Technological Relations at the Bronze Age Tell at Százhalombatta, Hungary. *Oxford Journal of Archaeology* 25(2): 127–147.

Sofaer, J. and Budden, S. 2013. Many Hands Make Light Work: Potting and Embodied Knowledge at the Bronze Age Tell at Százhalombatta, Hungary. In M. L. S. Sørensen and K. Rebay-Salisbury (eds), *Embodied Knowledge*. Oxford: Oxbow, pp. 117–127.

Sofaer, J. and Sofaer J. L. 2008. The Authenticity of Ambiguity: Writing the Dis/interest Project. In D. Arnold and J. Sofaer (eds), *Biographies and Space*. London: Routledge, pp. 168–193.

Sofaer, J. and Sørensen, M. L. S. 2002. Becoming Cultural: Society and the Incorporation of Bronze. In B. Ottaway and E. C. Wager (eds), *Metals and Society: Papers from a Session Held at the European Association of Archaeologists Sixth Annual Meeting in Lisbon 2000*. British Archaeological Reports International Series 1061. Oxford: Archaeopress, pp. 117–121.

Sofaer Derevenski, J. 2000. Rings of Life: The Role of Early Metalwork in Mediating the Gendered Life Course. *World Archaeology* 31(3): 389–406.

Teržan, B. 2005. Metamorpose – eine Vegetationsgottheit in der Spätbronzezeit. In B. Horejs, R. Jung, E. Kaiser, and B. Teržan (eds), *Interpretationsraum Bronzezeit. Bernard Hänsel von seinen Schülern gewidmet*. UPA 121: 241–261.

van der Leeuw, S. 1989. Risk, Perception, Innovation. In S. van der Leeuw and R. Torrence (eds), *What's New? A Closer Look at the Process of Innovation*. London: Unwin Hyman, pp. 300–329.

Wallaert- Pêtre, H. 2001. Learning How to Make the Right Pots: Apprenticeship Strategies and Material Culture, a Case Study in Handmade Pottery from Cameroon. *Journal of Anthropological Research* 57(4): 471–493.

Werry, M. and O'Gorman, R. 2012. The Anatomy of Failure: An Inventory. *Performance Research: A Journal of the Performing Arts* 17(1): 105–110.

Afterword

Bender Jørgensen, L., Sofaer, J., and Sørensen, M. L. S., with Appleby, G., Becker, S., Bergerbrant, S., Coxon, S., Grömer, K., Kaul, F., Maričević, D., Mihelić, S., Rast-Eicher, A., and Rösel-Mautendorfer, H. *Creativity in the Bronze Age*. Manuscript in preparation.

Benjamin, W. 1933 [1978]. *On the Mimetic Faculty*. In P. Demetz (ed), *Reflections: Essays Aphorisms, Autobiographical Writings*. Trans. E. Jephcott. New York: Schocken, pp. 720–722.

Brodsky, J. 1986. *Less than One. Selected Essays*. New York: Farrar, Straus, Giroux.

Crawford, M. 2011. *The Case for Working with Your Hands or Why Office Work Is Bad for Us and Fixing Things Feels Good*. London: Penguin Books.

Liep, J. 2001. Introduction. In J. Liep (ed), *Locating Cultural Creativity*. London: Pluto Press, pp. 1–13.

Pallasmaa, J. 2009. *The Thinking Hand. Existential and Embodied Wisdom in Architecture*. Chichester: John Wiley.

INDEX